Practical Rust Projects

Build Serverless, AI, Machine
Learning, Embedded, Game, and
Web Applications

Second Edition

Shing Lyu
Andrew Rzeznik

Apress®

Practical Rust Projects: Build Serverless, AI, Machine Learning, Embedded, Game, and Web Applications

Shing Lyu
Amsterdam, The Netherlands

Andrew Rzeznik
Arlington, MA, USA

ISBN-13 (pbk): 978-1-4842-9330-0
https://doi.org/10.1007/978-1-4842-9331-7

ISBN-13 (electronic): 978-1-4842-9331-7

Managing Director, Apress Media LLC: Welmoed Spahr
Acquisitions Editor: Steve Anglin
Development Editor: James Markham
Editorial Assistant: Gryffin Winkler
Copy Editor: April Rondeau

Cover designed by eStudioCalamar

Cover image designed by xb100 on freepik

Distributed to the book trade worldwide by Springer Science+Business Media New York, 1 New York Plaza, Suite 4600, New York, NY 10004-1562, USA. Phone 1-800-SPRINGER, fax (201) 348-4505, email orders-ny@ springer-sbm.com, or visit www.springeronline.com. Apress Media, LLC is a California LLC and the sole member (owner) is Springer Science+Business Media Finance Inc (SSBM Finance Inc). SSBM Finance Inc is a **Delaware** corporation.

For information on translations, please e-mail booktranslations@springernature.com; for reprint, paperback, or audio rights, please e-mail bookpermissions@springernature.com.

Apress titles may be purchased in bulk for academic, corporate, or promotional use. eBook versions and licenses are also available for most titles. For more information, reference our Print and eBook Bulk Sales web page at http://www.apress.com/bulk-sales.

Any source code or other supplementary material referenced by the author in this book is available to readers on GitHub (github.com/apress). For more detailed information, please visit http://www.apress.com/source-code.

Printed on acid-free paper

Table of Contents

About the Authors

Shing Lyu is a software engineer who is passionate about open source software. He's worked on Rust professionally at Mozilla on the Firefox (Gecko) and Servo browser engine project. Currently, he works at Amazon Web Services (AWS) as a solutions architect. Previously, Shing worked at DAZN, a sports streaming platform, as a backend developer, with a focus on AWS and serverless technology. Shing has worked for other world-famous brands such as Intel. He is also active in the open source community. Being one of the founders of the Taiwan Rust community, he loves to share his enthusiasm for Rust with people.

Andrew Rzeznik is a software development engineer at AWS Cryptography with interests in distributed systems, languages, tooling, Internet of Things (IoT), and low-level programming. His primary working language is Rust, but he considers himself a polyglot, having worked in C, C++, Python, Java, C#, and many others. Before AWS Andrew worked in various software positions, with a primary focus in factory automation. He developed robust yet accessible distributed machine control frameworks to bring advanced software patterns and techniques to manufacturing. He also served as a consultant, where he debugged manufacturing issues at various firms. Andrew received his PhD in mathematics from the Massachusetts Institute of Technology (MIT), where he wrote simulations for ocean mining plumes and tested them aboard a research vessel at sea.

About the Technical Reviewer

Satej Kumar Sahu works in the role of senior software data architect at Boeing. He is passionate about technology, people, and nature. He believes that through technology focused on sustainability and conscientious decision making each of us has the power to make this world a better place. In his free time, he can be seen reading books, playing basketball, and having fun with friends and family.

Introduction

Almost every programming language has one or more books about it that provide a deep dive into fundamental syntax, semantics, and functionality. These books are amazing as both an introduction and a reference. It's important to be able to dive deep and fully immerse yourself in a topic to gain a thorough understanding of it. Whenever I am starting to learn a new language, I look for this kind of foundational text to start my journey.

After completing this first stage, however, there is a question of where to move next. Sometimes you've learned a language for a very specific purpose, so you focus all your energies toward using the language for that task. But breadth of learning is also very important, and can sometimes be harder to find. The best programmers don't just know their own specialty, but also have a broad foundation of knowledge along with background on adjacent subjects. Learning different applications of a language can open your mind to new ideas both within that language and outside of it. It's also really fun to throw together a new project that does something you've never done before.

This book was created to provide some of these projects, which will let you take your core Rust knowledge and apply it to several different areas. Its goal is to expose you to new ideas and different ways of thinking, and show, not tell, you how Rust can be used.

One of the big reasons I was drawn to Rust as a programming language was how it embodies the "general purpose" paradigm. If you ask ten different people why they like the language, you'll frequently get ten different answers. Some people like it because it's low level; it compiles directly to machine code in the same way as C, with all of the fine control afforded there. However, some people like it because it's high level, with a strong type system and advanced macros for working with abstract constructs. Some people like Rust because it feels like a safer C++, while others learn it as a more performant alternative to Python. Some people like Rust for its large selection of available packages, while others like how powerful the core language feels even when the standard library has been disabled.

A lot of these different views are because Rust exists in a big ecosystem with wildly different applications, especially for being such a comparatively young language. On one end, it's possible to write tiny bare-metal programs whose compiled size can be measured in hundreds of bytes (not megabytes, not kilobytes, but bytes). On the other end, people are currently building operating systems, language compilers, and large distributed systems in Rust. This book was written to share with you a small set of these interesting applications, and hopefully show you the benefits (and joy) of writing them in Rust.

A drawback to the approach taken here is that we can't go into great depth on any of the topics. A whole book could be written for each single-chapter project we present here, diving deep into advanced theory, design, and tradeoffs. We chose to instead focus only on the core essence of each project, providing you with a scaffold that does something useful and that you can later extend with your own ideas. As any programmer knows, frequently the hardest parts of a new project are the initial setup, architecture, and library choices. We've tried to provide these components to you as a solid foundation for your projects, while also trying to include some interesting examples that touch on important issues in each of the topics.

We hope that this book lets you see the many faces of the Rust programming language, where it shines, and in some cases the places where a person like you can make things better. Many programmers feel that the gap between a novice and an expert is insurmountable, and that the people who build "real" production applications must have some unique gifts. Hopefully the examples here will help build your confidence and show you that anyone can build real, practical projects in Rust with a little guidance and determination.

Source Code

All code used in this book can be found at `github.com/apress/practical-rust-projects-2e`.

CHAPTER 1

Welcome to the World of Rust

If you're reading this book, you're probably as excited about Rust as we are. Since its first stable release in 2015, Rust has come a long way in terms of features and stability. Developers around the world are fascinated by how Rust can combine features that were once thought of as unavoidable trade-offs: performance with memory safety, and low-level control with productivity. Despite its infamous steep learning curve, Rust has gained popularity over the years. It was named the "most loved programming language" in a StackOverflow survey eight years in a row, from 2016 to 2023. In 2022, it was also named the "most wanted programming language," just beating out Python. Many big companies and organizations like Amazon, Facebook, Google, Microsoft, Dropbox, and npm use Rust in production. The Android platform supports writing native components in Rust, and, perhaps most interesting of all, Rust is the first language after C to be added to the Linux Kernel.

How large is the Rust ecosystem currently? If we take a look at crates.io, the official Rust crates (libraries) registry, there are over 100,000 crates and over fifty million downloads a day. There are 55 categories on crates.io,[1] ranging from command-line interfaces and cryptography to databases, games, operating systems, web programming, and more. What does it feel like to use these libraries? How does Rust's syntax and design philosophy affect the design of these crates? How can you get started writing some cool code with real use cases? This book will try to answer these questions.

---

[1] https://crates.io/categories

© Shing Lyu and Andrew Rzeznik 2023
S. Lyu and A. Rzeznik, *Practical Rust Projects*, https://doi.org/10.1007/978-1-4842-9331-7_1

1.1 Who Is This Book For?

This book will be useful for

- people who already know basic Rust syntax, but want to learn how to build applications in Rust;

- people who are considering using Rust to build production-ready systems and want a tour of some of the options; and

- people who wish to have a quick overview of high-level architecture and programming interface design in other fields.

You might have learned Rust out of curiosity. After finishing all the tutorials and beginner books, you might have been left wondering, "What should I do next? What can I build with Rust?" This book will walk you through a few different applications of Rust, which will help you move beyond basic language theory and into building real applications. Rust has a fascinating design and many interesting language features, but simply knowing how to write basic algorithms and data structures won't necessarily prepare you for building useful applications. We've tried to find the most production-ready but also modern Rust libraries to do the job, so you'll be able to judge if Rust is ready for the application you've envisioned. If it's not, you might find opportunities to contribute back to Rust's community by improving the existing libraries and frameworks, or by designing and building new ones.

You might have learned Rust for a specific project, like a CLI tool for work or an open-source browser engine that happens to use Rust. Once you master Rust for that domain, it's beneficial to learn Rust for other domains—say, building a game or a website. This will open you to new ideas that you can apply to the original domain. For example, by building a game, you'll know how game engine designers organize their code to make it decoupled and easy to maintain, while also being very performant. You may never build a game for work, but that knowledge might influence the architecture of your next project. As another example, learning how to cross-compile code to a Raspberry Pi might help you understand how compiling to WebAssembly works. This book aims to take you through a tour of various applications of Rust like this. You'll learn what their application programming interfaces (APIs)[2] look like and how they organize their code and architecture.

---

[2] We use the term "API" in a general sense. This includes the functions, structs, and command-line tools exposed by each library or framework.

1.2 Who Is This Book Not For?

This book might not be that useful for

- people who want to learn the Rust programming language itself;

- people who want to dive deep into one particular field; or

- people who are looking for the most experimental and cutting-edge Rust use cases.

This book is not a course on the Rust programming language itself, nor is it trying to teach Rust's syntax via examples. We'll focus on the applications themselves and their domain knowledge, assuming you already know Rust's syntax and language features (though we'll stop to review more advanced features as they are needed by a project). There are many excellent books on Rust itself, like *The Rust Programming Language* by Steve Klabnik and Carol Nichols. You can also find online books, interactive tutorials, and videos on the *Learn Rust* section of the official website.[3] Each of the topics in this book can easily be expanded into a book on its own, so we will try to give you a high-level understanding of the topic, but won't go too deep into any of them. We aim to give you a broad overview of what is possible with Rust and what the developer experience is like. Therefore, the examples are simplified so people without a background in that particular field can still get a taste of the mental models used. Also, we're not advocating that the methods presented in this book are the "best" or most trendy way of building those applications. We've tried to strike a balance between being modern and being pragmatic. In the end, each of the examples should give you the core of a functioning project, touch upon some common pain points, and show you how Rust can be used in a new domain.

1.3 Criteria for Selecting Libraries

Though Rust has already been used in many production-grade projects, it's still a relatively young language with constant innovation. This means it can sometimes be a challenge to select the libraries or frameworks to use in each chapter. There are experimental pure-Rust implementations for almost every domain, and just as many Rust bindings of popular libraries in other languages (especially in the C and C++ spaces). In some areas, a clear leader has emerged and a particular library acts as a

---

[3] https://www.rust-lang.org/learn

de-facto standard. In other areas, many proof of concept packages exist without any clear winner. The early adopters of Rust are usually adventurous developers; they are comfortable with rough edges in the libraries and find workarounds (the Rust ecosystem makes it easy to download and inspect the source code of any library used). Some libraries focus on innovation and experimentation, while others value stability and production readiness. In this book, we're trying to demonstrate the core concepts in each field, and how these translate into an idiomatic Rust API. Therefore, we select the libraries we use by the following criteria.

Pure Rust

We generally try to find libraries that are built purely in Rust. Rust's FFI (foreign function interface) allows you to call existing C libraries (and many other languages) from Rust. This in turn means that the easiest way to build Rust applications quickly is often to leverage existing libraries from other languages. These libraries are usually designed with other languages in mind, so wrapping them in Rust results in a weird and non-idiomatic Rust API. If there is a purely Rust library or a library that uses existing technology but is built from scratch using Rust, we tend to choose those.

Maturity

However, not every purely Rust library is very mature. Because many Rust libraries are built from a clean slate, the developers often try to experiment with the latest technology, and that might mean that the architecture and API design is very experimental and changes frequently. Some libraries show great potential in their early days, but then development slows down, and the projects eventually go into maintenance mode or are abandoned. We aim to build useful software rather than experiment with exciting technologies and throw the code away. Therefore, we need to be pragmatic and choose a library that is mature enough and uses widely accepted design patterns, rather than being dogmatic about using pure-Rust libraries. We chose to use a GTK+-based library in Chapter 3 for this reason.

Popularity

If two or more candidate libraries meet the preceding criteria, we'll choose the most popular one. The popularity is based on a combination of factors like the following:

- Number of downloads on crates.io

- Pace of development and releases

- Discussions on issue trackers and discussion forums

- Media coverage

Although popularity is not a guarantee of success, a popular project is more likely to have a big community that supports it and keeps it alive. This can help us find a library that has the most potential to stick around longer in the future. You are also more likely to get support and answers online.

1.4 How to Use This Book

The chapters in this book are independent of each other, so you may read them in any order you want. However, some of the ideas or design patterns are used in multiple chapters. We try to introduce these ideas in the chapter where the design originated, or where they make the most sense. For example, the concept of using event handlers to build a responsive user interface is introduced in the "Text-based User Interface" section in Chapter 3, and is then referenced in Chapter 7. So, reading the book from cover to cover might help you build up this knowledge in an incremental way.

Chapters Overview

In Chapter 2, we start with the easiest application we can build with Rust: a command-line interface (CLI). Building a CLI requires very minimal setup and background knowledge but can produce very powerful applications. We first introduce how to read raw arguments using the standard library, then we show how to use `Clap` to manage arguments better. We also see how to get features like generating a help message for free. Then we touch upon topics like piping, testing, and publishing the program to crates.io.

In Chapter 3, we build two-dimensional interfaces. We first build a text-based 2D interface using the `Cursive` text-based user interface system. This allows us to build interactive user interfaces like popups, buttons, and forms. The experience in the text-based user interface (TUI) paves the way for a graphical user interface (GUI). We'll be introducing the Rust bindings for the popular GTK+ 3 library, `gtk-rs`. We then build the same interactive form using the GUI library.

In Chapter 4, we compile Rust to WebAssembly, a combination of bytecode and sandboxed environment meant to run on platforms such as web browsers. We write some simple WebAssembly code to offload large, heavy operations in the browser from JavaScript to Rust. Then we explore `yew-rs`, a Rust front-end web framework that leverages WebAssembly to create responsive single-page applications. We create a single-page application that can receive and display user data, maintaining state in the web browser.

In Chapter 5, we explore Rust in the more traditional context of server-side rendered web pages and REST APIs. We recreate the web page from the previous chapter, except this time as a server-side page served by the Rust `actix-web` framework. We integrate a Postgres database to store and retrieve user-provided data. We then modify the project to use stand-alone REST APIs, which allows for programmatic calling of our APIs between different web services. We further refine our project to explore testing and error handling in the context of Rust.

In Chapter 6, we explore the cutting edge of web service development by deploying a REST API to AWS Lambda Functions and the AWS SDK for Rust. This lets us work with the web without individual servers. We use an AWS DynamoDB table to store user-provided info, and use an S3 Bucket to store larger files, with the Lambda functions interacting with both. We then use S3 to serve a static website with callbacks into our Lambda API, to give a complete website that deploys from a single project and scales to massive numbers of users.

In Chapter 7, we build a game in Rust. We use the Bevy game engine to make a cat volleyball game. You'll learn the design philosophy and architecture behind Bevy, called the entity-component system. You'll also learn how to create 2D games, rendering the characters and items with a spritesheet. We implement game logic like collision detection, keeping score, and adding sound effects and background music.

In Chapter 8, we connect the virtual world with the physical world by introducing physical computing on a Raspberry Pi development board. We start by installing a full operating system and the whole Rust toolchain on the device, and introduce how to use

Rust to control an LED and how to take inputs from a physical button. Then we show you how to cross-compile Rust on another computer to produce a binary that runs on a Raspberry Pi.

In Chapter 9, we shift our focus to artificial intelligence and machine learning. We show how to implement unsupervised and supervised machine learning models using the `linfa` and `rusty-machine` crates. For the unsupervised model we introduce K-means, and for the supervised model we demonstrate a neural network. We also show how to do some data-processing tasks like test data generation, reading/writing CSV files, and visualization.

Finally, in Chapter 10, we give a broad overview of other exciting fields in Rust that can't fit in this book. We point you to cool projects in areas like operating systems, programming languages, and distributed systems. This chapter acts as a guide book for your future exploration into the vast world of Rust.

1.5 Source Code

All source code for this book is available on GitHub: `https://www.github.com/apress/practical-rust-projects-2e`.

When we include source code in the book, we only highlight the parts that are relevant to the point being discussed. The non-relevant parts will be omitted with a comment like this:

```
// ...
```

Therefore, not all code examples can be compiled successfully. To check the fully working example, check the source code on GitHub.

Most of the examples are developed and tested on a Linux (Ubuntu 22.04) machine. The Rust version is `stable-x86_64-unknown-linux -gnu - rustc 1.68.2`. The stable version is used as much as possible, but certain libraries might require us to use the nightly version.

1.6 Topics Not Covered

We've chosen to leave out some important Rust development topics as they don't generally fit in with the subject of this book.

Firstly, we're not going to go in depth into general unit testing for every project (though we will cover some integration testing). Basic unit tests are covered in introductory Rust books, and you can read about advanced unit testing (like mocking dependencies) in various other places, so we won't cover it here. We also don't go very in depth into `cargo` usage and other build tools; while we do have to sometimes reach for a less commonly used command to build our projects, we don't spend a lot of time on the many features `cargo` has. Finally, we also don't go into any IDE setup or Rust syntax highlighting features. We assume you're already familiar with the basics of working with Rust, which includes some form of editor. Besides, people tend to have very different preferences for editors, and rather than trying to list all the options we've left it up to you.

With that, we're ready to go. Let's dive in and put the Rust language to work.

## CHAPTER 2

Building a Command-line Program

Command-line programs, also known as CLIs (command-line interfaces), are probably one of the most natural applications of Rust. A CLI is a piece of software that operates from the command line. You interact with it through textual input and output. When you compile your first "Hello World" program, you are already building a command-line program. A typical command-line program usually takes arguments, flags, and sometimes standard input as the input. It then executes its main algorithm and outputs to the standard output or file. All these operations are well supported by the Rust standard library and third-party crates on crates.io, the Rust community's package registry.

There are a few advantages to building a CLI in Rust. Firstly, the rich collection of libraries on crates.io will enable you to achieve many things without reinventing the wheel. Secondly, its outstanding performance and safety guarantees compared to other popular scripting languages let you mitigate many performance bottlenecks and bugs. Finally, Rust programs can be compiled into a single, small, binary-containing, platform-specific machine code file for easy distribution so users don't need to have a language runtime on their system.

One example Rust CLI is the `ripgrep`[1] project. It is a line-oriented search tool like GNU `grep`, `ack`, or The Silver Searcher. The `ripgrep` crate has exceptional performance. It outperforms C-based GNU `grep` in many benchmarks.[2] The project utilizes many existing libraries on crates.io, like the `regex` crate (regular expression parsing, compiling, and execution) and the `clap` crate (command-line argument parsing). This is a perfect example of how Rust can be productive and produce performant software.

---

[1] https://github.com/BurntSushi/ripgrep
[2] https://blog.burntsushi.net/ripgrep/

© Shing Lyu and Andrew Rzeznik 2023
S. Lyu and A. Rzeznik, *Practical Rust Projects*, https://doi.org/10.1007/978-1-4842-9331-7_2

2.1 What Are You Building?

Cowsay is a funny little command-line program originally written in Perl. It takes a text message and renders an ASCII-art cow (looks more like a horse to me, to be honest) saying that message in a speech bubble (Figure 2-1). Although this program seems pretty useless, it's still quite popular among Unix server administrators, who use it to print light-hearted welcome messages to the user.

```
% cowsay "Hello world"
 _____
< Hello world >
 -------------
               \   ^__^
                \  (oo)_____
                   (__)\       )\/\
                       ||----w |
                       ||     ||
```

Figure 2-1. *Example output of* cowsay

Cowsay has a very simple algorithm, so by using it as an example, you can focus on the mechanisms and tooling to build a command-line program. Since cats are the "unofficial mascot of the internet,"[3] you are going to build a catsay tool that makes a cat say our message. Its features will include the following:

- Take a message string as the positional argument.[4]

- Take a -h/--help flag to print a help message.

- Take a -d/--dead flag that makes the cat's eyes become xx, which is the comical expression of dead eyes.

- Print in color.

- Print the error message to STDERR for error handling.

---

[3] "Why The Internet Chose Cats." *Thought Catalog*. https://thoughtcatalog.com/leigh-alexander/2011/01/why-the-internet-chose-cats/

[4] A positional argument is a CLI argument that is denoted by its location relative to other arguments. For example, for the cli call mycli a b c, arguments a, b, and c are arguments in positions 1, 2, and 3. However, a CLI might have arguments like mycli --argument value. Here value is NOT a positional argument; instead, it acts as a keyword argument, and will be assigned to the same keyword --argument regardless of other arguments in the command.

- Accept STDIN for piping input and pipe the output to other programs.

- Perform integration tests.

- Package and publish to crates.io.

2.2 Creating a Binary Project

Although you can simply write a `.rs` file and compile it with `rustc`, handling dependencies this way would be a nightmare. Therefore, we are going to use Cargo, Rust's package manager, to manage Rust projects and handle the dependencies for us. Cargo is capable of creating two kinds of projects, binary and library. A library is used to build a package that is intended to be used a building block for other programs. A binary is a standalone program that is used independently, which is what you are building in this chapter. To create a binary program named `catsay`, run the following command in your terminal:

```
$ cargo new --bin catsay
```

The `--bin` flag stands for "binary," which tells Cargo to create the package as a binary executable. You can omit the flag because it is the default. Once the command runs, you should see the following output:

```
Created binary (application) 'catsay' package
```

The command creates a `catsay` folder and some basic files, including a `git` repo, as follows:

```
catsay
|-- Cargo.toml
|-- .git
|-- .gitignore
+-- src
    +-- main.rs
```

Open `main.rs` in any text editor of your choice, and you should see a Hello World program template created by `cargo`. To run the Hello World example, first move inside the 'catsay' folder by running:

```
$ cd catsay
```

Then, run this to ask `cargo` to compile and run the program:

```
$ cargo run
```

You should see output similar to this:

```
Compiling catsay v0.1.0
 Finished dev [unoptimized + debuginfo] target(s) in 1.77s
   Running 'target/debug/catsay'
Hello, world!
```

2.3 Reading Command-line Arguments with `std::env::args`

The first thing you are going to implement is the code to print an ASCII-art cat that says whatever string you pass to it as an argument. The expected output looks like this:

```
$ cargo run -- "Hello I'm a cat"
   Compiling catsay v0.1.0
    Finished dev [unoptimized + debuginfo] target(s) in 1.18s
     Running 'target/debug/catsay 'Hello I'\"m a cat"
Hello I'm a cat
 \
  \
    /\_/\
   ( o o )
   =( I )=
```

Note The `--` following `cargo run` signifies the end of options (to `cargo`); all the arguments following the `--` will be passed to the main program in `main.rs`, which gets compiled into the binary `target/debug/catsay`. The final line of the Cargo output you see before your program output starts will be the following:

```
Running 'target/debug/catsay 'Hello I'\"m a cat"
```

The input "Hello I'm a cat" is passed to target/debug/catsay. Also, keep in mind that the "Compiling ...," "Finished ...," and "Running ..." lines are the logs from Cargo itself. Our program's output starts after the "Running ..." line.

Printing the text and the cat is pretty straightforward with println!(), but how do you actually read the command-line argument? Thanks to the Rust standard library, you can use std::env::args() to read the arguments. Replace the code in src/main.rs as follows:

```
// src/main.rs
fn main() {
    let message = std::env::args().nth(1)
        .expect("Missing the message. Usage: catsay <message>");
    println!("{}", message);
    println!(" \\");
    println!("  \\");
    println!("     /\\_/\\");
    println!("    ( o o )");
    println!("    =( I )=");
}
```

The std::env::args() function returns an iterator to the command-line arguments. You can call the .nth() function on it to get the *n*th argument. The zeroth argument is the name of the binary itself, catsay. The first argument is the string argument you are looking for, so you can call .nth(1) to retrieve it. The .nth() function might fail (e.g., if *n* is larger than the number of arguments). Because it returns an Option, you need to call .unwrap() or .expect() to get the contained value. Then, assign this value to a variable named message and print it out using println!(), along with the cat ASCII-art.

2.4 Handling Complex Arguments with Clap

The std::env::args() works well for small programs with only a few options. But once we have more and more options, it becomes cumbersome to parse them by hand. For example, you might want to have flags that have both a long and a short form; e.g., --version and -v. The long form is great for readability, while the short form saves you a few keystrokes when you are already familiar with the options. Or we might have optional arguments that take values (e.g., `--option value`). These types of arguments are prevalent in command-line tools, but implementing them from scratch every time is a real pain. One solution is to use the `clap` crate.[5] You declare the arguments' names and types in Rust code or YAML, then `clap` generates the command-line parser based on your specification. It also adds a few common options like the `--help` message.

To make our life even easier, we are going to use the *derive* feature of the `clap` crate. The `derive` feature adds a `derive` macro that automatically generates some parsing code on any struct. You can define a struct containing the arguments' names and type definitions, and then annotate it with `#[derive(Parser)]`. A macro defined by the `clap` crate automatically generates the required parser code for the struct from command-line arguments. The parser outputs the parsed arguments in the struct format you defined. It's much more declarative than writing all the parsing code by hand, and the parser output struct is easier to manipulate than individual variables.

To use `clap`, add the `clap` crate to the `[dependencies]` section in the `Cargo.toml` file by running

```
cargo add clap --features derive
```

Your Cargo.toml should look like the following (with some additional possible comments). Make sure that the Clap version is the same. You can always manually modify it if you messed up the preceding command, or if you don't feel like running it:

```
# Cargo.toml
[package]
name = "catsay"
version = "0.1.0"
edition = "2021"
[dependencies]
clap = { version = "4.2.1", features = ["derive"] }
```

Once you have added the dependency, change `src/main.rs` to the following:

```
// src/main.rs

use clap::Parser;

#[derive(Parser)]
```

---

[5] "Clap" stands for Command Line Argument Parser. https://clap.rs/

```
struct Options {
    message: String // [1]
}

fn main() {
    let options = Options::parse(); // [2]
    let message = options.message;
    println!("{}", message);
    // ... print the cat
}
```

In [1], you define a struct named Options (not to be confused with std::option::Option) that has one String field called message. The struct is annotated with the custom derive attribute #[derive(Parser)], indicating the struct is our command-line arguments definition. The Parser derive macro generates the argument parser accordingly. To use this parser to parse the arguments in main(), you call Options::parse(), which returns an Options struct populated with the parsed argument values. You can then access an individual argument by accessing the corresponding field of that struct (e.g., options.message).

Let's see how that looks in action. One nice thing you get for free from clap is an automatically generated --help command:

```
$ cargo run -- --help
    Finished dev [unoptimized + debuginfo] target(s) in 0.11s
     Running 'target/debug/catsay --help'
Usage: catsay <MESSAGE>

Arguments:
  <MESSAGE>

Options:
  -h, --help Print help
```

As you can see in the help message, there is a positional argument named <MESSAGE> under the Arguments section.

If you forget to provide the message argument, clap is smart enough to show an error message:

```
$ cargo run
```

```
    Finished dev [unoptimized + debuginfo] target(s) in 0.11s
     Running 'target/debug/catsay'
error: The following required arguments were not provided:
    <MESSAGE>

Usage: catsay <MESSAGE>

For more information, try '--help'.
```

However, the current help message only tells you that there is an argument called message, but does not say what it is for. It is also unclear to a new user what the format of the argument should be. To improve the help message, you can include a description for that field and add a default value. If the user does not provide the message argument, the default value will be used. The default value also serves as an example for the format of the field. To add the description and the default value for the message argument, modify the Options struct in src/main.rs as follows:

```
// src/main.rs

// ...
struct Options{
  #[clap(default_value = "Meow!")]
  /// What does the cat say?
  message: String,
}

// ...
```

The default value is set by annotating the field with #[clap(default_value=" Meow!")]. The next line looks like a comment in Rust, but it starts with a triple "/" instead of double. This is a documentation comment, which is usually used for Rust documentation (e.g., for generating documentation using the rustdoc tools). Clap uses it as the description for that field.

The help message now becomes:

```
Usage: catsay [MESSAGE]
```

Arguments:

[MESSAGE] What does the cat say? [default: Meow!]

Options:

-h, --help Print help

2.5 Adding Binary Flags

Clap also makes it easy to add *binary flags*, also known as toggles or switches, used to toggle a feature on and off. Cowsay has a flag called --dead (-d), which changes the cow's eye from an o symbol to x, a classic comical expression of dead characters. You can easily implement this by adding the following field to the Options struct in src/main.rs:

```
// src/main.rs
// ...
struct Options {
    // ...
    #[clap(short = 'd', long = "dead")]
    /// Make the cat appear dead
    dead: bool,
}
```

You add a field of type bool named dead. You can assign the long and short versions of the flag by annotating the field with:

```
#[clap(short = 'd', long= "dead")]
```

If you run cargo run -- --help now, the help message should include the newly added --dead flag:

```
Options:
  -d, --dead Make the cat appear dead
  -h, --help Print help
```

For now the flag is not doing anything. To change the behavior of the application based on the flag, you can modify the main() function in src/main.rs as follows:

```
// src/main.rs
//...
fn main() {
    let options = Options::parse();
    let message = options.message;

    let eye = if options.dead { "x" } else { "o" }; // [1]

    println!("{}", message);
    println!(" \\");
    println!(" \\");
    println!(" /\\_/\\");
    println!(" ( {eye} {eye} )"); // [2]
    println!(" =( I )=");
}
```

When a flag has the bool type, its value is determined by its presence. If the flag is present, its value will be true, otherwise, the value will be false. In [1] you assign the eye variable to either "o" or "x" based on whether options.dead is true or false. Then, in [2] you use println!() to substitute the "{eye}" part with the desired eye character.

Boolean options will be true if the flag is supplied or false otherwise, but there are other types of arguments. Another common case is taking a name and a value (e.g., -- name value). This will be discussed shortly in section 2.8. Let's first shift our focus to handling the output.

2.6 Printing to STDERR

Up until now, you've generated output using println!(), which prints to the standard output (STDOUT). However, in Unix-like systems, there is also the standard error (STDERR) stream for printing errors. Rust provides a STDERR equivalent of println!(), called eprintln!(). (The e prefix stands for "error.") For example, you can print an error if the user tries to make the cat say "Woof":

```
// src/main.rs
fn main() {
```

```rust
    // ...
    if message.to_lowercase() == "woof" {
        eprintln!("A cat shouldn't bark like a dog.")
    }
    // ...
}
```

You can test by redirecting the STDOUT and STDERR to separate files:

```
cargo run "woof" 1> stdout.txt 2> stderr.txt
```

You can print the content of these files using the `cat` command:

```
$ cat stdout.txt
woof
 \
  \
    /\_/\
   ( o o )
   =( I )=

$ cat stderr.txt
   Compiling catsay v0.1.0 (~/catsay)
    Finished dev [unoptimized + debuginfo] target(s) in 1.89s
     Running 'target/debug/catsay woof'
A cat shouldn't bark like a dog.
```

An interesting fact is that `cargo run` prints its log (i.e., the "Compiling…, Finished…" message) to STDERR. That's why you'll see the `cargo` logs before your own error message in the `stderr.txt` file. If you wish to print without a new line at the end of each line, you can use `print!()` and `eprint!()` instead.

2.7 Printing with Color

Nowadays, terminals (or terminal emulators) are usually capable of printing in color. So you can make `catsay` more colorful by using the `colored` crate. First, run

```
cargo add colored
```

to add the crate to the `Cargo.toml` file.

The crate should be added to your `Cargo.toml` file; confirm that the version matches the following:

```
// Cargo.toml
[dependencies]
// ...
colored = "2.0.0"
```

The `colored` crate defines a `Colorize` trait, which is implemented on a `&str` and `String`. This trait provides various chainable coloring functions, as follows:

- Coloring the text: `.red()`, `.green()`, `.blue()`, etc.

- Coloring the background: `.on_red()` (i.e., text on red background), `.on_green ()`, `.on_blue()`, etc.

- Brighter version: `.bright_red()`, `.on_bright_green()`, etc.

- Styling: `.bold()`, `.underline()`, `.italic()`, etc.

Modify `src/main.rs` as follows to use these coloring functions:

```
// src/main.rs
use colored::Colorize;
//...

fn main() {
    // ...
    println!(
        "{}",
        message.bright_yellow().underline().on_purple()
    );
    println!(" \\");
    println!(" \\");
    println!(" /\\_/\\");
    println!(" ( {eye} {eye} )", eye=eye.red().bold());
    println!(" =( I )=");
}
```

This makes the message text turn bright yellow with an underline, on a purple background. The cat's eyes are bloody red and bold. Run `cargo run` and the output should look like Figure 2-2.

```
% cargo run --
    Finished dev [unoptimized + debuginfo] target(s) in 0.06s
     Running `target/debug/catsay`
Meow!
  \
   \
     /\_/\
    ( o o )
    =( I )=
```

Figure 2-2. *Example output of the colored catsay*

2.8 Reading the Cat Picture from a File

Another common operation in command-line applications is reading from a file. Cowsay has an -f option that allows you to pass in a custom cow picture file. You are going to implement a simplified version of this to learn how to read files in Rust.

First, add an optional argument so we can specify the path of the picture file:

```
// src/main.rs
// ...
#[derive(Parser)]
struct Options {
    // ...

    #[clap(short = 'f', long = "file")]
    /// Load the cat picture from the specified file
    catfile: Option<std::path::PathBuf>,
}
// ...
```

There are a few important points about this code snippet:

- In the #[clap(...)] annotation, the short and long versions of the option (-f/--file) are named differently from the field name (catfile) in the Options struct. You can name the options and flags in user-friendly terms while keeping the variable names meaningful.

21

- Inside the Option<T> we use a std::path::PathBuf instead of a raw string. PathBuf can help us handle paths to files more robustly because it hides away many differences in how the operating systems represent paths (like forward versus back slashes).

- This catfile option is optional, so it's wrapped in an Option<T>. If the field is not provided, it will simply be an Option::None.

Note   There are other option types, like Vec<T>, which represents a list of arguments, and u64, which indicates the number of occurrences of a parameter; for example -v, -vv, and -vvv, which are commonly used to set the verbosity level.

Now if you run cargo run -- --help again, you should see a new section called "OPTIONS":

```
$ cargo run -- --help
...
Usage: catsay [OPTIONS] [MESSAGE]

Arguments:
  [MESSAGE]  What does the cat say? [default: Meow!]

Options:
  -d, --dead             Make the cat appears dead
  -f, --file <CATFILE>   Load the cat picture from the specified file
  -h, --help             Print help
```

Once you have the --file options in place, you can read the file at the specified path in main() to load the external file and render it. Modify src/main.rs as follows:

```
// src/main.rs

fn main() {
  // ...

  match &options.catfile {
    Some(path) => {
```

```rust
    let cat_template = std::fs::read_to_string(path)
      .expect(
        &format!("could not read file {:?}", path)
      );
    let eye = format!("{}", eye.red().bold());
    let cat_picture = cat_template.replace("{eye}", &eye);
    println!(
      "{}",
      message.bright_yellow().underline().on_purple()
    );
    println!("{}", &cat_picture);
  },
  None => {
    // ... print the cat as before
  }
 }
}
```

In this example, you use a match statement to check whether the options.catfile is a Some(PathBuf) or None. If it's None, just print out the default cat as before. But if it is a Some(PathBuf), use std::fs::read_to_string(path) to read the file contents to a string. You can see an example catfile in Listing 2-1. To support different eyes, a placeholder {eye} is written in place of the eyes. But you cannot simply use format!() to replace it with o or x, because format!() needs to know the formatting string at compile-time, but the cat_template string is loaded at runtime. Therefore, you need to use the String.replace() function to replace the eye placeholder with either o or x.

Listing 2-1. An example catfile

```
 \
  \                     / )
   \ (\__/)         ( (
     ){eye} {eye} (          ) )
   ={  Y   }=       / /
    )     `-------/ /
   (             /
    \            |
   ,'\        ,    ,'
   `-'\  ,---\   | \
     _) )    `. \ /
    (_/        ) )
              (_/
```

To test this out, save an example `catfile` like the one included here at the top directory of your project as `catfile.txt` and then run the following:

`cargo run -- -f catfile.txt`

2.9 Handling Errors

Until now, you have always used `unwrap()` or `expect()` on functions that might fail (e.g., `std::fs::read_to_string`). When the return value is a `Result:: Err`, using `unwrap()` on it causes the program to crash with `panic!()`. This is not always desirable, because you lose the ability to recover from the failure or provide a better error message so the user can figure out what happened. The `human_panic` crate[6] can help you produce a more human-readable panic message, but it's still hard-crashing the program. A better way is to use the `?` operator.

By changing `std::fs::read_to_string(path).expect(...)` to `std:: fs::read_to_string(path)?` (notice the `?` at the end), the code will behave like the following (Note: this change by itself won't compile yet):

`let cat_template = match std::fs::read_to_string(path) {`

---

[6]`https://github.com/rust-cli/human-panic`

```
    Ok(file_content) => file_content,
    Err(e) => return e.into(), // e: std::io::Error
};
```

The ? operator performs a match on the Result returned by read_to_string(). If the value is Ok(), it unwraps the value inside it. If the value is Err(), the function early returns with the error wrapped inside, possibly converted into the error type of the wrapping function. This is particularly useful if you have multiple potential points of failure in your function. Any one of them failing will cause an early return with the Err(), and the function caller can then handle the error or further escalate the error to its caller.

However, you might notice that the main() function currently doesn't return anything, and if you just start using the ? operator, the code won't compile. By using the ? operator, the main() function might return a std::io::Error. To handle this case, its function signature must be changed to fn main() -> Result<(), Box<dyn std::error::Error>>. If the main() function finishes successfully, it does not return anything; therefore, the type for T in Result<T, E> is (). The E is a weird-looking Box<dyn std::error::Error>. This is a boxed trait object, which means any type that implements the std::error::Error trait can be used here. You can think of the type as a container that holds any type that implements the std::error::Error trait. By using this trait object, you can use multiple ?'s in the main() function, with each returning a different kind of error, and they all will be placed inside the Box. Also, don't forget to return an Ok(()) at the end of the function to satisfy T in the function signature. Modify the src/main.rs file so the main() function has the correct function signature, as follows:

```
// src/main.rs
// ...
fn main() -> Result<(), Box<dyn std::error::Error>> {
    // ...
    let cat_template = std::fs::read_to_string(path)?
    // ...
    Ok(())
}
```

If you trigger an error now by providing an invalid file path, you should get this error message:

```
cargo run -- -f no/such/file.txt
    Finished dev [unoptimized + debuginfo] target(s) in 0.05s
     Running 'target/debug/catsay -f no/such/file.txt'
Error: Os { code: 2, kind: NotFound, message: "No such file or
    directory" }
```

If you want to define a more user-friendly error, you can use the anyhow crate (Listing 2.9). First, add the anyhow crate by running `cargo add anyhow`. It should be added to the `Cargo.toml` file like so:

```
// Cargo.toml
[package]
// ...

[dependencies]
// ...
anyhow = "1.0.70"
```

The anyhow crate provides a Context trait, which wraps the original error with a human-readable and user-facing explanation of the error, called context. You can choose to look into the machine-readable error to try to recover from it or simply present the human-readable context to the user. To use Context, you can call the `with_context()` function on `std::result::Result` so you can define a context message. This is how you can modify `src/main.rs` to add a context to the error:

```
// main.rs
use anyhow::{Context, Result};
// ...

fn main() -> Result<()> {
    // ...
    std::fs::read_to_string(path).with_context(
        || format!("Could not read file {:?}", path)
```

```
    )?
    // ...
    Ok(())
}
```

Notice that the E type in Result<T, E> is now gone. In actuality, the Result from std is shadowed by anyhow::Result. This struct contains the std::io::Error from read_to_string() and the "could not read file *filename*" error message (i.e., the context). The anyhow crate allows you to ignore the specifics of what error type you want to use, and easily put all the information in a single Result type with different context data.

Now the error message looks better:

```
$ cargo run -- -f no/such/file.txt

// ... regular cargo compile output
Error: Could not read file "catfiles.txt"

Caused by:
    No such file or directory (os error 2)
```

Tip   The anyhow crate and its context are much more than just printing a human-friendly error message. If we have a function call chain, we can have a nested chain of errors; each has a context that is relevant to the layer of abstraction. It also gives ergonomic ways to manipulate the chain of errors and backtraces. It also allows easier downcasting from a generic Error to a specific type, compared to the built-in std::error::Error. It's worth considering using anyhow if your command-line program grows more and more complex.

2.10 Piping to Other Commands

Piping is one of the most powerful features in Unix-like operating systems, in which the text output of one command can be sent directly to another command as an input. This allows a command-line program to be designed in a modular way and multiple programs to work together easily without specialized protocols. To make the catsay tool pipe-friendly, you need to make some modifications to the program.

Piping to STDOUT Without Color

The first obstacle in piping the output to other programs comes from the coloring. In a previous section, you used the `colored` crate to add color to the STDOUT output. It works by adding ANSI color escape codes to the output, and the terminal interprets these color codes and applies the colors onto the text. You can see the raw color codes by piping the output to a file:

```
cargo run > output.txt
```

The content of the `output.txt` should look like this:

```
^[[4;45;93mMeow!^[[0m
 \
  \
    /\_/\
   ( ^[[1;31mo^[[0m ^[[1;31mo^[[0m )
   =( I )=
```

While not all command-line tools handle these color codes, many do (and in fact, depending on your development environment, you might have a hard time finding a text editor that will show you the file as just shown). They may treat the color codes as raw characters, which would result in unexpected behavior. To avoid this kind of situation, you can set the NO_COLOR environment variable to 1 to turn off the coloring. This NO_COLOR environment variable is an informal standard[7] to toggle coloring on and off. The `colored` crate and many other command-line tools or libraries have already implemented this standard.

If you run NO_COLOR=1 cargo run, you should not see colors anymore. If you pipe the output to a file, you'll also notice that the color code is no longer present. This should come in handy if you wish to pipe a colored output to other command-line programs.

---

[7] https://no-color.org/

Accepting STDIN

Taking input from STDIN is another way to interact with other programs. You can make catsay take a string from STDIN as the message argument. You can create a switch --stdin that enables this behavior. For example, you can receive a string from the echo command-line tool, which prints a string to STDOUT:

```
echo -n "Hello world" | catsay --stdin
```

The -n flag for echo is to tell echo not to add a new line to the end of its STDOUT output.

You can add a Boolean flag --stdin into the Options struct in src/main.rs:

```
// src/main.rs
#[derive(Parser)]
struct Options {
    // ...
    #[clap(short = 'i', long = "stdin")]
    /// Read the message from STDIN instead of the argument
    stdin: bool,
}
```

Then in the main() function, whenever options.stdin is true (i.e., when --stdin is present), you need to read the message from STDIN. If options.stdin is false, keep the old behavior and read from the argument options.message. Modify the src/main.rs as follows to implement this new logic:

```
// src/main.rs
use std::io::{self, Read};
// ...

fn main() -> Result<()> {
    let options = Options::parse();
    let mut message = String::new(); // [2]
    if options.stdin {
        io::stdin().read_to_string(&mut message)?; // [1]
```

```
    } else {
        message = options.message;
    };

    // ...
}
```

On line [1], you read from STDIN and store it in a string `message`, using `io::stdin().read_to_string()`. The `read_to_string()` function does not return the string. Instead, it copies the string into the `&mut String` argument passed to it. Because the argument needs to be mutable so the function can modify it, you have to add a `mut` on [2].

This allows you to read the message from the standard input. Being able to interact with other programs through piping will make your program much more flexible and expandable. If you now pipe the output of `echo` into `catsay` you should be able to see something like this:

```
$ echo -n "Hello World" | cargo run -- --stdin
    Finished dev [unoptimized + debuginfo] target(s) in 0.03s
      Running 'target/debug/catsay --stdin'
Meow!
 \
  \
    /\_/\
   ( o o )
   =( I )=
```

2.11 Integration Testing

Automated testing is a vital tool to improve code quality and catch bugs early. Until now you have written everything in the `main()` function in `src/main.rs`. But that's not very testable. To unit test the business logic, it's better to split the functionality into a separate library crate, and let our `main.rs` file import and use that crate. Then you can unit test the other crate internally, which contains most of the business logic. These kinds of unit tests are relatively easy to write. You can follow the official Rust documentation or any introductory Rust book/course to learn how to unit test your code. In this section, we are going to focus on how to write an integration test that is specific to command-line programs.

Testing a command-line program usually involves running the command, then verifying its return code and its STDOUT/STDERR output. This can be easily done by writing a shell script. But writing a shell script means that you have to implement your own assertion and test result aggregation and reporting, which Rust already supports in its unit testing framework. The `std::process::Command` struct and `assert_cmd`[8] crate are going to help to test the program.

First, run the command

```
$ cargo add assert_cmd
```

to add the new crate. It should match the version here (update this if it does not match):

```
# Cargo.toml
[package]
name = "catsay"
version = "0.1.0"
edition = "2021"

[dependencies]
// ...
assert_cmd = "2.0.10"
```

Next, create a folder called `tests` in the project's root directory to hold the tests. Then, create a file named `integration_test.rs`, and paste following code into it:

```
// tests/integration\_test.rs
use std::process::Command; // Run programs
use assert_cmd::prelude::*; // Add methods on commands

#[test]
fn run_with_defaults() {
    Command::cargo_bin("catsay")
        .expect("binary exists")
        .assert()
        .success();
}
```

---

[8] https://crates.io/crates/assert_cmd

You brought in two different modules with the use command: the std::process::Command and assert_cmd::prelude::*. The std::process::Command crate gives you a Command struct that can help us run a program in a newly spawned process. The assert_cmd::prelude::* module imports a few useful traits that extend Command to be more suitable for integration testing, like cargo_bin(), assert(), and success(), which will be discussed shortly.

In the test function run_with_defaults(), you first initialize the command using Command::cargo_bin(), which takes a cargo-built binary name, in this case, "catsay." It will return an Err(CargoError) in cases like if the binary doesn't exist. Therefore, you need to unwrap it with .expect(). Then you call assert() on the command, which produces an Assert struct. The Assert struct gives you various utility functions for assertions of the status and output of the executed command. In this example, a very basic assertion success(), which checks if the command succeeded or not, is used.

You can run this test by running cargo test in the terminal. You should get an output like this:

```
$ cargo test
   Compiling catsay v0.1.0
    Finished dev [unoptimized + debuginfo] target(s) in 1.04s
     Running target/debug/deps/catsay-bf24a9cbada6cbf2

running 0 tests

test result: ok. 0 passed; 0 failed; 0 ignored; 0 measured; 0 filtered out

     Running target/debug/deps/integration_test- cce770f212f0b7be

running 1 test
test run_with_defaults ... ok

test result: ok. 1 passed; 0 failed; 0 ignored; 0 measured; 0 filterd out
```

The test you just wrote was not very exciting, nor did it test much more than making sure the code runs. The next step is to check the STDOUT and see if it contains the expected output. When you run the catsay program without any argument, it prints out a cat saying "Meow!", so you can verify if there is the string "Meow!" in the standard output. To do this, you can use the stdout() function from assert_cmd to get the STDOUT output. Then, use the utilities provided by the predicates crate to verify if the STDOUT string contains what you are looking for.

Add the predicates crate by running the following:

```
$ cargo add predicates
```

The Cargo.toml file should now look like this:

```
// Cargo.toml
[package]
// ...

[dependencies]
// ...
predicates = "3.0.2"
```

Then, modify tests/integration_test.rs as follows:

```
// tests/integration_test.rs
// ...
use predicates::prelude::*;

#[test]
fn run_with_defaults() {
    Command::cargo_bin("catsay")
        .expect("binary exists")
        .assert()
        .success()
        .stdout(predicate::str::contains("Meow!"));
}
```

You can test not only positive cases but also negative cases and error handling. For example, the next example checks if an invalid -f argument is handled correctly by the program:

```
#[test]
fn fail_on_non_existing_file()
    -> Result<(), Box<dyn std::error::Error>> {
    Command::cargo_bin("catsay")
        .expect("binary exists")
        .args(&["-f", "no/such/file.txt"])
        .assert()
```

```
        .failure();
    Ok(())
}
```

You pass an invalid file no/such/file.txt to the -f argument using the .args() function. This is equivalent to calling catsay -f no/such/file.txt. It is expected that the program will exit with an error because it fails to read the file. Therefore, you call .assert().failure() to check whether it actually fails.

2.12 Publishing and Distributing the Program

Once you are happy with the program, you might want to package it in a way that anyone can easily install and use it as a command in their shell. There are several ways you can do this. Each method has some trade-offs between the ease of use from the user's perspective and the effort to publish from the developer's perspective.

Install from Source

If you run cargo install –path ./ in the project folder, Cargo will compile the code in release mode, then install it into the ~/.cargo/bin folder. You can then append this path to your PATH environment variable, and the catsay command should be available in your shell.

Tip   The location where Cargo installs your program can be overridden by setting the CARGO_HOME environment variable. By default it's set to $HOME/.cargo.

You can publish the code onto any public code repository service like GitHub, or even publish it as a tarball on a web page you manage, then ask your user to download the source code and run cargo install --path ./. But there are several drawbacks to this method:

- It's hard for the user to find the program themselves.

- The user needs the Rust toolchain and a powerful computer to compile the source code.

- It requires knowledge of how to download the source code and compile it.

- It's difficult to manage different versions of the program, and upgrading is hard.

Publish to crates.io

Nowadays, most Rust programmers find packages on crates.io. So, to make your program easier to find, you can publish it to crates.io. It's very easy to publish your program on crates.io, and users can easily run `cargo install <crate name>` to download and install it.

To be able to publish on crates.io, you need to have an account and get an access token. Here are the steps to acquire one:

- Open `https://crates.io` in a browser.

- Click the **Log in with GitHub** link (You need a GitHub account. If you don't have one, sign up at `https://github.com/signup` first.)

- Add an email address and verify it.

- Once logged in to `crate.io`, click on your avatar on the top right and select Account Settings.

- Under the **API Tokens** section, you can generate a token with **New Token**. Copy that token and keep it handy.

Once you get the token, you can run `cargo login <token>` (replace `<token>` with the token you just created) to allow Cargo to access crates.io on your behalf. Then you can run `cargo package` in the project directory, which will package your program into a format that crates.io accepts. You can check the `target/package` folder to see what was generated.

There's one more step you need to take to publish to `crates.io`; you need to add a license and description field to the `Cargo.toml` file, and commit all of your code into your local git repository (if you need to, install git with `sudo apt install git`). The MIT/Apache licenses effectively let anyone use your code for any reason without having to keep it open source; if you're interested in what licenses are out there and available you can take a look at `https://choosealicense.com/licenses/`.

```
# Cargo.toml
[package]
// ...
license = "MIT OR Apache-2.0"
description = "A catsay cli"

// ...
```

Once the package is ready, simply run `cargo publish` to publish it to crates.io.

Keep in mind that once the code is uploaded to crates.io, it stays there forever and can't be removed or overwritten. To update the code, you need to increase the version number in `Cargo.toml` and publish a new version. If you accidentally publish a broken version, you can use the `cargo yank` command to "yank" it. That means your users can no longer create new dependencies against that version, but existing ones still work. And even though the version is yanked, the code still stays public. So never publish any secret (e.g., a password, an access token, or any personal information) in your crates.io package.

Although publishing to crates.io solves the discoverability issue and takes away the burden for the users to manually download your code, the code is still compiled from scratch every time a user installs. So the user still needs to have the full Rust toolchain installed on their machine. To make it even easier for the users, we can pre-compile the project into binaries and release them directly.

Building Binaries for Distribution

Rust compiles to machine code and by default links statically, so it doesn't require a heavy runtime like a Java virtual machine or a Python interpreter. If you run `cargo build --release`, Cargo compiles your program in release mode, which means a higher level of optimization and less verbose logging than the default debug mode. You'll find the built binary in `target/release/catsay`. This binary can then be shared with a user using the same platform as yours. They can execute it directly without installing anything.

Notice the assumption about ""using the same platform." This is because the binary might not run on another CPU architecture and operating system combination. In theory, you can cross-compile for a different target platform. For example, if you are running a Linux machine with an x86_64 CPU, we can compile our program for an embedded device with an ARM processor. Cross-compilation is generally simple with Rust, and there are many resources built right into Cargo; see `https://rust-lang.`

github.io/rustup/cross-compilation.html. There is also the cross[9] project, which solves this problem by wrapping all the cross-compilation environments into Docker images. This spins up a lightweight virtual machine in Docker, with all the cross-compilation toolchain and libraries configured to cross-compile the most portable binaries.

Alternatively, you can also use cargo-zigbuild.[10] This crate uses Zig, another programming language famous for its cross-compile capability, as a linker for Cargo. This makes cross-compiling much easier.

If you don't wish to set up a Linux machine with Docker just for the compilation, you can easily offload that task to a hosted continuous integration (CI) service. Nowadays, you can easily get free access to CI services like Aws CodePipelines and connect them with GitHub. The trust[11] project provides templates to set up Travis CI and AppVeyor CI pipelines to build your binaries. For Linux builds, it actually uses cross underneath. For Windows builds, it relies on the Windows-based AppVeyor CI.

Once the binaries are built, you can put them online for users to download. But usually different platforms have their specific package format, which comes with package repositories and package managers. Users can effortlessly search, download, install, and update binaries using them. For example, macOS has Homebrew formulae, Debian uses apt for .deb packages, and RedHat Linux hat uses yum for .rpm packages. It's a good idea to submit your program into each package repository for discoverability and easier updating. Different platforms have different ways of packaging and submission, so they are out of scope for this book. You can find some helper tools on crates.io to help you pack for a specific format; for example, cargo-deb and cargo-rpm.

---

[9] https://github.com/rust-embedded/cross
[10] https://crates.io/crates/cargo-zigbuild
[11] https://github.com/japaric/trust

2.13 Conclusion

In this chapter, you learned how to build a command-line program in Rust. You started with how to create a binary project and read simple command-line arguments. Then you improved the command-line parser and started to parse more complex arguments with Clap. You looked at how to add positional arguments, binary flags, and options; and how to add description and default values to them. You also learned how to build common command-line features like coloring, reading from a file, accepting standard input, and output to standard output and standard error. Then you ran integration tests on your command-line program. Finally, you saw various ways to publish and distribute your program.

## CHAPTER 3

Creating Graphical User Interfaces (GUIs)

Command-line tools are handy in situations that don't require too much visual interaction, like batch processing. But because a command-line program can only handle text input/output and files, it is not ideal if 3D (or even 2D) visual interaction is required. So, in this chapter you'll break out of the constraints of the command line and implement graphical user interfaces (GUIs).

The goal of this chapter is to show you how to build a cross-platform desktop application with a GUI. Although there are frameworks like Electron,[1] which allows you to build a desktop app in HTML, CSS, and JavaScript, they are actually wrapping a browser engine inside. Therefore, the developer experience will be closer to building a website or web app than to coding a native desktop application. In this chapter, you'll use the GTK framework, which showcases the experience of building a native application in Rust.

As a bridge between command-line programs and actual GUI apps, you'll first learn about the text-based user interface (TUI). A TUI looks like a GUI, but it's drawn with text characters. Thus, it can be created in a terminal environment. But because a TUI draws with text characters, the resolution is low, and the screen real estate is very limited. Nevertheless, a TUI is a good way to understand the high-level concept of event-driven architecture that is common in GUI programs. Once you acquire the knowledge of how a TUI program is structured, you can apply that knowledge in implementing a full-fledged GUI program in GTK.

---

[1] https://electronjs.org/

© Shing Lyu and Andrew Rzeznik 2023
S. Lyu and A. Rzeznik, *Practical Rust Projects*, https://doi.org/10.1007/978-1-4842-9331-7_3

3.1 What Are You Building?

To avoid the distraction of complex business logic and to focus on the structure of the code, you'll build a simplified version of the catsay program as a TUI and GUI. For the TUI, you'll build the following:

- An interactive form to receive the message. (Figure 3-1)

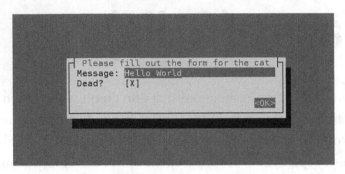

Figure 3-1. *The input form of the TUI program*

- A checkbox for the --dead option.
- A dialog box that shows a cat saying the message. (Figure 3-2)

Figure 3-2. *The dialog box of the TUI program*

You'll then build a GUI that has the same input as the TUI program. But this time, instead of the ASCII-art cat, a photo of a real cat will be used (Figure 3-3).

Figure 3-3. *The GUI program with a photo of a cat (cat image from* `https://pix-abay.com/photos/cat-kitten-to-sit-isolated-red-2669554/,` `Pixabay license)`

You'll be building the GUI using gtk3-rs, which is a Rust binding for the GTK3 library and its underlying libraries. You'll first build the GUI in pure Rust code and then switch to Glade, a user interface design tool that can help you design the layout in a more intuitive and easy-to-manage way.

3.2 Building a Text-based User Interface

In Chapter 2, you used `println!()` for most of the output. The problem with it is that you can only output one line at a time. Although you can create ASCII-art images by carefully aligning the lines you print, it is hard to scale if you want to draw windows, dialog boxes, and buttons—not to mention handle keyboard input and mouse clicks and have the UI react to these inputs. Thankfully, a category of libraries known as text-based user interface libraries can help you build UI components easily. One example is the ncurses library for Unix-like systems. The ncurses name stands for "new curses" because it was the "new" (in the 1990s) version of the old curses library in System V Release 4.0 (SVr4). You'll be using the cursive crate. It hides away many low-level details, so it's very easy to work with.

The cursive crate provides an abstraction layer over different TUI backend libraries. In this chapter, you'll use the default ncurses backend for simplicity, but if you need cross-system support for Windows and/or macOS, you can choose other backends, like pancurses or crossterm. To use ncurses you need to install it on your system. On Ubuntu, run the following command in the shell:

```
$ sudo apt install libncursesw5-dev
```

You can create a new project with cargo new and add the cursive crate to Cargo.toml by running these commands:

```
$ cargo new catsay-tui
$ cd catsay-tui
$ cargo add cursive
```

The Cargo.toml file should contain the cursive crate in the dependencies section. The version of cursive in your application may be different; you should double-check the version and set it to match the example.

```
# Cargo.toml
# ...
[dependencies]
cursive = "0.20.0"
```

Now, replace the src/main.rs file with this minimal skeleton code:

```
// src/main.rs

fn main() {
    let mut siv = cursive::default();

    siv.run(); // starting the event loop
}
```

In the main() function, you create a Cursive root object with cursive::default() and start the event loop with siv.run(). The event loop is a fundamental concept in building user interfaces. For a command-line program, interactions are usually limited to one input and one output at a time. If you need to take user input, you have to pause the execution of the program and wait for the user input to finish. No other operations or output can be processed at that time. But a GUI program might be listening to multiple inputs from the keyboard and mouse. Since you can't predict which input will be triggered first, the program (conceptually) runs in an infinite loop that handles whatever input that is triggered first. If you have registered an event handler for that particular event, then the event loop will invoke the handler when that event happens. For example, if you have an OK button in a dialog box, clicking it will trigger a button-click event, which might be handled by a handler function that closes this dialog box.

3.3 Showing a Dialog Box

If you now run `cargo run`, you will see a blue screen (Figure 3-4). But that's not very exciting. To close the program you have to press `Ctrl+C` in the terminal where you are running `cargo run`, which will send an interrupt signal and force it to terminate. To display the cat ASCII-art on the screen, you can add the code listed below to `src/main.rs`:

Figure 3-4. *An empty* `Cursive` *screen*

```
// src/main.rs

use cursive::views::TextView;

fn main() {
    let mut siv = cursive::default();
```

```
    let cat_text = "Meow!
 \\
 \\
   /\\_/\\
   ( o o )
   =( I )=";

    // Declaring the app layout
    siv.add_layer(TextView::new(cat_text));

    siv.run();
}
```

Notice that before calling `siv.run()`, you set up the content of the app with the following:

```
siv.add_layer(TextView::new(cat_text));
```

You created a TextView to hold the cat ASCII-art. Views are the main building blocks of a cursive TUI program. There are many pre-built views in the cursive::views module; for example, buttons, checkboxes, dialogs, progress bars, etc. You can also implement custom views by implementing the View trait on your struct. TextView is used to hold a static text, which was passed in as a constructor parameter. But the newly created TextView is not visible yet because it is not part of the main program. You can add it as a layer to the main cursive program, siv, by calling siv.add_layer(). Cursive uses layers to create a stacked view of the components (i.e., Views). Layers are stacked together such that the top-most one will be active and can receive input. They are also rendered with a shadow, so they look like 3D layers stacked together. You can see a TextView in action in Figure 3-5.

Figure 3-5. *A TextView showing the cat ASCII-art*

3.4 Handling Simple Keyboard Inputs

Up until now the TUI program has only produced output and can't handle any input.
A good starting point for input is to make the program respond to the ESC key press
by closing itself after cleaning up its state gracefully (currently the only way to close
our program is by using Ctrl+C or closing the containing terminal, both of which will
abruptly stop the program without any cleanup). Modify the src/main.rs file as follows:

```
// src/main.rs
// ...
use cursive::event::Key;

fn main() {
    let mut siv = cursive::default();
    let cat_text = // ...

    siv.add_layer(TextView::new(cat_text));

    // Listen to Key::Esc and quit
    siv.add_global_callback(Key::Esc, |s| s.quit());

    siv.run();
}
```

In the code, you set up a global callback with siv.add_global_callback(). This
function takes two arguments: an event and a callback function. Whenever the event
occurs, the callback function will be executed. The cursive::event::Key::Esc is
assigned as the event, which is triggered when the ESC key is pressed. In the callback
argument, you passed a closure, |s| s.quit(). The s argument is a mutable reference to
the Cursive struct itself, so s.quit() will gracefully quit the program.

The callback does not execute right away. The siv.add_global_callback() function
also does not block the execution. The line simply registers the callback and continues
the execution of the program. When the next line siv.run() is executed, the event loop
starts and waits for keypresses and mouse clicks. By using a non-blocking event-based
architecture, the user interface becomes more responsive to user input, and you are not
limited to one kind of interaction at a time. You can set up multiple event handlers so
they can handle different kinds of events regardless of the order. You will see more event
handlers in the coming sections.

3.5 Adding a Dialog

To give the program a more sophisticated look and feel, you can wrap the TextView with a Dialog (Figure 3-5). Change the file src/main.rs like this:

```
// src/main.rs
use cursive::views::{Dialog, TextView};

fn main() {
    let mut siv = cursive::default();
    let cat_text = // ...

    siv.add_layer(
        Dialog::around(TextView::new(cat_text))
            .button("OK", |s| s.quit())
    );

    siv.run();
}
```

You use Dialog::around() to wrap the TextView, which will add a Dialog around the TextView (Figure 3-6). You can also add a button to the dialog with the label "OK" and a callback (|s| s.quit()). This callback will be triggered when the button is clicked. One nice feature of Cursive is that it supports keyboard and mouse interaction out-of-the-box, so you can close the program by either hitting the ENTER (Return) key when the focus is on the button or by double-clicking the button with a mouse.

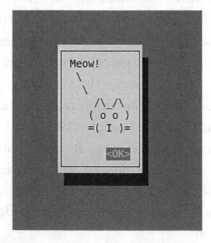

Figure 3-6. *Displaying a dialog with an OK button*

Since it's very common to wrap a `TextView` inside `Dialog` to show a text dialog, `cursive` offers a shorthand syntax, `Dialog::text()`. So, you can rewrite the line in `src/main.rs` like this:

```
siv.add_layer(
    Dialog::text(cat_text).button("OK", |s| s.quit())
);
```

3.6 Multi-step Dialogs

You are not limited to just one static layer at a time. You can actually build a multistep flow. In the first step, the user is prompted to fill in a form and press "OK," then you hide the form and display the cat ASCII-art using the information provided in the form. Modify the `src/main.rs` file like in Listing 3-1.

Listing 3-1. Multi-step form

```
// src/main.rs

use cursive::traits::Nameable;
use cursive::views::{Checkbox, Dialog, EditView, ListView};
use cursive::Cursive;

// Wrap all form fields value in one struct
// so we can pass them around easily
struct CatsayOptions<'a> {
    message: &'a str,
    dead: bool,
}

fn input_step(siv: &mut Cursive) {
    siv.add_layer(
        Dialog::new()
            .title("Please fill out the form for the cat")
            .content(
                ListView::new()
                    .child(
                        "Message:",
```

```rust
                    EditView::new().with_name("message")
                )
                .child(
                    "Dead?",
                    Checkbox::new().with_name("dead")
                ),
            )
        .button("OK", |s| {
            let message = s
                .call_on_name(
                    "message",
                    |t: &mut EditView| t.get_content()
                ).unwrap();
            let is_dead = s
                .call_on_name(
                    "dead",
                    |t: &mut Checkbox| t.is_checked()
                ).unwrap();
            let options = CatsayOptions {
                message: &message,
                dead: is_dead,
            };
            result_step(s, &options) // [2]
        }),
    );
}

fn result_step(siv: &mut Cursive, options: &CatsayOptions) {
    let eye = if options.dead { "x" } else { "o" };

    let cat_text = format!(
        "{msg}
```

```
      \\
       \\
        /\\_/\\
      ( {eye} {eye} )
      =( I )=",
          msg = options.message,
          eye = eye
      );

      siv.pop_layer(); // [3]
      siv.add_layer( // [4]
          Dialog::text(cat_text)
              .title("The cat says...")
              .button("OK", |s| s.quit()),
      );
}

fn main() {
    let mut siv = cursive::default();

    input_step(&mut siv); // [1]
    siv.run();
}
```

This example is slightly more complex, so let's break it down a little bit. The following is the high-level flow:

- main(): Creates Cursive object and calls input_step()

- input_step(): Sets up the form layout and callbacks

- result_step(): When "OK" is clicked, hides the form and shows the cat dialog

In the main() function, instead of directly setting up the layout with add_layer(), you move all the layout code into the input_step(&mut siv) function ([1]).

Inside input_step() you set up a form, which will be discussed in detail later. Notice that it has a button called "OK." In the callback function of the button, you call result_step(s, &options)([2]), which handles the next step.

In result_step(), you first hide the form by calling siv.pop_layer() ([3]). This "pops" the existing layer (i.e., the form layer) from the layers stack, and then you add the layer that displays the cat in a TextView ([4]). These actions combined allow for a nice dialog that works the user through multiple stages.

3.7 Reading User Input

Now you understand how the program goes from one layer to another, but how does the user's input (the message and the "Dead?" flag) get carried from the form to the cat picture dialog? If you take a closer look at the input_step() in Listing 3-1, you will find that the step consists of two parts. First, you set up the input fields with the following code:

```
siv.add_layer(
    Dialog::new()
        .title("Please fill out the form for the cat")
        .content(
            ListView::new()
                .child(
                    "Message:",
                    EditView::new().with_id("message")
                )
                .child(
                    "Dead?",
                    Checkbox::new().with_id("dead")
                ),
        )
)
```

As before, you create a layer and add a Dialog element to it. You set the content of the Dialog using .content(). Inside the Dialog you create two input elements, an EditView and a Checkbox. To place them properly, you wrap them in a ListView, which is a layout container that will display its children in a scrollable list. Notice that you call .with_name() on the EditView and Checkbox, which gives each of them a unique name that you can use to identify and retrieve them later.

Then you add a button to the Dialog like so:

```
Dialog::new()
    .title(...)
    .content(...)
    .button("OK", |s| {
        let message = s
            .call_on_name(
                "message",
                |t: &mut EditView| t.get_content()
            ).unwrap();
        let is_dead = s
            .call_on_name(
                "dead",
                |t: &mut Checkbox| t.is_checked()
            ).unwrap();
        let options = CatsayOptions {
            message: &message,
            dead: is_dead,
        };
        result_step(s, &options)
    }),
```

In this button's callback, you read the message and the status of the "Dead?" flag, collect them into a CatsayOptions struct, then pass the CatsayOptions struct to the result_step() to display the final output. This is when the names come in handy. The first argument ("message") of the s.call_on_name() call is the name you just set for the first widget. call_on_name() will try to find the element and pass its mutable reference into the callback closure (the second argument). Inside the closure you use t.get_content() (where t is &mut EditView) to get the text inside the EditView. You might fail to find any element with the given name, in which case call_on_name() returns an Option wrapping the return value of the closure, which is why you have to unwrap it to get the actual string. You do similarly for the Checkbox. By calling is_checked() on a Checkbox, it will return a Boolean indicating whether the checkbox is checked or not.

Then you simply wrap the two values into a `CatsayOptions` struct so you can pass them to the `result_step()`. Inside the `result_step()` (Listing 3-1), you display the cat ASCII-art in a `Dialog` using the options from the previous step.

There are many more callbacks and UI patterns to talk about. But a TUI is relatively limited due to its low resolution. There is very limited space on the screen if you have to render each pixel as a character. Also, it's not very aesthetically pleasing for modern users, sometimes even a little bit intimidating. However, a TUI is still very useful if you want to build some small tools that require simple interactions. Also, it might be useful on servers with only SSH access. Due to these limitations, you are going to conclude the journey in TUIs and move on to a GUI, or graphical user interface.

3.8 Moving to Graphical User Interfaces (GUIs)

In the next half of this chapter, you'll be building a GUI version of the TUI program you just built. This time you'll be able to display a real cat photo! For this purpose, you are going to use the `gtk` crate, which is a Rust binding for the GTK3 library. GTK, originally known as GTK+ and GIMP Toolkit, is a free and open-source widget toolkit for building GUIs. It is written in C and supports multiple platforms, like Linux, Microsoft Windows, and macOS. It provides many UI widgets out of the box so you can easily assemble them into a GUI program. Many popular programs like the GNOME desktop environment use it.

Note   Currently, there are two active versions of GTK: GTK3 and GTK4. GTK4 has quite a few breaking changes from GTK3, so it requires quite some effort to migrate from GTK3 to GTK4. At the time of writing, GTK4 doesn't have an official visual user interface designer tool like Glade, which will be discussed in the "Using Glade to Design the UI" section. Also, GTK3 is still being actively maintained and has a long track record of powering popular GUI programs like the GNOME desktop environment. Therefore, we are sticking with GTK3 in this book.

The Rust bindings for GTK3 are in the `gtk` crate on crates.io, while the GTK4 binding is in the `gtk4` crate. Do not confuse it with the name `gtk-rs`, which is the umbrella project that covers `gtk` and `gtk4`. Sometimes the projects are referred to as `gtk3-rs` and `gtk4-rs`, which are their GitHub repository names.

There are many other GUI toolkits for Rust, but you'll use `gtk-rs` for its popularity and maturity. It's one of the most downloaded GUI crates on crates.io, and it is one of the most mature libraries in the domain because of the maturity of GTK itself. It can potentially support cross-platform development (by installing GTK libraries for the target platform). An additional benefit of using `gtk-rs` is its nice documentation and community support. Because it's a wrapper around the C-based GTK library, whenever the Rust documentation is not clear, you can always find the C documentation and many discussions online. We'll discuss alternatives in the section "Alternatives."

3.9 Creating a Window

First, you'll create a window with GTK. `Gtk3-rs` relies on the system GTK library. To install it on Ubuntu,[2] run the following command in a terminal:

```
$ sudo apt install libgtk-3-dev
```

Then, create a new project with `cargo` and add gtk as a dependency:

```
$ cargo new catsay-gui
$ cd catsay-gui
$ cargo add gtk --features v3_24
```

Then add the gtk crate to `Cargo.toml` by directly editing the file:

```
# Cargo.toml
[package]
name = "catsay-gui"
version = "0.1.0"
edition = "2021"

[dependencies.gtk]
gtk = { version = "0.17.1", features = ["v3_24"] }
```

---

[2] You can find installation instructions for other platforms here: `https://www.gtk.org/docs/installations/`.

Because gtk3-rs relies on the system gtk library, it uses the Cargo "feature" to control which version of the system gtk library it is targeting. Therefore, we use an advanced Cargo.toml syntax to pass these version configurations to the gtk dependency. The version = "0.17.1" is specifying the version of the gtk crate itself, while the features=["v3_24"] line is specifying the version of the system gtk library. In case you don't know which version of the system gtk library was installed, you can run the following command to find out:

```
$ apt list libgtk-3-0
# OR
$ dpkg -l libgtk-3-0
```

You now have done the groundwork and are ready to code. Open the src/main.rs file and copy-paste the following code:

```
// src/main.rs

use gtk::prelude::*;
use gtk::{Application, ApplicationWindow};

fn main() {
    let app = Application::new(
        Some("com.shinglyu.catsay-gui"),
        Default::default()
    );

    app.connect_activate(|app| {
        let window = ApplicationWindow::new(app);
        window.set_title("Catsay");
        window.set_default_size(350, 70);

        window.show_all();
    });
    app.run();
}
```

You might notice that the code has a very similar structure to that of the TUI program. First, you created a GTK application using Application::new(). You have to set an application ID in the first argument. A GTK application ID follows the "reverse DNS" style.

So, let's say the application has a public website at `https://catsay-gui.shinglyu.com`; you should use `com.shinglyu.catsay-gui` for the ID. When the application starts up, the `activate` event is triggered. You should set up the application's content inside the `activate` event handler. In this case, you create an `ApplicationWindow` and set its title and size. Then `window.show_all()` shows the window that was initially hidden when created. Finally, `app.run()` starts the main event loop of the application and shows the window.

Now if you run `cargo run`, you should see an empty window like in Figure 3-7.

Figure 3-7. *An empty GTK window*

3.10 Displaying an Image

Now put a cat image in the window by adding the code in Listing 3-2 to `src/main.rs`.

Listing 3-2. Showing text and a cat picture

```
// src/main.rs
use gtk::{Application, ApplicationWindow,
    Box as GtkBox, Image, Label, Orientation};
// ...

fn main() {
    // ...

    app.connect_activate(|app| {
        let window = ApplicationWindow::new(app);

        // ...

        // [1]
        let layout_box = GtkBox::new(Orientation::Vertical, 0);

        let label = Label::new(
            Some("Meow!\n      \\\n        \\")
```

```
    );
    layout_box.add(&label);

    // [2]
    let cat_image = Image::from_file(
        "./images/cat.png"
    );
    layout_box.add(&cat_image);

    window.add(&layout_box); // [3]

    window.show_all();
});

// ...
}
```

Figure 3-8. *Displaying the text and text image in a GTK window*

The code example is trying to display a text (Label) and an image (Image). But to properly control the layout, you need to wrap them in a GtkBox. This is not a std::box::Box that you are probably already familiar with. A GtkBox is a container that can display widgets in a single row or column. On line [1], you create a box with Orientation::Vertical, which displays the widgets from top to bottom in a vertical column. The second parameter 0 is the spacing between each widget, which is set to none.

Then you create the text in a Label, which is similar to TextView in the TUI example. You also created an Image using Image::from_file(). This creates a GTK image widget that shows a PNG file. You need to create a folder in the same project called images and put the cat.png image in there. These two elements are not showing yet, and you have to add them to the container with layout_box.add(&label) and layout_box.add(&cat_image), then add the layout box to the window (window.add(&layout_box)).

Before you can run this code, you should create the top-level directory images and then save an image as images/cat.png. Now run cargo run, and the new window should look like Figure 3-8.

Tip   You defined the layout of the widgets in Rust code. But sometimes, when the widgets are positioned incorrectly, it's pretty hard to figure out why they go astray just by reading the code. GTK3 has a visual debugger so you can see the widget tree and have them highlighted in the application window. Simply run your GTK application with the environment variable GTK_DEBUG set to interactive. For example, GTK_DEBUG=interactive cargo run. You'll see the program starts along with the debugger window (Figure 3-9). In the Objects tab in the debugger, you can see the hierarchy of the widgets. If you click on one of the widgets, that widget will flash in the main application window to show its position and size. In Figure 3-10 the GtkLabel widget is selected, and you can see it is being highlighted. This can help us debug and tweak the layout of the widgets much easier.

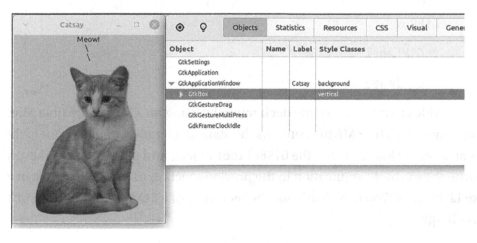

Figure 3-9. *GTK debugger that highlights the GtkBox*

Figure 3-10. GTK debugger that highlights the GtkLabel

3.11 Using Glade to Design the UI

In Listing 3-2, you built the UI procedurally. That means you have to use code to do everything, including creating widgets, putting them in containers, putting containers into bigger containers, attaching them to the window, and displaying them. This way of working is very error-prone and hard to maintain as the program grows larger. An alternative is to define the UI layout declaratively and let GTK figure out how to create the underlying widgets and containers. The hierarchy of the widgets should be like the following:

- GtkApplicationWindow
  - GtkBox
    * GtkLabel
    * GtkImage

GTK provides a way to make the declaration by using an XML (eXtensible Markup Language) markup. The XML file contains the static declaration of the layout of the widgets and can be loaded using the GTKBuilder object, and it builds the UI at runtime. If you write the example application in the previous section in the XML format, it will look like Listing 3-3. You can clearly see the hierarchy of a GtkBox containing a GtkLabel and a GtkImage.

Listing 3-3. An example of Glade XML

```xml
<?xml version="1.0" encoding="UTF-8"?>
<interface>
  <requires lib="gtk+" version="3.12"/>
  <object class="GtkApplicationWindow" id="applicationwindow1">
    <child>
      <object class="GtkBox" id="box1">
        <property name="orientation">vertical</property>
        <child>
          <object class="GtkLabel" id="label1">
            <property name="label" translatable="yes">
                Meow!
            </property>
          </object>
        </child>
        <child>
          <object class="GtkImage" id="image1">
            <property name="pixbuf">./images/cat.png</property>
          </object>
        </child>
      </object>
    </child>
  </object>
</interface>
```

But writing this XML by hand is very tedious. Instead, you can use Glade (Figure 3-11), the UI design tool that comes with GTK3, to generate the XML. You can install Glade with this command on Ubuntu: `sudo apt install glade`. In Glade, you can drag and drop widgets in a WYSIWYG (What-You-See-Is-What-You-Get) editor. You can also tweak the parameters of individual widgets and get instant feedback. With Glade (and the XML layout definition), you can separate the visual presentation from the behavior. You can keep most of the visual design and layout in the XML and leave only event handler logic in Rust code.

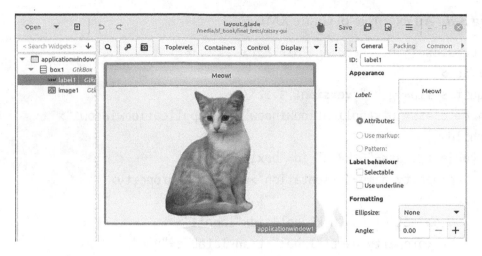

Figure 3-11. *Glade UI design tool*

So, let's build a simple form with Glade. You can start by playing around with the Glade UI design tool, looking at the example in Listing 3-3. Laying out basic forms in Glade, you can drag and drop a form that looks like Figure 3-12; its widgets are organized as in Figure 3-13. Then you can click the menu **File**, then **Save as…** to save this to a new XML file. You won't actually use this file (to ensure the demo works properly you'll copy-paste the XML file in Listing 3-4), so you can save it wherever just to practice.

Figure 3-12. *Building the form with Glade*

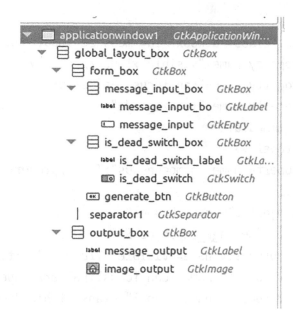

Figure 3-13. *Widget hierarchy of the form*

Listing 3-4. Glade layout XML

```xml
<?xml version="1.0" encoding="UTF-8"?>
<!-- Generated with glade 3.18.3 -->
<interface>
  <requires lib="gtk+" version="3.12"/>
  <object class="GtkApplicationWindow" id="applicationwindow1">
    <property name="can_focus">False</property>
    <property name="title" translatable="yes">Catsay</property>
    <child>
      <object class="GtkBox" id="global_layout_box">
        <property name="visible">True</property>
        <property name="can_focus">False</property>
        <property name="orientation">vertical</property>
        <child>
          <object class="GtkBox" id="form_box">
            <property name="visible">True</property>
            <property name="can_focus">False</property>
            <property name="orientation">vertical</property>
```

```
<child>
  <object class="GtkBox" id="message_input_box">
    <property name="visible">True</property>
    <property name="can_focus">False</property>
    <property name="resize_mode">
        immediate
    </property>
    <property name="homogeneous">True</property>
    <child>
      <object class="GtkLabel"
        id="message_input_bo">
        <property name="visible">True</property>
        <property name="can_focus">False</property>
        <property name="label" translatable="yes">
            What does the cat say:
        </property>
      </object>
      <packing>
        <property name="expand">False</property>
        <property name="fill">True</property>
        <property name="position">0</property>
      </packing>
    </child>
    <child>
      <object class="GtkEntry" id="message_input">
        <property name="visible">True</property>
        <property name="can_focus">True</property>
      </object>
      <packing>
        <property name="expand">False</property>
        <property name="fill">True</property>
        <property name="position">1</property>
      </packing>
    </child>
  </object>
```

```
    <packing>
      <property name="expand">False</property>
      <property name="fill">True</property>
      <property name="position">0</property>
    </packing>
  </child>
  <child>
    <object class="GtkBox" id="is_dead_switch_box">
      <property name="visible">True</property>
      <property name="can_focus">False</property>
      <property name="homogeneous">True</property>
      <child>
        <object class="GtkLabel"
          id="is_dead_switch_label">
          <property name="visible">True</property>
          <property name="can_focus">False</property>
          <property name="label" translatable="yes">
              Dead?
          </property>
        </object>
        <packing>
          <property name="expand">False</property>
          <property name="fill">True</property>
          <property name="position">0</property>
        </packing>
      </child>
      <child>
        <object class="GtkSwitch" id="is_dead_switch">
          <property name="visible">True</property>
          <property name="can_focus">True</property>
        </object>
        <packing>
          <property name="expand">False</property>
          <property name="fill">True</property>
          <property name="position">1</property>
```

```
              </packing>
            </child>
          </object>
          <packing>
            <property name="expand">False</property>
            <property name="fill">True</property>
            <property name="position">1</property>
          </packing>
        </child>
        <child>
          <object class="GtkButton" id="generate_btn">
            <property name="label" translatable="yes">
                Generate
            </property>
            <property name="visible">True</property>
            <property name="can_focus">True</property>
            <property name="receives_default">
                True
            </property>
          </object>
          <packing>
            <property name="expand">False</property>
            <property name="fill">True</property>
            <property name="position">2</property>
          </packing>
        </child>
      </object>
      <packing>
        <property name="expand">False</property>
        <property name="fill">True</property>
        <property name="position">0</property>
      </packing>
    </child>
    <child>
      <object class="GtkSeparator" id="separator1">
```

```
            <property name="visible">True</property>
            <property name="can_focus">False</property>
          </object>
          <packing>
            <property name="expand">False</property>
            <property name="fill">True</property>
            <property name="position">1</property>
          </packing>
        </child>
        <child>
          <object class="GtkBox" id="output_box">
            <property name="visible">True</property>
            <property name="can_focus">False</property>
            <property name="orientation">vertical</property>
            <child>
              <object class="GtkLabel" id="message_output">
                <property name="visible">True</property>
                <property name="can_focus">False</property>
                <property name="ellipsize">end</property>
              </object>
              <packing>
                <property name="expand">False</property>
                <property name="fill">True</property>
                <property name="position">0</property>
              </packing>
            </child>
            <child>
              <object class="GtkImage" id="image_output">
                <property name="can_focus">False</property>
                <property name="pixbuf">images/cat.png</property>
              </object>
              <packing>
                <property name="expand">False</property>
                <property name="fill">True</property>
                <property name="position">1</property>
```

```
            </packing>
          </child>
        </object>
        <packing>
          <property name="expand">False</property>
          <property name="fill">True</property>
          <property name="position">2</property>
        </packing>
      </child>
    </object>
  </child>
</object>
</interface>
```

Now you can start a new project for the Glade-based GUI. Create a new Rust project and then add the gtk crate as before:

```
$ cargo new catsay-gui-glade
$ cargo add gtk –features v3_24
```

Then, copy the `layout.glade` file in Listing 3-4 into the `catsay-gui-glade/src/` folder. Also, copy and paste the following code into `src/main.rs`:

```
// src/main.rs

use gtk::prelude::*;

fn build_ui(app: &gtk::Application) {
    let glade_src = include_str!("layout.glade");
    let builder = gtk::Builder::from_string(glade_src);

    let window: gtk::Window = builder.object(
        "applicationwindow1"
    ).unwrap();
    window.set_application(Some(app));

    window.show_all();
}
```

```
fn main() {
    let application = gtk::Application::new(
        Some("com.catsay-gui-glade"),
        Default::default()
    );

    application.connect_activate(build_ui);

    application.run();
}
```

For this example, you should make sure the cat.png file is in the folder catsay-gui-glade/images. If you run the program with cargo run, you should see a GTK application that looks like Figure 3-14. Note you'll see a few warnings; you can ignore those for this example.

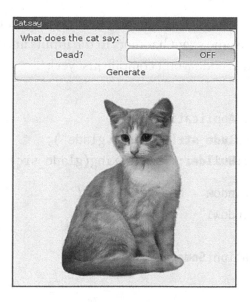

Figure 3-14. *GTK application created by Glade*

Notice how the connect_active() handler is much simpler than the previous example where you set up the app layout by code. You no longer need to build up the widget hierarchy inside Rust code. Instead, you load the Glade XML file using include_str!() in the build_ui() function. The built-in macro include_str!() loads a file into the string variable glade_src. You then use gtk::Builder::from_string() to build the GTK program using the Glade XML definition string. However, because you are not building the widgets in Rust code, you don't have any Rust variable that points to the individual widgets, so you cannot call functions like `window.show_all()`, because the `window` is not defined. You can identify the widgets by their IDs inside the application built by the builder. In Listing 3-4, the `ApplicationWindow` has an `id="applicationwindow1"` that was auto-generated by Glade. You can use `builder.object("applicationwindow1")` to get the widget. Because you might provide an ID that doesn't exist, the function returns an `Option`, so please remember to `unwrap()` it, and to handle the error cases properly. The window created by the builder also doesn't know which `gtk::Application` it belongs to. You have to use `window.set_application(app)` to associate the application with the window. To do this you pass the `gtk::Application` created in the `main()` function into the `build_ui()` function.

3.12 Accepting Inputs and Button Clicks

You can add interactivity to the GTK application in a way similar to what you did for the TUI application. Let's add some event handlers to the inputs and buttons in the `build_ui()` function (note that this code won't compile just yet):

```
// src/main.rs
fn build_ui(app: &gtk::Application) {
    let glade_src = include_str!("layout.glade");
    let builder = gtk::Builder::from_string(glade_src);

    let window: gtk::Window = builder.object(
        "applicationwindow1"
    ).unwrap();
    window.set_application(Some(app));

    // Inputs
    let message_input: gtk::Entry = builder.object(
        "message_input"
    ).unwrap();

    // Submit button
    let button: gtk::Button = builder.object(
        "generate_btn"
    ).unwrap();
```

```
// Outputs
let message_output: gtk::Label = builder.object(
    "message_output"
).unwrap();
let image_output: gtk::Image = builder.object(
    "image_output"
).unwrap();

button.connect_clicked(|_| {
    message_output.set_text(&format!(
        "{}\n \\\n \\",
        message_input.text().as_str()
    ));
    image_output.show();
});

window.show_all();
image_output.hide();
}
```

First, you get the handles for all the widgets you need using the `builder.object()` function, just like you did for getting the `ApplicationWindow`:

```
let message_input: gtk::Entry = builder.object(
    "message_input"
).unwrap();
```

You have to create a callback function on the **Generate** button to show the cat and the text message. You call `button.connect_clicked()` to set the callback for the button's clicked event:

```
button.connect_clicked(|_| {
    message_output.set_text(&format!(
        "{}\n        \\\n        \\",
        message_input.text().as_str()
    ));
    image_output.show();
});
```

The callback is a closure, in which you do the following:

- Read the input from message_input.text() (text() returns a glib::
  GString, so you convert it to &str using .as_str()).

- Set the message_output text using the text in message_input.

- Show the image with image_output.show().

You also want the cat image to remain hidden until you click the **Generate** button. So you call image_output.hide() right after window.show_all(). The order is important here because you first show everything and then hide the image. If you hide the image first, then call window.show_all(), the image will be shown again.

Although the structure of the code looks OK, the code won't compile. You'll receive the following error when you try to compile via cargo build:

```
error[E0373]: closure may outlive the current function, but it borrows
'image_output', which is owned by the current function
  --> src/main.rs:36:28
   |
36 |      button.connect_clicked(|_| {
   |                                 ^^^ may outlive borrowed value 'image_output'
...
41 |          image_output.show();
   |          ------------ 'image_output' is borrowed here
   |
note: function requires argument type to outlive ''static'
  --> src/main.rs:36:5
   |
36 | /       button.connect_clicked(|_| {
37 | |           message_output.set_text(&format!(
38 | |             "{}\n       \\\n        \\",
39 | |             message_input.text().as_str()
40 | |           ));
41 | |           image_output.show();
42 | |       });
   | |_____^
```

```
help: to force the closure to take ownership of 'image_output' (and any
other referenced variables), use the 'move' keyword
   |
36 |     button.connect_clicked(move |_| {
   |                            ++++
```

This is because once the callback function is set, it might get triggered at any time during the application's lifetime. But by the time the callback is triggered, the build_ ui() function is probably already finished and the image_output variable has gone out of scope. To mitigate this, you have to move the ownership of the variable to the closure, so the closure can keep it alive. But if you simply add a move keyword to the closure, the image_output variable won't be accessible after you move it into the closure, because the ownership has already been moved to the closure. For example:

```
let image_output: gtk::Image = builder.get_object(
    "image_output"
    ).unwrap();

button.connect_clicked(move |_| {
    // ...
    image_output.show();
});

image_output.hide(); // This will fail!
// error[E0382]: borrow of moved value: 'image_output'
```

However, because gtk3-rs is a wrapper around the C GTK library, doing a Rust clone on a gtk3-rs object only copies the pointer. So, since it's not a costly, deep clone of the whole data structure, you can simply clone the handle and move it into the closure.[3] You can see here how we create the image_output_clone and then call show on it inside the closure:

```
let image_output: gtk::Image = builder.get_object(
    "image_output"
).unwrap();
```

---

[3] We are not cloning the message_input and message_output simply because we don't need to use them after defining the callback function. But if you need to use them after moving them into the callback, you should clone them just like you did for image_output.

71

```rust
let image_output_clone = image_output.clone(); // low-cost clone

button.connect_clicked(move |_| {
    message_output.set_text(&format!(
        "{}\n    \\\n    \\",
        message_input.text().as_str()
    ));
    // the clone is moved into the closure
    image_output_clone.show();
});

image_output.hide(); // you still keep the ownership of it
Ok(())
```

3.13 Reading a gtk::Switch

There is only one thing missing in the Glade-based design—the "Dead?" switch. The code change is pretty straightforward. Modify the src/main.rs file as follows:

```rust
// src/main.rs
fn build_ui(app: &gtk::Application) {
    // ...
    let is_dead_switch: gtk::Switch = builder.object(
        "is_dead_switch"
    ).unwrap();

    let image_output: gtk::Image = builder.object(
        "image_output"
    ).unwrap();
    let image_output_clone = image_output.clone();

    button.connect_clicked(move |_| {
        // ...
        let is_dead = is_dead_switch.is_active();
```

```
    if is_dead {
        image_output_clone.set_from_file(
            Some("./images/cat_dead.png")
        )
    } else {
        image_output_clone.set_from_file(
            Some("./images/cat.png")
        )
    }
    image_output_clone.show();
});

window.show_all();
image_output.hide();
}
```

As before, you get the handle of the switch with the following code:

```
let is_dead_switch: gtk::Switch = builder.object(
    "is_dead_switch"
).unwrap();
```

Then you can check if it's activated or not by reading is_dead_switch.is_active(). Based on whether it's true or false you can load different cat images using image_output_clone.set_from_file(). This allows you to change the image at runtime. Note that you'll also need to add the image images/cat_dead.png.

Finally, the end product will look like Figure 3-15 to Figure 3-17.

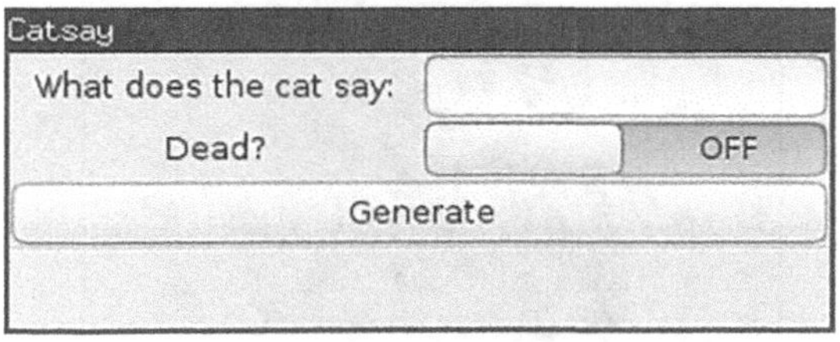

Figure 3-15. *The form created with Glade*

Figure 3-16. *After clicking **Generate** with **Dead?** off*

Figure 3-17. *After clicking **Generate** with **Dead?** on*

3.14 Alternatives

This concludes the journey from building a text-based user interface (TUI) to creating a graphical user interface (GUI). You learned the ncurses-based TUI library and GTK-based GUI library because they are mature and stable. And the corresponding Rust library is also more production-ready. However, there are many exciting new Rust libraries out there that provide a more idiomatic Rust interface or better cross-platform support.

On the TUI side, tui-rs is also a good alternative to Cursive, but it doesn't support input handling out of the box, so it's better suited for building applications that don't require user interaction, like a monitoring dashboard. There are also some pure-Rust alternatives, like termion[4] (part of ReduxOS) and crossterm,[5] which provide backends to tui-rs. If you are looking for cross-system support, including Linux and Windows, pancurses[6] is an abstraction layer above the platform-specific layers. It uses ncurses-rs[7] for Linux and pdcurses-sys[8] for Windows underneath.

On the GUI side, there are many different crates with different design philosophies. Since GUI is a very mature field in software development, there are many existing GUI frameworks there were not designed specifically for Rust. But there are Rust bindings to these crates. Choosing this kind of library will give you the maturity and stability of the underlying GUI framework, but the API might not be that Rusty. These libraries include Qt, a cross-platform GUI library written in C++. There are Rust bindings for it, like

---

[4] https://crates.io/crates/termion
[5] https://crates.io/crates/crossterm
[6] https://crates.io/crates/pancurses
[7] https://crates.io/crates/ncurses-rs
[8] https://crates.io/crates/pdcurses-sys

Ritual[9] and QMetaObject.[10] Other bindings include FLTK[11] (for the C++-based FLTK[12]), iui[13] (for libui[14]), sciter-rs[15] (for Sciter[16]), and Slint[17] (for Slint,[18] formerly known as SixtyFPS).

Another popular source of design inspiration comes from Elm, a functional programming language that compiles to JavaScript. It is used to build web apps, but its main design principle, the Elm Architecture, inspires a few Rust GUI libraries, like Relm[19] and iced.[20] The Yew library in Chapter 4 is also based on the Elm architecture.

The GTK library you learned in this chapter belongs to a category of GUI libraries called *retained-mode GUI*. There is another category called *immediate-mode GUI*. In a retained-mode GUI library, you create widgets, like a button, then attach callbacks on them. The button stays around (i.e., is retained) and expects click events. But in an immediate-mode GUI, the button is redrawn every time a new frame is rendered. This is a common design pattern in game GUIs. Immediate-mode GUI results in simpler code. For example, the retained widgets and callbacks creates lifetime headaches for Rust. But managing the layout is generally harder in immediate-mode than in retained-mode. Immediate-mode Rust GUI libraries include egui[21] and imgui[22] (bindings for Dear ImGui, a C++ immediate-mode GUI library).

There are also projects that aim to create Rust-native GUI libraries, like Druid[23] and OrbTk,[24] which is part of the ReduxOS project.

---

[9] https://rust-qt.github.io/qt/
[10] https://crates.io/crates/qmetaobject
[11] https://crates.io/crates/fltk
[12] https://www.fltk.org/
[13] https://crates.io/crates/iui
[14] https://github.com/andlabs/libui
[15] https://crates.io/crates/sciter-rs
[16] https://sciter.com/
[17] https://crates.io/crates/slint
[18] https://slint-ui.com/
[19] https://crates.io/crates/relm
[20] https://crates.io/crates/iced
[21] https://crates.io/crates/egui
[22] https://crates.io/crates/imgui
[23] https://crates.io/crates/druid
[24] https://crates.io/crates/orbtk

It is worth mentioning Tauri.[25] Tauri is not strictly a GUI library; it allows you to build a desktop application and define the user interface using any web-based technology. The UI is rendered by an embedded web browser engine, and the frontend interacts with the Rust-based core that controls the native platform. This is similar to the concept of the popular Electron framework.

There are so many options for building TUIs and GUIs in Rust. Based on the complexity of your project and your preferred API design, you can almost always find a library that suits your project needs.

3.15 Conclusion

In this chapter you created three projects to act as visual interfaces for a simple `catsay` program. The first application, `catsay-tui`, used `ncurses` to create a text-based user interface. You learned how to handle input and output with text-based user interfaces and how to customize them with multi-step dialogs. Then you moved to a full GUI, creating the `catsay-gui` project that used `gtk` bindings to create a simple GUI from Rust. After this, you moved on to the `catsay-gui-glade` project, where you used a more complicated XML-based editor to define the UI presentation, and then linked in behavior from the Rust side.

---

[25] `https://tauri.studio/`

## CHAPTER 4

High-Performance Web Frontend Using WebAssembly

We've just seen how Rust can help us write a graphical user interface as a desktop program. But what if we wanted to write interactive websites? Rust also excels in this domain. With the introduction of *WebAssembly*[1] (abbreviated *Wasm*), you can compile a Rust program to run in a browser alongside JavaScript.

4.1 What Is WebAssembly?

WebAssembly is an open standard for a binary instruction format that runs on a stack-based virtual machine. Its original design goal was to provide near-native performance in web browsers. You can think of it as an assembly language for the web. WebAssembly is a World Wide Web Consortium (W3C) recommendation, and it's implemented in all major browsers.

WebAssembly is designed to run at near-native speed. It doesn't require you to use a garbage collector (GC).[2] It can be a compile target for many languages, like C, C++, and Rust. Therefore, you can write frontend applications in the high-level programming language you prefer and get predictable performance.

---

[1] https://webassembly.org/

[2] Although there are discussions under way to add GC as an optional feature.

© Shing Lyu and Andrew Rzeznik 2023
S. Lyu and A. Rzeznik, *Practical Rust Projects*, https://doi.org/10.1007/978-1-4842-9331-7_4

There are a few reasons why you might want to use Rust to compile to WebAssembly:

- Enjoy the high-level syntax and low-level control of Rust in browsers.

- Save bandwidth while downloading the small .wasm binary because of Rust's minimal runtime.

- Reuse the extensive collection of existing Rust libraries.

- Use familiar frontend web tools, like ES6 modules, npm, and webpack, through the wasm-pack toolchain.

There are also some common misconceptions about WebAssembly:

- WebAssembly is not aiming to replace JavaScript. It is designed to run alongside JavaScript and simplify some tasks in the browser, along with providing extra performance where needed.

- WebAssembly is not limited to only the browser, although that was the initial target. The WebAssembly runtime can potentially run anywhere, like on servers or in Internet of Things (IoT) devices. These applications also benefit from the isolation guarantees of the runtime. This usage as a more secure container/virtual machine technology is currently seeing a lot of growth.[3]

A common use for WebAssembly is to speed up a performance bottleneck in JavaScript-based web applications. The user interface (UI) can be built in HTML, CSS, and JavaScript, with CPU-intensive tasks or functions being written in WebAssembly. The result of the computation can then be passed back to JavaScript for display.

Some frameworks take this idea a step further and let you write your whole frontend application in Rust, like Sycamore, Yew, or Percy. They usually take inspiration from other popular frontend frameworks, like React and Elm, and use a Virtual DOM.[4] The Rust code is compiled to Wasm and rendered to the screen by finding any difference between the virtual and real DOMs and then making adjustments to the real DOM accordingly. This is a relatively efficient and fast method, as only changes need to be re-rendered.

---

[3] https://www.docker.com/blog/why-containers-and-webassembly-work-well-together/
[4] https://reactjs.org/docs/faq-internals.html#what-is-the-virtual-dom

4.2 What Are You Building?

First, you'll be building a simple Hello World application. This application will create a browser `alert()` from Rust. This example will show you the process of getting a WebAssembly program up and running. You'll also learn how WebAssembly works with JavaScript.

In the `catsay` example from Chapter 3, you wrote an application to add text to a cat photo. This application used a previously chosen cat, but now you might want to have a website where you can upload different cat photos to use for different applications (the internet can always use more cat photos). Some of these photos could be very large, however, which would use up a lot of bandwidth and future storage space. You'll be building a frontend application for reducing the size of a cat image for upload. Since reducing the size of an image is a CPU-intensive job, it makes sense to implement the resize algorithm in WebAssembly.

Once you have a basic understanding of how WebAssembly can work with JavaScript, you can start to use a fully Rust-based frontend web framework. You'll first start with a hello-world-style example to get familiar with the setup and build process. This example will have a button that can increase a counter.

Finally, you'll be building a simple Catdex application that will let you interactively add cat images to and remove them from a single-page application with the Yew[5] framework.

4.3 Hello WebAssembly!

There are quite a few steps to running a Hello World program in WebAssembly. Conceptually, this is how you get some Rust code running in the browser as WebAssembly:

1. Write the Rust code to expose functionality to JavaScript, and to handle data passing between JavaScript and Wasm.

---

[5] https://yew.rs

2. Use the compiler toolchain to compile Rust code into a
    `.wasm` binary.

3. Serve the `.wasm` file on a web server

4. Write an HTML and JavaScript page to load this `.wasm` file.

5. In the JavaScript file, `fetch`[6] the `.wasm` file and use the
    `WebAssembly.instantiateStreaming()`[7] API to compile and
    instantiate the `.wasm` module.

6. In JavaScript, make calls to the functions that the `.wasm` module
    exports.

These steps are tedious and do not feel as ergonomic as what `cargo` or npm[8] offer. Thankfully, there is a tool called `wasm-pack` that bundles many other tools that make this process smoother. Also, to avoid writing boilerplate code, you can use the template `wasm-pack-template`[9] to quickly generate a project.

Setting Up the Development Environment

To set up `wasm-pack`, head to `https://rustwasm.github.io/wasm-pack/installer/`. For Linux, it's as simple as executing the following command in the terminal[10]:

```
curl https://rustwasm.github.io/wasm-pack/installer/init.sh -sSf | sh
```

---

[6] Fetch is a web API that allows you to download additional resources. It's a successor of the old `XMLHttpRequest`.

[7] Check `https://developer.mozilla.org/en-US/docs/WebAssembly/Loading_and_running` for more detail.

[8] npm is the de facto standard package manager used for JavaScript development, similar to how cargo is the package manager used for Rust development (`https://www.npmjs.com/`).

[9] `https://github.com/rustwasm/wasm-pack-template`

[10] `curl` is a popular command-line HTTP client. If you don't have it yet you can almost certainly find it in your Linux distribution's package directory.

Wasm-pack helps you package the project into an npm (Node Package Manager) package, so developers who are familiar with modern JavaScript development can easily pick it up. To properly create and publish the package, you need to install the command-line npm using the following steps (if you are not using Ubuntu you can find directions for installing npm on your platform at https://nodejs.org/en/download). For this chapter, we use npm version 8.5.1, though any newer version should work fine.

```
sudo apt update
sudo apt install npm
```

Creating the Project

Now you have all the required tools installed. You can start creating the project by running the following:

```
wasm-pack new hello-wasm
```

You should see the following code in the terminal:

```
[INFO]: Installing cargo-generate...
 Generating a new rustwasm project with name 'hello-wasm'...
 Creating project called 'hello-wasm'...
 Done! New project created /home/user/hello-wasm
[INFO]: Generated new project at /hello-wasm
```

Internally, this command makes `cargo-generate` download the `wasm-pack-template` from GitHub and create a project locally. `Cargo-generate` will ask you for the project name; you can name it "hello-wasm." After `cargo-generate` finishes, you'll see a `hello-wasm` folder in the current directory.

In the `hello-wasm` folder, you'll find a fairly typical Cargo library project, with a `Cargo.toml` and `src/lib.rs`. But if you look closely at the `Cargo.toml` file's contents listed below, you'll see it has a few interesting features:[11]

[package]
```
name = "hello-wasm"
version = "0.1.0"
```

---

[11] The `wasm-pack-template` is being updated from time to time. The versions of the dependencies might be newer than the ones listed here.

```
edition = "2018"

[lib]
crate-type = ["cdylib", "rlib"]

[features]
default = ["console_error_panic_hook"]

[dependencies]
wasm-bindgen = "0.2.63"

# The 'console_error_panic_hook' crate provides better debugging
# of panics by logging them with 'console.error'. This is great
# for development, but requires all the 'std::fmt' and
# 'std::panicking' infrastructure, so isn't great for code size
# when deploying.
console_error_panic_hook = {version = "0.1.6", optional = true}

# 'wee_alloc' is a tiny allocator for wasm that is only ~1K in
# code size compared to the default allocator's ~10K. It is
# slower than the default allocator, however.
#
# Unfortunately, 'wee_alloc' requires nightly Rust when
# targeting wasm for now.
wee_alloc = { version = "0.4.5", optional = true }

[dev-dependencies]
wasm-bindgen-test = "0.3.13"

[profile.release]
# Tell 'rustc' to optimize for small code size.
opt-level = "s"
```

You should also make sure that you change the Rust edition in the Cargo.toml file to 2021. This will ensure you're using the newest version of all the available crates.

The crate-type is cdylib (**C D**ynamic **Lib**rary) and rlib (**R**ust **Lib**rary). Cdylib ensures that the output is a dynamic library that follows the C FFI convention. All the Rust-specific information is stripped away. This will help the "Low Level Virtual Machine" (LLVM) compiler that compiles your code to Wasm understand the exported interfaces. Rlib is added for running unit tests; it's not required for compiling to WebAssembly.

Since browsers will download the .wasm binary through the internet, it's crucial to keep the binary size small so that the download is fast. You'll notice that in [profile.release], the opt-level options are set to s, which means optimize for small code size. The template also chooses to use a custom memory allocator wee_alloc that is optimized for code size.

The template also adds the wasm-bindgen crate, which is used to generate binding between WebAssembly and JavaScript. You can see the wasm-bindgen crate being used in the src/lib.rs file:

```
mod utils;

use wasm_bindgen::prelude::*;

// When the 'wee_alloc' feature is enabled, use 'wee_alloc'
// as the global allocator.
#[cfg(feature = "wee_alloc")]
#[global_allocator]
static ALLOC: wee_alloc::WeeAlloc = wee_alloc::WeeAlloc::INIT;

#[wasm_bindgen]
extern {
    fn alert(s: &str);
}

#[wasm_bindgen]
pub fn greet() {
    alert("Hello, hello-wasm!");
}
```

The first few lines of src/lib.rs set up the wee_alloc allocator, which we don't need to go into more detail about here.

The next two blocks are the key to this Hello World example. What this file is trying to do is as follows:

1. Expose the JavaScript DOM API window.alert() to Rust/Wasm.

2. Expose a Wasm function named greet() to JavaScript.

3. When JavaScript calls the greet() Wasm function, call the alert() function from Wasm to display a pop-up message in the browser.

The following block in Listing 4-3 exposes the `window.alert()` function to Wasm:

```
#[wasm_bindgen]
extern {
    fn alert(s: &str);
}
```

The `extern` block tells Rust this function exists somewhere and can be called via a foreign function interface (FFI). Rust can then call this foreign JavaScript function defined elsewhere.

Notice that the `alert` function takes a `&str`. This matches the JavaScript `alert`, which takes a JS `String`. However, in Wasm's specification, you are only allowed to pass integers and floating-point numbers between JavaScript and Wasm. So, how can you pass a `&str` as the parameter? This is the magic of `wasm_bindgen`. The `#[wasm_bindgen]` attribute tells `wasm_bindgen` to create a binding. The `Wasm_bindgen` crate generates Wasm code that encodes the `&str` into an integer array, passes it to JavaScript, then generates JavaScript code that converts the integer array back into a JavaScript string. This is because in Rust `String` is UTF-8 encoded, meaning that each character is between 1 and 4 bytes and the common Latin alphabet/ASCII keyset takes 1 byte per character. On the other hand, JavaScript holds strings in the UTF-16 format, where each character is either 2 or 4 bytes (Figure 4-1). An array of integers is used as a simple set of bytes that can be passed between the two languages. This is just one example of the complexities of converting data representations between two programming languages, and a good example of why it's useful to have a good library to handle these conversions.

`Wasm_bindgen` also works the other way around: you can expose a Rust function using `pub fn greet()` and annotate it with the `#[wasm_bindgen]` attribute. `Wasm_bindgen` will compile this function to Wasm and expose it to JavaScript.

Note   You might be wondering what's the purpose of `src/utils.rs` and the `console_error_panic_hook` feature defined in `Cargo.toml`. When Rust code panics, you'll only see a generic Wasm error message in the browser's console. The `console_error_panic_hook` feature prints a more informative error message about the panic to the browser's console, which helps you with debugging. The `console_error_panic_hook` needs to be explicitly initialized once, and so the `src/utils.rs` provides a small function to do that.

If you now run `wasm-pack build`, `wasm-pack` will ensure that you have the correct toolchain (for example, download the correct compilation target with rustup) and compile your code to Wasm. You'll see the output in the `pkg` folder. `Wasm-pack` generates a few files:

- `hello_wasm_bg.wasm`: The compiled Wasm binary, containing the Rust function you exposed.

- `hello_wasm.js`: Some JavaScript binding wrapper around the Wasm functions that makes passing values easier.

- `hello_wasm_bg.d.ts`: TypeScript type definitions. Useful if you want to develop the frontend in TypeScript.

- `hello_wasm_bg.js`: Generated JavaScript bindings; we won't be directly working with this file.

- `hello_wasm.d.ts`: TypeScript definitions.

- `package.json`: The npm project metadata file. This will be useful when you publish the package to npm.

- `README.md`: A short introductory note to the package user. It will be shown on the npm website if you publish this package.

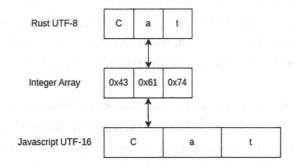

Figure 4-1. *Conversion between Rust UTF-8 and JavaScript UTF-16 strings*

Note   TypeScript is a programming language that builds on JavaScript by adding static type definitions. As a Rust developer, you already know the power of static types. Since the Rust code you write for Wasm is typed, it makes sense to use it with TypeScript instead of JavaScript to enjoy the power of end-to-end static typing.

Wasm-pack doesn't force you to use TypeScript, so it generates a .js file containing the implementation, and a .d.ts definition file that contains TypeScript type definitions. If the frontend uses JavaScript, it can use the .js file only and ignore the .d.ts file. But if the frontend uses TypeScript it can reference the .d.ts file to enforce the types.

Because TypeScript is a topic that deserves its own book, we'll stick with JavaScript here.

Creating the Frontend

Now you have the Wasm package ready, but how do you make it work on a web page? Since Wasm does not support the ECMAScript 6 (ES6, the formal name for the Javascript standard) import statement yet, you'll have to perform a fetch to download the .wasm file, then call the WebAssembly.instantiateStreaming() web API to instantiate it. This is quite cumbersome and doesn't feel natural to the npm-style workflow. Instead, you can use Webpack to simplify the way you import the Wasm package into a JavaScript application.

Webpack is a versatile tool for bundling your JavaScript files. It can analyze the dependency of your various JavaScript files and packages installed from npm and package them into a single .js file. This reduces the overhead of downloading multiple JavaScript files, and reduces the risk of missing dependencies in runtime. The most important feature you want from Webpack is using the ES6 import statement to import a Wasm package. This allows you to avoid all the boilerplate code of fetching the .wasm file and instantiating it.

Webpack requires some configuration to work with Wasm. To save you this trouble, you are going to use another template, `create-wasm-app`.[12] This template creates a frontend web page project with Webpack configuration for Wasm. To initiate a project based on this template, simply run the following command in the command line inside the `hello-wasm` folder:

```
npm init wasm-app client
```

This will ask you to install `create-wasm-app`; go ahead and approve the installation. The command will then download the `create-wasm-app` template[13] and create the project in a folder called `client`.

Tip   When you run `cargo generate`, Cargo will initialize a git project in the created project directory. When you run `npm init wasm-app client`, npm will also initialize a separate git repository inside the `client` folder. You end up with two git repositories, one inside the other. If you want to version control the whole project in one git repository, you can delete the inner `client/.git` folder.

Since this template creates a frontend project, there should be an HTML file as the entry point. You can find an `index.html` file in the `client` folder, shown below:

```html
<!DOCTYPE html>
<html>
  <head>
    <meta charset="utf-8">
    <title>Hello wasm-pack!</title>
  </head>
  <body>
    <noscript>
      This page contains webassembly and javascript content,
      please enable javascript in your browser.
    </noscript>
```

---

[12] https://github.com/rustwasm/create-wasm-app

[13] An npm template, officially called an *initializer*, is an npm package with a prefix `create-` in the name. The command `npm init foo` is a shorthand for `npm init create-foo`. npm will look for the npm package named `create-foo`.

```html
  <script src="./bootstrap.js"></script>
  </body>
</html>
```

The index.html file is a very minimal HTML page. It includes the bootstrap.js file with a <script> tag. This needs to be imported as below:

```js
// A dependency graph that contains any wasm must
// all be imported asynchronously. This 'bootstrap.js'
// file does the single async import, so that no one
// else needs to worry about it again.
import("./index.js")
  .catch(e => console.error("Error importing 'index.js':", e));
```

This bootstrap.js file imports the index.js file asynchronously. This is a limitation of Webpack v4; the file can not be imported synchronously. The index.js file below is what actually uses the Wasm package.

```js
import * as wasm from "hello-wasm-pack";

wasm.greet();
```

In index.js, the template imports a demo Wasm package on npm called hello-wasm-pack. But you want to use the Wasm project you just built in the parent directly. How do you change that? You'll need to open the package.json file and add a dependencies section:

```json
{
  "name": "create-wasm-app",
  // ...
  "dependencies": {
    "hello-wasm": "file:../pkg"
  },
  "devDependencies": {
    // Removed the hello-wasm-pack package
    "webpack": "^4.29.3",
    "webpack-cli": "^3.1.0",
    "webpack-dev-server": "^3.1.5",
```

```
    "copy-webpack-plugin": "^5.0.0"
  }
}
```

In dependencies, you defined a new package called hello-wasm, and the file:../
pkg means the package is located in the pkg folder, one directory up from the current
file's location (this means the pkg folder in the hello-wasm directory). Don't forget to
remove the unused hello-wasm-pack demo package from devDependencies as well.

Then you can go back to index.js and change the first line to:

```
import * as wasm from "hello-wasm";
```

This will load the hello-wasm package. The next line calls the greet function you
exported from Rust:

```
wasm.greet();
```

As mentioned before, the import statement won't work without Webpack. This
template already has all the Webpack configuration you need, including the following:

- webpack.config.js: Webpack-specific configurations.

- package.json

  - devDependencies: This section specifies all the dependencies, like webpack,
    webpack-cli, webpack-dev-server, and copy-webpack-plugin.

  - scripts: This section provides two commands:

    * build: Use Webpack to bundle the source code into the ./dist[14] folder.

    * start: Start a development server that will bundle the code and serve it
      right away. It also monitors source code changes and re-bundles if needed.

You need to install Webpack and its dependencies by going into the client folder
and running the following command sequence:

```
npm install
npm run build
npm run start
```

---

[14] This is the default location, so you won't find that mentioned in the code or configuration.

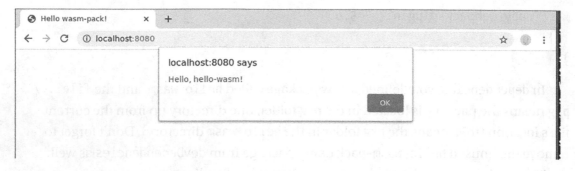

Figure 4-2. *The pop-up alert*

Running npm install will install the packages. Then you should run npm run build to build the package. Once the dependencies are installed and the package is built, you can run npm run start, which will call webpack-dev-server. This development server runs Webpack to bundle your code whenever your code changes, and serves it at the address http://localhost:8080. When you open that URL in a web browser, you should see an alert pop up with the message "Hello, hello-wasm!" (Figure 4-2).

The development server, as the name suggests, is for development only. If you want to put this website into production, you'll have to

- run npm run build, and

- deploy to a production-ready web server the files created in the './dist' folder.

As a final note, it's worth mentioning the command npm audit and its specialization npm audit fix. Too often security is put off with the excuse that it's only a small toy project, only to have that toy project result in a Common Vulnerabilities and Exposures report (CVE)[15] and a flurry of exploits and patching. The npm audit command checks your npm dependencies and ensures that none of the versions in your project are using known vulnerabilities, and the npm audit fix command will update them. This is one small step that helps prevent deploying a vulnerable web app that could lead to a data breach.

---

[15] https://www.cve.org/About/Overview

4.4 Resizing an Image with WebAssembly

The Hello World project you just implemented might seem a bit trivial. Why should JavaScript call Wasm, then let Wasm call the JavaScript web API `alert`, instead of just letting JavaScript call `alert` directly? Well, now that you've got a simple example running, you can dive deeper with a project that showcases the power of Wasm. Wasm is best suited for replacing performance bottlenecks in JavaScript applications. Because Wasm is designed to run at near-native speed, it makes sense to offload performance-critical parts of a JavaScript application to Wasm, while keeping the rest in JavaScript for flexibility and ease of development. And while we'll focus on the performance use case here, the integration of WebAssembly in the Rust ecosystem means that a huge number of general Rust utility crates can be compiled into the web browser with it. The ability to use relatively arbitrary Rust code (anything that generally doesn't use CPU- or OS-specific features) in the web browser opens up a whole world that was previously limited to JavaScript libraries. After you've worked through this example, we encourage you to try your favorite Rust library and see if you can get it working in a browser using WebAssembly.

A common performance-critical job is image processing, especially in frontend applications. Image-processing algorithms are usually computationally intensive, and performing those computations in Wasm instead of JavaScript can frequently result in a good performance improvement.

Following up on the CLI and GUI programs for working with cat images, you're going to build a very basic image-processing tool using JavaScript and Wasm. Let's start with one of the simplest types of image manipulation functionality: resizing.

The most common way to represent an image on a computer is to store the color values of each pixel. As you might have learned in basic physics class, different colors can be created by adding red, green, and blue lights together at different intensities. If you represent each color component's intensity with an 8-bit integer, you can represent $2^8 \times 2^8 \times 2^8 = 256 \times 256 \times 256 = 1{,}677{,}216$ different colors.

The simplest way to store an image is using triplets of 8-bit numbers to represent each pixel (so a total of 24 bits or 3 bytes per pixel). With this naive format a single HD resolution image (1920x1080 pixels) would take up almost 6 megabytes. To save storage space, images are usually stored in some form of more advanced compressed format. There are hundreds of file formats for storing image data, with some of the most common being PNG, JPEG, and GIF. Since this is not a book on digital image processing, you are going to rely on an existing Rust crate called `image` to handle all the nitty-gritty of image formats. The `image` crate not only helps you read and write various image formats, it also provides several image-processing algorithms, like resize, rotate, invert, etc. This also demonstrates one of the benefits of compiling Rust to Wasm: you can build on top of Rust's vibrant crates ecosystem for reliable and high-performance libraries.

First, you need to create a Wasm project using the same command as before:

```
wasm-pack new wasm-image-processing
```

This time, you can name the project `wasm-image-processing`. Then you can add the `image` crate to the [dependencies] section in the `Cargo.toml` by running the following command in your new `wasm-image-processing` directory:

```
cargo add image
```

```
[package]
name = "wasm-image-processing"
//...
edition = "2021"
//...

[dependencies]
wasm-bindgen = "0.2.63"
image = "0.24.5"
// ... Other dependencies ...
```

You'll want to make sure that the versions for the dependencies in `Cargo.toml` match the versions specified to ensure the code doesn't have any issues with newer versions. You also should make sure that `edition = "2021"` is specified in the `Cargo.toml` file.

Let's first think about what the API exposing the JavaScript should look like. The first feature you want to expose to JavaScript is a function that can resize an image. To make this example easier, you can make the function shrink the image by half, so you don't have to deal with passing different resize ratios.

Before we dive deep into the Rust side of things, you'll need to figure out what you need to scaffold out on the JavaScript side. Since the main thing you'll use Rust for is resizing an image, you should figure out the type for the `original_image` and the image it returns. You can take a hint from the resize function you'll be using from the image crate. The function is located in image::imageops, and its function signature is shown in Listing 4-4.[16]

```rust
pub fn resize<I: GenericImageView>(
    image: &I,
    nwidth: u32,
    nheight: u32,
    filter: FilterType
) -> ImageBuffer<I::Pixel, Vec<<I::Pixel as Pixel>::Subpixel>>
where
    I::Pixel: 'static,
    <I::Pixel as Pixel>::Subpixel: 'static,
```

The image parameter takes an image that implements the GenericImageView trait. So you know you need some kind of image data that can be transformed into a type that implements GenericImageView. The return type is an ImageBuffer, which can be transformed into something that JavaScript can interpret as an image. It also takes the new width (nwidth) and new height (nheight) as u32's. The final parameter filter takes an enum FilterType. This allows you to select which algorithm to use to scale down the image. You can choose the Nearest Neighbor algorithm[17] for its simplicity and speed.

Now you know that you need a type that can be transformed into another type that implements the GenericImageView trait. You are ready to move to the JavaScript frontend and see if there's an appropriate type there that can be sent to the Wasm backend. You can create a frontend project inside the current wasm-image-processing folder as before:

```
npm init wasm-app client
```

Inside the client/index.html file, you can copy and paste the following HTML code (Listing 4-4):

```html
<!DOCTYPE html>
<html>
  <head>
```

---

[16] https://docs.rs/image/0.23.3/image/imageops/fn.resize.html

[17] https://en.wikipedia.org/wiki/Image_scaling#Nearest-neighbor_interpolation

```
    <meta charset="utf-8">
    <title>Cat image processor</title>
  </head>
  <body>
    <noscript>
      This page contains webassembly and javascript content,
      please enable javascript in your browser.
      </noscript>

    <input type="file"
     name="image-upload"
     id="image-upload"
     value=""
    >
    <br>
    <button id="shrink">Shrink</button>
    <br>
    <canvas id="preview"></canvas>
    <script src="./bootstrap.js"></script>
  </body>
</html>
```

The page consists of the following elements:

- `<input type="file">`: This is the file selector that allows you to select an image from your computer.

- `<button>Shrink</button>`: When this button is clicked, you should call the Wasm function to shrink the image.

- `<canvas>`: This canvas is used the display the image.

The `<canvas>` is an HTML element that can be used to draw images with JavaScript. You can render an image onto it using JavaScript APIs. It also provides some APIs to read the rendered image data, which will be handy for converting an image into something Rust/Wasm can understand.

Let's break this process into three steps:

1. Use the `<input type="file">` element to load a local image onto the `<canvas>`.

2. Extract the image data from the `<canvas>` and pass it to Wasm for resizing.

3. Receive the resized image data from Wasm and display it onto the `<canvas>`.

Loading an Image File onto the `<canvas>`

You can load the image file onto the `<canvas>` just with JavaScript. Open the `index.js`[18] and add the code in Listing 4-4 (and while you're at it, remove the `wasm.greet()` line added by the template).

```javascript
function setup(event) {
  const fileInput = document.getElementById('image-upload')
  fileInput.addEventListener('change', function(event) {
    const file = event.target.files[0]
    const imageUrl = window.URL.createObjectURL(file)

    const image = new Image()
    image.src = imageUrl

    image.addEventListener('load', (loadEvent) => {
      const canvas = document.getElementById('preview')
      canvas.width = image.naturalWidth
      canvas.height = image.naturalHeight
      canvas.getContext('2d').drawImage(
        image,
        0,
        0,
        canvas.width,
        canvas.height
      )
```

---

[18] This file is loaded in `index.html` through `bootstrap.js`, thanks to the template.

```
    })
  })
}

if (document.readState !== 'loading') {
  setup()
} else {
  window.addEventListener('DOMContentLoaded', setup);
}
```

This code defines a setup() function. The function is called immediately if the page is loaded (document.readyState !== 'loading'); otherwise, it will be called when the DOMContentLoaded event fires.

In the setup() function, you monitor the change event on the <input type=" file">. Whenever the user selects a new file with the <input>, the change will fire. The <input type="file"> has an attribute .files, which returns a list of files you selected as JavaScript File objects. You can reach this FileList by referencing the event.target object (i.e., the <input type="file">).

To draw the image file onto the <canvas>, you need to convert it to an HTMLImageElement (which is a JavaScript representation of an <img> element). When writing HTML, you set the src attribute on the <img> element to specify the URL of the image. But the file you just loaded is from a local file system; how can you get a URL for it? The window.URL.createObjectURL()[19] method is designed for exactly this purpose. It takes a File object as input and returns a temporary URL for the object. The URL's lifetime is tied to the document in which it was created. With this the following code turns the loaded image file into an HTMLImageElement:

```
const file = event.target.files[0]
const imageUrl = window.URL.createObjectURL(file)

const image = new Image()
image.src = imageUrl
```

After you set the src attribute and the file is loaded, a load event will fire. In Listing 4-4, the code listens for the load event and draws the image onto the canvas. Because you didn't specify the width and height of the <canvas> element in HTML,

---

[19] https://developer.mozilla.org/en-US/docs/Web/API/URL/createObjectURL

it has a default pixel size of 300 x 150. The image might have a different size, so you can set the canvas's width and height to the naturalWidth and naturalHeight of the HTMLImageElement. These two values represent the intrinsic size of the image.

Finally, you can draw the image onto the <canvas>. But you can't draw directly to the HTMLCanvasElement (i.e., the return value of document.getElementById ('preview')). You'll first need to get a 2D drawing context by calling canvas.getContext('2d'). Only after that can you call the .drawImage() function on that context. The drawImage() function can take the following arguments:

- image: the HTMLImageElement you created from the file.

- dx: the x-axis coordinate of the top-left corner of the image's position.

- dy: the y-axis coordinate of the top-left corner of the image's position.

Both dx and dy are set to 0 so the image's top-left corner matches the canvas's top-left corner.

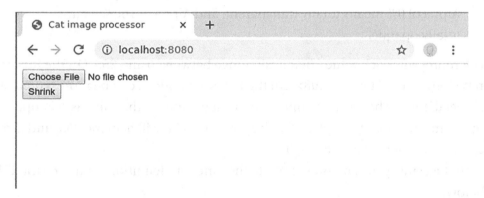

Figure 4-3. *Loading a local image onto the <canvas>*

To test this code, run wasm-pack build in the wasm-image-processing folder, which generates the Wasm module for the client to consume. This should build with some warnings for now. Then run npm install followed by npm run start inside the wasm-image-processing/client directory. The pre-configured webpack-dev-server will start running. You can open a browser and visit http://localhost:8080 to see the page in action (Figure 4-3). You should be able to upload an image and have it display in the browser, but the shrink button will currently do nothing.

Passing the Image to Wasm

You now have a basic JavaScript application that can load an image onto a <canvas>, but how do we get this data into our Wasm code? As mentioned before, images can be represented as a collection of pixels; each pixel's color can be represented by integers. Both JavaScript and Rust are very adept at working with arrays of integers, so we'll use this format to pass data between the JavaScript and Rust code.

You learned before that a pixel can be represented with three pieces of color data: Red, Green, and Blue values, each as an 8-bit u8. In this case we are going to add a little bit of additional information and use the following modified format:

- R: the intensity of the red channel

- G: the intensity of the green channel

- B: the intensity of the blue channel

- A: the Alpha channel, meaning the transparency of the pixel.
  Alpha of 0% means totally transparent, and Alpha of 100% means
  totally opaque.

If a u8 represents each value, then it can range between 0 and 255. On the Rust side, this can be represented by a Vec<u8>. On the JavaScript side, it can be represented by a Uint8ClampedArray. The term "clamped" in the name means the value is "clamped" to the range from 0 to 255. If you set a value larger than 255 it will become 255, and if you set a negative number it will become 0.

On the Rust side, you can now complete the function definition, updating the lib.rs file as below:

```
use image::{RgbaImage};
use image::imageops;

use wasm_bindgen::prelude::*;

// When the 'wee_alloc' feature is enabled, use 'wee_alloc'
// as the global allocator.
#[cfg(feature = "wee_alloc")]
#[global_allocator]
static ALLOC: wee_alloc::WeeAlloc = wee_alloc::WeeAlloc::INIT;

#[wasm_bindgen]
```

```rust
pub fn shrink_by_half(
    original_image: Vec<u8>,
    width: u32,
    height: u32
) -> Vec<u8> {
    let image: RgbaImage =
        image::ImageBuffer::from_vec(
            width, height, original_image
        ).unwrap();
    let output_image = imageops::resize(
        &image,
        width / 2,
        height / 2,
        imageops::FilterType::Nearest
    );

    output_image.into_vec()
}
```

The original_image parameter is a 1D Vec<u8>. To reconstruct an 2D image from a 1D array, you need to also pass the width and height.[20] You can use the image::ImageBuffer::from_vec() function to turn the Vec<u8> back into an RgbaImage. Because the RgbaImage type implements the GenericImageView trait, you can pass this RgbaImage to imageops::resize to resize the image. Once you've received the resized image, it can then be turned back into a Vec<u8> with .into_vec() and returned to JavaScript.

On the frontend page, you can add an event listener on the "Shrink" button, so it triggers a call to shrink_by_half() Wasm function. You can modify the index.js file to follow the code below, adding the import to the top of the file and the additional code to the setup function:

---

[20] In theory you only need to pass either the width or the height, because the other one can be calculated from the size of the array and the specified dimension. But passing in both in this example helps makes your code simpler and easier to read.

```javascript
import * as wasmImage from "wasm-image-processing"

function setup(event) {
  // ... Previous code in setup function...
  //
  const shrinkButton = document.getElementById('shrink')
  shrinkButton.addEventListener('click', function(event) {
      const canvas = document.getElementById('preview')
      const canvasContext = canvas.getContext('2d')
      const imageBuffer = canvasContext.getImageData(
          0, 0, canvas.width, canvas.height
      ).data

      const outputBuffer = wasmImage.shrink_by_half(
          imageBuffer, canvas.width, canvas.height
      )

      const u8OutputBuffer = new ImageData(
          new Uint8ClampedArray(outputBuffer), canvas.width / 2
)
canvasContext.clearRect(
0, 0, canvas.width, canvas.height
      );

      canvas.width = canvas.width / 2
          canvas.height = canvas.height / 2
      canvasContext.putImageData(u8OutputBuffer, 0, 0)
  })
}

// ...
```

Notice that you imported the wasm-image-processing, which is the crate in the top-level folder. When the button is clicked, you need to first get the 2D context from the canvas. The context exposes a function getImageData, which can retrieve part of the canvas as an ImageData object. The first two parameters specify the X and Y coordinates of the top-right corner of the area you want to retrieve. The next two parameters specify the width and height of that area. Here you get the whole canvas. The ImageData has a read-only `data` attribute that contains the `Uint8ClampedArray` representation of the RGBA values.

You can pass this `Uint8ClampedArray` to the `wasmImage.shrink_by_half()` Wasm function imported at the beginning of the file. The return value will be a `Vec<u8>` representation of the shrunken image. You can convert it back to `Uint8ClampedArray` and wrap it in an `ImageData`.

To show this shrunken image on the `<canvas>`, you can follow the three steps shown in the code:

1. Clear the canvas with `clearRect()`.

2. Set the canvas size to the new shrunken size.

3. Draw the new `ImageData` onto the `<canvas>` using `putImageData()`.

As a final modification, you need to ensure that the `package.json` file in the `client` directory has the Rust-generated Wasm as a dependency. While at it, you can also remove the `hello-wasm-pack` dev dependency:

```
{
  "name": "create-wasm-app",
  // ...
  "dependencies": {
    "wasm-image-processing": "file:../pkg"
  },
  "devDependencies": {
    // remove hello-wasm-pack
    "webpack": "^4.29.3",
    "webpack-cli": "^3.1.0",
    "webpack-dev-server": "^3.1.5",
    "copy-webpack-plugin": "^5.0.0"
  }
}
```

To test this application, follow these steps:

1. In the wasm-image-processing folder, run wasm-pack build. This compiles the Rust code into Wasm, located in the pkg folder.

2. Change directories to the client folder, run npm install && npm run start.

3. Open a browser, go to http://localhost:8080 (Figure 4-3).

4. Click the "Choose File" button. A file selector window will pop up. Select an image file (PNG) from your computer (Figure 4-4).

5. Click the "Shrink" button. See Figure 4-5.

Figure 4-4. *File selected*

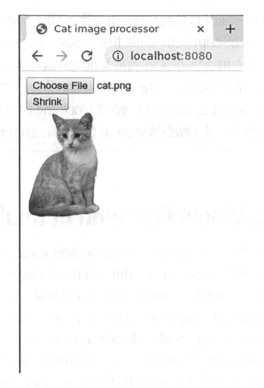

Figure 4-5. *After clicking the Shrink button*

Note   The method shown in this section is not the most efficient way of moving data between JavaScript and Wasm. As a general rule you want to avoid unnecessary copying between JavaScript memory and the WebAssembly linear memory. Quoting from the official *Rust and WebAssembly* book[21]:

... a good JavaScript-WebAssembly interface design is often one where large, long-lived data structures are implemented as Rust types that live in the WebAssembly linear memory and are exposed to JavaScript as opaque handles. JavaScript calls exported WebAssembly functions that take these opaque handles, transform their data, perform heavy computations, query the data, and ultimately return a small, copy-able result.

Therefore you might want to try loading the image directly in Rust/Wasm, like this great open-source project demonstrates: `https://www.imagproc.com/main`.

---

[21] `https://rustwasm.github.io/book/game-of-life/implementing.html`

Another potential improvement is that you can offload the computation to a Web Worker. Currently, our JavaScript code calls the image-processing function on the main event loop. While the image-processing function is running, it might block further user interaction. Web Workers are a web technology that allows you to run scripts in a background thread so that they won't block the user interface event loop. You can also find an example of a Web Worker in the `www.imageproc.com` code.

4.5 Writing the Whole Frontend in Rust

Up until now, you've been building a web page in JavaScript and calling Wasm functions when needed. But is it possible to write everything in Rust? The answer is yes, but it relies on a programming pattern called the Virtual Document Object Model *(Virtual DOM)*.

The Virtual DOM is a concept popularized by the popular JavaScript framework React.[22] When you build a web page in plain JavaScript and need to change something on the screen, you need to call many DOM APIs *imperatively*. That means you need to say, "Get me this <p> element and change its text to 'foobar,' then get that button and turn it red." But as a page grows more and more complicated this approach can lead to chaos and human errors (a.k.a. bugs). Instead, React uses a *declarative* approach. You instead say, ""I want this <p> to contain 'foobar,' and I want the button to be red," and React needs to figure out how to get the page from the current state to your desired state.

Whenever the desired state changes, React will "render" the page to a Virtual DOM, which is an in-memory representation of the real DOM. The Virtual DOM can figure out which parts of the page changed compared to the previous state, and calls the DOM API to update (or *reconcile* in React terminology) only the required parts of the real DOM. This allows the developer to focus on the overall UI declaration instead of worrying about which parts of the DOM to update.

If you build a Virtual DOM in Rust and compile it to Wasm, you can write the rest of the page in Rust, which interacts with the Virtual DOM. Then the Virtual DOM uses crates like `web-sys` to interact with the real DOM API to reconcile the difference. There have been many different Rust frameworks that support this architecture. You'll use one

---

[22] https://reactjs.org/docs/faq-internals.html#what-is-the-virtual-dom

of the most popular frameworks called Yew.[23] Yew is heavily influenced by the design of React and Elm[24]; feel free to examine these other frameworks to better understand the general idea of the Virtual DOMs and the reactive architecture paradigm.

4.6 A Hello World Example

First, you'll set up a minimal Hello World project with Yew. Unlike your previous project where we used wasm-pack, you can get everything you need using only Cargo and some add-ons (meaning we won't have any npm calls here). Run the following commands to download the helper programs and create the new Rust crate:

```
$ cargo new hello-yew-world
$ cd hello-yew-world
$ cargo add yew --features csr
```

Now you should move into the new hello-yew-world directory created and update the Cargo.toml file to follow Listing 4-6. Just as in other projects, make sure that the dependency versions in your file match those listed here.

```
[package]
name = "yew-app"
version = "0.1.0"
edition = "2021"

[dependencies]
yew = { version = "0.20.0", features = ["csr"] }
```

With the dependency imported you can now update your main.rs file to follow the code below. You start by importing the yew::prelude::* to bring in the commonly used features.

```
use yew::prelude::*;

#[function_component(App)]
fn app() -> Html {
```

---

[23] https://yew.rs/docs/

[24] Another popular web framework/language for building frontend applications

```rust
    html! { <Button value=0/> }
}

#[derive(Properties, PartialEq)]
struct ButtonProp {
    value: i64
}

#[function_component(Button)]
fn increment_button(button: &ButtonProp) -> Html {
    let counter = use_state(|| button.value);
    let on_click = {
        let counter = counter.clone();
        move |_| {
            let new_value = *counter + 1;
            counter.set(new_value);
        }
    };
    html! {
        <div>
            <button onclick={on_click}>
                { "+1" }
            </button>
            <p>{*counter}</p>
        </div>
    }
}

fn main() {
    yew::Renderer::<App>::new().render();
}
```

Finally, to actually run the project, you need to add an index.html file in the hello-yew-world directory. This file should match that listed below. This index file will serve as the extremely basic bare-bones HTML skeleton that the rest of your Rust code will add to:

```html
<!DOCTYPE html>
<html lang="en">
```

```
    <head> </head>
    <body></body>
</html>
```

Now you've got all the basic files set, and you are ready to build the project. For this you need to install `trunk` using `cargo`:

```
$ cargo install trunk
```

The `trunk` package is a Wasm web application bundler. Now you can simultaneously build and run your app using the command

```
$ trunk serve --open
```

which will build your project, start a web server, and open a web browser to connect to this server at the local host address `http://127.0.0.1:8080` (see Figure 4-6). The `trunk` package will also automatically recompile and reload your web page as you make changes to the Rust code, giving you a fast feedback loop to iterate on design changes. Note you must connect via `http` and not `https`. Some web browsers (like Chrome) will by default switch to `https` so it may seem like your code is not loading. In this case, just type the address directly into the search bar while `trunk` is running in the background.

The core of this example is in `src/main.rs`, which defines two components, one called App and one called Button.

Just like a standard Rust program, your Yew app starts by calling the `main()` function, defined in `src/main.rs`. This function contains a single line,

```
yew::Renderer::<App>::new().render();
```

This line starts the Yew application by mounting the `app::App` component onto the `<body>` of the HTML page.

Our App is defined by the following function:

```
#[function_component(App)]
fn app() -> Html {
    html! { <Button value=0/> }
}
```

This is called a "functional component" in yew. It's created by writing a function that returns the `Html` type, and then annotating the function with a `#[function_component(Name)]` attribute where `Name` is the name you assign to the component. The body of the function defines the html to return for this component.

The `html!{}` macro allows you to write HTML syntax inside Rust, similar to JSX[25] in React. This `app()` function defines the HTML that will render a `<Button value=0/>`. Let's examine the button component now to see how it works.

First, the `Button` component has a `value` property that defines its start value. More generally, properties (or props) are how parent components pass information down to child components, including both initial static values and values that can change over time. You represent a component's properties in Yew as a struct.

Figure 4-6. *Browser brought up by* `trunk serve - open`

```
#[derive(Properties, PartialEq)]
struct ButtonProp {
    value: i64
}
```

The `ButtonProp` struct contains fields for each property of the `Button` component. Note the derived attributes. The `Properties` attribute is needed to let Yew know that this struct represents properties of the component, and `PartialEq` is required by the Yew framework for any properties.

Finally, we can get to the actual function that defines our component:

---

[25] https://reactjs.org/docs/glossary.html#jsx

```rust
#[function_component(Button)]
fn increment_button(button: &ButtonProp) -> Html {
    let counter = use_state(|| button.value);
    let on_click = {
        let counter = counter.clone();
        move |_| {
            let new_value = *counter + 1;
            counter.set(new_value);
        }
    };
    html! {
        <div>
            <button onclick={on_click}>
                { "+1" }
            </button>
            <p>{*counter}</p>
        </div>
    }
}
```

The `increment_button` function takes a single argument of type `&ButtonProp`, which provides the properties for our component. The first line in the function defines a counter using the `use_state` function. The return value of `use_state` is what Yew calls a "hook." The hook stores state (with the initial state determined by evaluating the closure provided to `use_state`). Why can't you use a regular variable that holds a value? First, since our entire component is defined in a function, any local variable would be dropped as soon as the function completed. Creating a hook tells the Yew framework to create a place to store the state information required for this component (in our case, a simple counter). Second, whenever the value in the hook is updated, Yew is aware which components display data based on that hook, and it can trigger a rerender of only those components. This is the critical idea behind the reactive programming paradigm (most well known from React web framework). The programmer defines components and the data they depend on, and then lets the framework figure out which components need to be updated/rerendered as different pieces of data change. Yew's version of hooks closely follows the idea behind the original React implementation.

After the hook we define a callback `on_click`. To properly set up this callback, a new scope is defined with curly brackets `{...}` and then the counter is cloned and assigned to a new variable that shadows itself from the outer scope. Hooks are reference-counted and work similar to `Arc`'s from Rust's standard library. We initially set up a new scope here and clone the `counter` hook in order to move ownership of this cloned hook into the callback. If we didn't have the inner scope and moved our counter into the callback directly, we wouldn't have been able to refer to it in the `html!` macro afterward. The callback itself simply dereferences the counter (retrieving its value), adds one, and then uses the `set` method on the counter to update its value. This `set` method ties into the rest of the Yew framework and will automatically trigger a rerender of any component that displays data from that hook.

Finally, let's move on to the `html!` macro. Notice that the text inside the `<p>` is not hardcoded, but refers to a variable `*counter`, wrapped inside a pair of curly brackets. This tells Yew to substitute the text with the value inside the hook when the component is rendered. The callback `on_click` is also attached to the button here. Now, whenever the `counter` changes value (for example due to the `on_click` callback), Yew will update the component in the virtual DOM, and the Virtual DOM will reconcile the change to the DOM and show it on screen.

At this point you can call `trunk serve --open` on the command line, and a web browser should open displaying your page. Every time you click the button the counter will increment by one.

4.7 A Cat Management Application

Now that you've gotten a basic Yew application under your belt, you can create something a bit more complicated. In the game *Pokémon*, there is a device called a Pokédex, which is an index/encyclopedia of all Pokémon. In the rest of this chapter, we are going to build a (you guessed it) cat index called Catdex. The Catdex should have the following features:

- Showing a list of cats. This demonstrates how to render a list using a template.

- Uploading new cats. This shows how we can take input and store state in our application.

- Delete a specific cat. This shows how we can use props to pass information to child components, and callbacks to pass it back up to parents.

Let's take a quick detour regarding the terminology referencing "props" and "callbacks." The term "props" is short for "properties," and is a term used in many UI frameworks. We won't go into extreme technical detail on this, so for our purposes you can think of props as the input arguments to your UI components. They are set up to pass parent component data down to child components, and critically to automatically and efficiently be able to update the child components upon a change. Callbacks are a more familiar concept. A parent component passes a function or closure down to a child. When the child then needs to pass information back to the parent, it calls the callback with the information to be passed up to the parent as arguments. These two concepts together make up the core means of communication between different components that don't involve some shared global state.

In this section, we're focusing on how the preceding set of operations can be done in a client-side application, but you'll see in the next chapter how a similar application can be created using server-side methods.

First, let's create a new project and bring in our Yew dependency with

```
$ cargo new catdex-yew
$ cd catdex-yew
$ cargo add yew --features csr
```

You should add an `index.html` file at the top level of the project exactly like you did in the previous project; you can once again use the index used previously.

Next, let's clean up `src/main.rs` to build up a skeleton Yew component for displaying a list of cats:

```rust
use yew::prelude::*;

#[function_component(App)]
fn app() -> Html {
    let cat_list = use_state(|| Vec::<CatDetails>::new());

    let on_change = {
        let cat_list = cat_list.clone();
        // ...
    };

    html! {
        <div>
```

```rust
            <h1>{"Catdex"}</h1>
            <input
                type="file"
                accept="image/*"
                onchange={on_change}
            />
            <section class="cats">
                { for cat_list.iter().map(cat) }
            </section>
        </div>
    }
}

#[derive(Clone)]
struct CatDetails {
    name: String,
    image: Vec<u8>,
}

fn cat(file: &CatDetails) -> Html {
    // ...
}

fn main() {
    yew::Renderer::<App>::new().render();
}
```

In the App component function you use a hook use_state to hold the current list
of CatDetails, which includes the cats' names and their image data. You also have a
callback on_change (which we'll fill in momentarily), which will trigger upon changes to
the file input. We then have an html! macro that provides the basic skeleton, including a
file input to upload files, and then a section that iterates over the list of cats. Note how we
can directly use a for iterator in the html! block to template out multiple HTML entries.
In this case, the cat function provides a simple way of converting CatDetails to HTML
and can be applied to each CatDetails to generate the HTML to display that specific cat.
CatDetails itself simply stores the name of a cat and its image.

You can flesh out this skeleton by starting with the cat function below. For this to work, you'll need to pull in the base64 crate with cargo add base64. The Vec<u8> of binary image data can then be base-64 encoded and displayed as an image.

```
use base64::{engine::general_purpose, Engine};
// ...

fn cat(cat: &CatDetails) -> Html {
    html! {
        <article class="cat">
            <h3>{ format!( "{}", cat.name )}</h3>
            <img src={
                format!("data:image;base64,{}",
                general_purpose::STANDARD.encode(&cat.image))
            } />
        </article>
    }
}
```

The final and trickiest part of this initial setup is uploading the files and saving them in the cat list. You can look at the rust code below to go over the final steps. Note quite a few additional crates are needed for these finals steps, and these crates can be added to Cargo with the following commands:

```
$ cargo add js-sys
$ cargo add gloo-file --features futures
$ cargo add wasm-bindgen-futures
$ cargo add web-sys
```

We've already seen web-sys before as a library to access low-level JavaScript primitives from Rust. The js-sys crate is similar, while the gloo_file crate provides a higher level of abstraction around the traditional JavaScript interfaces. All three of these are needed in one form or another to work with the files being loaded into the browser. Finally, because at the time of writing Yew does not support direct use of async in hooks, we need to use a local async executor to run the read_as_bytes function that will actually read the file's contents into memory.

```rust
use std::ops::Deref;
use gloo_file::File;
use wasm_bindgen_futures::spawn_local;
use web_sys::{FileList, HtmlInputElement};

// ...

fn app() -> Html {
  // ...

  let on_change = {
    let cat_list = cat_list.clone();
    move |e: Event| {
      let cat_list = cat_list.clone();
      spawn_local(async move {
        let input: HtmlInputElement = e.target_unchecked_into();
        let files = upload_file(input.files());
        let mut interior_cat_list = cat_list.deref().clone();

        for file in files {
          let new_details = CatDetails {
            name: file.name(),
            image: gloo_file::futures::read_as_bytes(&file)
              .await
              .unwrap(),
          };
          interior_cat_list.push(new_details)
        }
        cat_list.set(interior_cat_list);
      })
    }
  };
  // ..
}

// ...
```

```rust
fn upload_file(files: Option<FileList>) -> Vec<File> {
    files
        .map(|files| {
        js_sys::try_iter(&files)
            .unwrap()
            .unwrap()
            .map(|v| web_sys::File::from(v.unwrap()))
            .map(File::from)
            .collect()
    })
    .unwrap_or_default()
}

// ...
```

Catdex

Figure 4-7. Uploading images

The on_change callback needs a few levels of nested closures to get lifetimes to work out properly. First, the cat_list is cloned so that the cloned copy can be passed into the actual callback, which starts on the line with move |e: Event|. We need to again clone the cat_list inside the closure because of its being passed into the async block used in spawn_local. There, we convert the event into the HtmlInputElement that we know it was emitted from, and pass its file list into the upload_file helper function. This function extracts the File types from the list and converts them into a Vec<File>, which is easier to work with in Rust. This vector in turn is iterated upon in order to pull out the name and read in the bytes. To get that data into our hook, we first clone the current state in the hook, push the new cat onto the back of the vector, and then set the hook state to the newly enlarged vector with the additional cat. This process can be a little performance intensive (copying all cat image data just to add a new cat is a lot of extra work), and Yew has other hooks that are more complicated but can be optimized for modifying larger data like images without copies. For now you can stick to the simple use_state hook since the performance is still pretty good and it keeps this example a bit simpler.

CSS Styling

We've got a basic example, but it's pretty bland, and the cat images can end up all different sizes, with each image loading in a vertical list at its native size. We want our Catdex to have nice clean cats arrayed in a regular grid. For this we can bring in some CSS to spruce things up.

Yew itself doesn't have an official CSS support built into its crate. However, there is a large ecosystem of crates that allow CSS to be integrated into a Yew project. For this project you'll use the stylist crate with the yew and parser features enabled:

```
$ cargo add stylist --features yew
$ cargo add stylist --features parser
```

The changes needed to get added styling are relatively minor. We'll only perform them on our App component, but in general you can apply styling individually on any component as desired.

```
// ...

use stylist::{yew::styled_component, Style};
```

```rust
#[styled_component(App)]
fn app() -> Html {
    const CSS: &str = include_str!("index.css");
    let stylesheet = Style::new(CSS).unwrap();

    // ...
    html! {
        <div class= {stylesheet}>
            <h1>{format!("Catdex")}</h1>
            <label for="file-upload"/>
            <input
                id="file-upload"
                type="file"
                accept="image/*"
                onchange={on_change}
            />
            <section class="cats">
                { for cat_list.iter().map(cat) }
            </section>
        </div>
    }
}
```

Figure 4-8. *The Catdex with CSS added for styling*

119

In our Rust code we've replaced `function_component` with `styled_component`. We then use the (`include_str!`) macro to load `index.css` from the `src` folder, and then convert this string into a stylesheet. Finally, the top-level `div` is provided with this stylesheet as a class attribute. These relatively simple steps allow any component to have it's own styling, and for parent components to apply their styling to children in the normal cascading manner. You can see the result of these added sheets in Figure 4-8.

```
.cats {
    display: flex;
}

.cat {
    border: 1px solid grey;
    min-width: 200px;
    min-height: 350px;
    margin: 5px;
    padding: 5px;
    text-align: center;
}

.cat > img {
    width: 190px;
}
```

At this point you can once again run `trunk serve --open` and you should see the page load. Try uploading a few cats and see how the styling boxes and sizes them.

Deleting Files

There's a glaring issue with the current page design: You can add cats to your page, but you can't delete any of the cats that you've added (say, because of a mistaken upload). It's time to fix that.

First, we need to create a callback in our top-level App component that will remove a cat from the cat list when provided with the file name:

```
// ...
fn app() -> Html {
```

```rust
let delete_cat = {
  let cat_list = cat_list.clone();
  Callback::from(move |name: String| {
    let interior_cat_list = cat_list.deref().clone();
    let new_cat_list: Vec<_> = interior_cat_list
        .into_iter()
        .filter(|cat| cat.name != name).collect();
    cat_list.set(new_cat_list);
  })
};

html! {
  <div class= {stylesheet}>
    <h1>{"Catdex"}</h1>
    <input
      type="file"
      accept="image/*"
      onchange={on_change}
    />
    <section class="cats">
      { for cat_list.iter().map(
          |val| cat(val, delete_cat.clone())
      ) }
    </section>
  </div>
  }

}

// ...
```

Creating a Yew Callback requires passing it a closure that will run when the callback is triggered. Like we did when creating a closure to add cats, here we make a clone of the cat_list and pass it into the closure. The closure itself is relatively straightforward: given the name of a cat to be removed, the closure will search the cat list and remove that cat, collecting the remaining cats and using them to set the hook with a new cat list. This callback can then be passed to the cat function to be added to each cat being displayed

Next, you'll need a button component that will trigger this callback when clicked. Similar to the button in the Hello World example, the code below creates a Button functional component that can be embedded in the larger app. Using the props on the component, you can pass in the button text, the name to be emitted to the callback, and the callback to be triggered. This general button component will trigger the callback on a click, emitting whatever string has been set in name. The cat function is modified to also accept a callback in addition to CatDetails, and the button is added to the article for each cat. Note critically how data goes down to child components and up to parent components: Setting values in properties will allow a parent component to set the values of a child, while providing callbacks in properties gives a method for child components to send information back to parents.

```rust
#[derive(Properties, PartialEq)]
struct ButtonProp {
  text: String,
  name: String,
  on_click: Callback<String>
}

#[function_component(Button)]
fn delete_button(button: &ButtonProp) -> Html {
  let on_click = {
    let name = button.name.clone();
    let callback = button.on_click.clone();
    move |_| {
      callback.emit(name.clone())
    }
  };
  html! {
    <div>
      <button onclick={on_click}>
        { {button.text.clone()} }
      </button>
    </div>
  }
}
```

```
fn cat(cat: &CatDetails, callback: Callback<String>) -> Html {
  html! {
    <article class="cat">
      <h3>{ format!( "{}", cat.name )}</h3>
      <Button text= {"Delete".to_string()}
        name={cat.name.clone()}
        on_click={callback}
      />
      <img src={format!(
        "data:image;base64,{}",
        general_purpose::STANDARD.encode(&cat.image)
      )} />
    </article>
  }
}
```

The final result with the interactive Delete buttons can be seen in Figure 4-9. After adding cats, clicking the Delete button will remove the cat from the page.

Figure 4-9. *The Catdex with delete functionality*

4.8 Wasm Alternatives

WebAssembly is a versatile platform for many applications, so there are many different tools and frameworks that focus on different topics.

The tools introduced in this chapter are mostly maintained by the Rust and WebAssembly Working Group.[26] That includes the web-sys and js-sys crates. But web-sys provides a very low-level API, which might not be user friendly. Their APIs are also a direct mapping to JavaScript APIs, so the syntax is not idiomatic Rust. It also uses a different build system called cargo-web,[27] which doesn't rely on npm and web-pack like wasm-bindgen. Stdweb has had wasm-bindgen compatibility since version 0.4.16. You can start using stdweb in wasm-bindgen-based projects, and it can be built using wasm-bindgen tooling. We ended up using trunk[28] for packaging and deployment, as it's the default suggested tool for building and deploying Yew applications.

There has also been an effort from the Rust and WebAssembly Working Group to build a high-level toolkit, called gloo,[29] which we used here for file handling. While development on gloo is a bit slower than that on some of the other low-level libraries, it's still an important and useful library and does see updates.

There are also many frontend frameworks similar to Yew. They are mostly inspired by popular frontend frameworks and patterns in other languages, like Elm, React, and Redux. Just to name a few (in alphabetical order):

- Darco[30]: Inspired by Elm and Redux.

- Percy[31]: Supports isomorphic web application, meaning the same code runs both on the server side and client side.

- Seed[32]: Inspired by Elm, React, and Redux

- Smithy[33]

---

[26] https://github.com/rustwasm/team

[27] https://github.com/koute/cargo-web

[28] https://trunkrs.dev/

[29] https://github.com/rustwasm/gloo

[30] https://github.com/utkarshkukreti/draco

[31] https://github.com/chinedufn/percy

[32] https://seed-rs.org/

[33] https://github.com/rbalicki2/smithy

- rust-dominator[34]

- squark[35]

- willow[36]: Inspired by Elm

But WebAssembly is not limited to the browser only. In theory, the Wasm runtime can be embedded (or run stand-alone) almost everywhere. Some interesting examples include:

- Serve as backend web servers

- Power Istio[37] plugins

- Run on Internet of Things devices

- Drive robots

There is a cross-industry alliance called the Bytecode Alliance[38] that is driving the development of WebAssembly foundation outside of the browser. Their projects include the following:

- Wasmtime[39]: a Wasm runtime

- Cranelift[40]: A code generator that powers Wasmtime

- Lucet[41]: A Wasm compiler and runtime that allows you to execute untrusted Wasm code in a sandbox

- WAMR[42]: WebAssembly Micro Runtime

Many of these projects are built with Rust or work with Rust. So, if you are interested in the development of WebAssembly, you should keep a close eye on their development.

---

[34] https://github.com/Pauan/rust-dominator

[35] https://github.com/rail44/squark

[36] https://github.com/sindreij/willow

[37] Istio is a service mesh, which allows you to control, manage, and observe the network traffic between a network of microservices.

[38] https://bytecodealliance.org/

[39] https://wasmtime.dev/

[40] https://github.com/bytecodealliance/wasmtime/tree/master/cranelift

[41] https://github.com/bytecodealliance/lucet/

[42] https://github.com/bytecodealliance/wasm-micro-runtime

4.9 Conclusion

In this chapter you learned how to compile Rust to WebAssembly and leverage it on the web. You started with a simple Hello World project that showed you how you can trigger browser functionality from Rust. You then used Rust to compile a Wasm module that took over some heavier computational lifting from a JavaScript image-resizing frontend. From this you moved to writing the entire frontend in Rust using the yew crate, creating an application that can load, display, and delete cat images from a web page. In the next couple of chapters you'll see new ways of working with Rust on the web focused more on the backend.

CHAPTER 5

REST APIs

You've just completed building a web page frontend in Rust. But the web is massive, in content types, technologies used, and raw quantity. At the time of writing this book there are over 1.8 billion websites on the World Wide Web. And if you look at job boards for software developers, web developers take up a large proportion of the open positions. Since you've seen how Rust can replace JavaScript frameworks in the frontend, the next obvious question is what can it do on the backend (i.e., server side)? There are already many established programming languages for building backend applications: Java, PHP, Python, Ruby, Node.js, and Go, to name a few of the popular ones. But Rust's popularity for backend development has been growing recently, thanks largely to a few major features that are hard to find together in other available languages, as follows:

- Security

- Concurrency

- Low-level control

Web security has only increased in importance in recent years after multiple high-profile hacks were featured on the news. Having good developer coding practices can have a large effect on the types of bugs that may arise, as can the language choices made for backend development. Rust prevents a large class of vulnerabilities thanks to its robust type system and borrow checker, like null-pointer errors or use-after-free memory corruption. By having Rust check your code at compile time, you can prevent many runtime vulnerabilities that might otherwise go undetected and end up exploited by malicious parties. Safe Rust guarantees memory safety, meaning if you don't use the `unsafe` keyword in your code, you shouldn't have any bugs related to accessing or misinterpreting low-level computer memory (which are possible and common in languages like C or C++).

But security isn't the only thing that makes Rust a good choice. Popular websites need to handle a large number of concurrent users, so concurrency and efficiency are crucial for web server software. Rust's focus on "fearless concurrency" makes it easier

127

© Shing Lyu and Andrew Rzeznik 2023
S. Lyu and A. Rzeznik, *Practical Rust Projects*, https://doi.org/10.1007/978-1-4842-9331-7_5

to handle a large number of concurrent requests. The powerful `async/await` syntax also makes asynchronous Input/Ouput (async I/O) more accessible to the average Rust programmer. On top of thread safety and async I/O, Rust's ability to control low-level CPU and memory opens up the possibility of squeezing more performance out of the server hardware.

Rust also has a vibrant ecosystem that provides both high-level frameworks and low-level control over networking, database access, and type-safe templating. It's hard to find any other programming language that supports security, performance, and control at the level of Rust, especially with its great existing ecosystem. We are going to leverage this as we explore how to build a REST API and web server in Rust.

In the previous chapter, you learned how to build an interactive frontend website that leverages the powerful yew.rs framework. You packaged an initial set of cats with the app and allowed users to add new cats, but refreshing the page brought users back to the initial app state. In most web applications, the frontend makes requests to one or more backend servers to get information or submit forms. The most common way to retrieve information from or send information to a web server is via a REST API,[1] which defines a standard method of communication on the web. The core ideas of a REST API are very simple: A server exposes endpoints that allow a client to either send or request information via an HTTP request. There are a lot of design principles suggested about what should and shouldn't go into a REST API, but the core point is that the API is stateless. Any single request receives a response only based on the parameters of that request, and not based on the particular client or any of its previous requests. The API might have some state due to changing information in a database, but it doesn't require a complicated series of requests and responses to get to that data. If you know the right information to put in your request, you can always get what you want back in a single response.

A benefit of this architecture for the development team is that the backend and frontend can be built independently. The team only needs to negotiate an API contract and not step on each other's toes. The frontend also doesn't need to be served by the application server. Instead, it can be deployed in a separate server or a managed service like AWS S3, and be served through a CDN for maximum performance. The frontend can even asynchronously make REST calls to the backend to get data while displaying nice interactive screens, without having to reload an entire page.

---

[1] You can also use other protocols, like SOAP, GraphQL, or gRPC, but we'll stick with REST in this chapter.

Note this design (a JavaScript frontend and REST API backend) is not the only way websites can be created. You could render all the HTML on the server and send it along with the data as a single package when a user visits your website. Such server-side rendering does have some benefits, such as with search engine optimization.[2] A simple server-rendered HTML page can also be faster to load and requires less processing power on the client side, and is useful for quick debugging information. Still, most flagship web applications tend to choose some flavor of JavaScript frontend and REST API backend as a basis for their web services.

5.1 What Are You Building?

In this chapter, you'll build a web server that serves a REST API. This API will work with the same type of cat information that you used in the previous frontend chapter, but this time with a focus on getting that information to and from a server. After you get the end-points working, you'll update your server with additional features that are important for a production-grade application, like input validation, error handling, logging, and testing. You'll be building the following:

- A RESTful API that returns a list of cats from a database in JSON format

- A frontend in HTML and JavaScript that consumes the API to display cats

- Integration tests for the list of cats' API endpoint

- An API endpoint to POST a new cat to the database

- An API endpoint that returns a cat's detail in JSON, given that cat's ID

- Input validation to check the ID is valid, and that returns a 400 Bad Request response if not

---

[2] Since the server renders the full page, the web crawlers employed by search engines don't have to run any JavaScript to render such pages, making it easier and faster to extract pertinent information from them and build and index. But in recent years this hasn't been as much of a benefit as the large players in the search engine space have made their web crawlers more capable.

- Custom error handling to prevent users from seeing unexpected errors from the server

- Logging using the `Logging` middleware

- Enabling HTTPS

We'll be using the `Actix-web` framework (version 4) as our web framework. As a backend web framework, `Actix-web` focuses on receiving and responding to HTTP requests. The data in an HTTP response can take many forms. If serving a REST API, the body is commonly (but not always) JSON data. If the response is a more standard web page, the body can contain some mix of HTML rendered on the server itself and JavaScript that will render the page in the browser. After a quick HTML example, you'll be spending most of the time in this chapter focusing on a REST API. We'll also need a database to store our cat pictures. For that we'll use the `PostgreSQL` database through the `Diesel` ORM and `r2d2` connection pool. Since the focus of this chapter is backend development, we'll write our test page for the API in simple vanilla JavaScript. In a production application, we'd probably call our API from some framework-based frontend app (like what you built in the previous chapter), but here we'll stick to the backend to not get distracted.

5.2 Hello Backend World!

To start an Actix application, you first need to create an empty project with `cargo`, then add `actix-web` as a dependency. Run the following commands in your terminal:

```
$ cargo new catdex-api
$ cd catdex-api
$ cargo add actix-web
```

Once `cargo` has added the dependency, your `Cargo.toml` should look like Listing 5-1. If the version numbers don't match, you should replace them in your file with those listed here.

Listing 5-1. Cargo.toml for a Hello World Actix application

```
[package]
name = "catdex-api"
# ...

[dependencies]
actix-web = "4.3.1"
```

Now, open the `src/main.rs` file and copy Listing 5-2 into it.

Listing 5-2. Hello World Actix application

```rust
use actix_web::{web, App, HttpResponse, HttpServer, Responder};

async fn hello() -> impl Responder {
    HttpResponse::Ok().body("Hello world")
}

#[actix_web::main]
async fn main() -> std::io::Result<()> {
    println!("Listening on port 8080");
    HttpServer::new(|| {
        App::new()
            .route("/hello", web::get().to(hello))
    })
    .bind("127.0.0.1:8080")?
    .run()
    .await
}
```

The core of Listing 5-2 is the `App` builder in the `main()` function. The `App` struct uses the builder pattern to build a new application instance. When you call `route()`, you specify which handler should be called when the user visits a specific path under the website. In this example, when the user visits `/hello` with an HTTP GET method (`web::get()`), it invokes the `hello()` handler.

The hello() handler is an async function that returns something that implements a Responder trait. A Responder is something that can be converted into an HTTP response. It's implemented on common types like &str, String, and &[u8] slices. In this simple example, we respond with an HttpResponse::Ok() (i.e., status code 200) and the string body "Hello world."

An HttpServer wraps the App. It handles the incoming requests and passes them to the App. You bind() an address (127.0.0.1:8080) to the server so it will listen on the specific IP and port. Finally, you call run() to start the server and await on it. Notice that the HttpServer doesn't take an App instance. Instead, it takes an App factory, which is a simple closure that creates a new App instance when called. This is because the HttpServer will create multiple worker threads, each running one instance of the App. This way it can better utilize multiple CPU cores and achieve higher scalability.

You might also notice that the main() function is annotated with #[actix_web::main] attribute macro. This attribute tells Actix to execute the main() function in the actix_rt runtime, which is built on top of the popular Tokio[3] runtime. The actix_rt::main macro is re-exposed in the actix_web crate as actix_web::main, which is why we didn't need to add actix_rt as a dependency.

Note   You might have noticed that the functions in the Hello World program all have async in front, and you need to put .await after them when calling. This is an important language feature that makes it possible to build highly efficient web servers. When you call a normal (i.e., blocking) function, the whole thread blocks and waits for the function to return. But if the function is async, it immediately returns a Future instead of blocking. While you .await that Future, the program asynchronously waits for it to complete, which allows other tasks on the same thread to make progress.

This is extremely important for building web servers. A modern web server usually needs to handle a large number of clients at the same time. If the server only processes one thing at a time and blocks whenever it's waiting for I/O (input/output), like in a socket communication, it will essentially be doing nothing as it waits on a single message. One way to solve this is to use an operating system (OS) construct called a *process*. A process is an instance of a program, and the OS

---

[3] https://tokio.rs/

allows you to start multiple processes (like when you open up multiple separate web browsers). This way, you can have one process handling one client. But processes have a high overhead so it won't scale very well (just like having many different web browser windows open can slow down your system).

Another alternative is to use several *threads*. A thread is a series of instructions (and their surrounding execution context) that can run independent of other threads. Threads and processes are implemented differently in each operating system, but in general a thread is a component of a process. Threads in the same process share some common resources like memory space, so they have a lower overhead to run than a process (which as a general rule shares nothing with other duplicate processes). Therefore, we can run more threads than processes on the same hardware, serving more clients.

However, because network I/O is much slower than CPU, most of the time the threads are sitting idle, waiting for network I/O (such as waiting for the result of a request to the database). Although threads are lighter than processes, they still have some overhead. By using async/await, we can potentially serve multiple clients per thread. When the server is waiting for a client's network I/O, it can yield the execution to other clients served by the same thread. As soon as the current task gets stuck waiting for something that generally takes a long time (like a network request), it informs the runtime. The runtime can then check if any new network responses came in that other tasks were waiting on, and if one did, the appropriate tasks gets resumed with the result of that task. All this can happen on a single thread, meaning that there is no superfluous thread context switching at the operating system level. This in turn generally translates to better performance.

This is an overly simplified explanation of async/await and how it can help web development. If you wish to learn more about the history and rationale of Rust's async/await design, you can watch Steve Klabnik's talk, "Rust's Journey to Async/await."[4] You can also read the *Asynchronous Programming in Rust* book.[5]

---

[4]https://www.infoq.com/presentations/rust-2019/
[5]https://rust-lang.github.io/async-book/01_getting_started/01_chapter.html

To run this example, simply run the command `cargo run` in the terminal under this project directory. A web server will start on `127.0.0.1:8080` as we specified. Once the server is running, open a web browser and go to `http://127.0.0.1:8080/hello`, and you'll see the text "Hello world" (Figure 5-1).

Figure 5-1. *Web server responding "Hello world"*

Building out an `actix-web` project (and many other backend web framework projects) at its core is defining functions to handle requests, and mapping these functions to routes in the main application. Over the rest of this chapter we will add additional handlers with their own routes.

5.3 Serving Static Files

In the Hello World example we respond with a simple string. But most web services are built with HTML (as we saw in the previous chapter) or JSON (as we'll see here). You could write HTML as a very long string in the Rust code and serve it that way, but this would quickly become very hard to manage. A more common technique is to store any HTML responses as separate `.html` files and serve them with the web server. An HTML file usually also references other CSS, JavaScript, or media files (e.g., images, videos). Actix allows you to serve all these files easily without explicitly writing code to read the file from disk.

You can create a folder called "static" in your project with the `mkdir static` command, which will hold the static files. Within this folder you should also create a css folder with `mkdir static/css`. Then you can add the files `static/index.html` (Listing 5-3) and `static/css/index.css` (Listing 5-4) to your project. Since there is no JavaScript in there yet, the page won't show any cats.

Listing 5-3. index.html

```html
<!DOCTYPE html>
<html>
  <head>
    <meta charset="UTF-8" />
    <title>Catdex</title>
    <link
      rel="stylesheet"
      href="static/css/index.css"
      type="text/css"
    >
  </head>
  <body>
    <h1>Catdex</h1>

    <section class="cats">
      <p>No cats yet</p>
    </section>
  </body>
</html>
```

Listing 5-4. index.css

```css
.cats {
  display: flex;
}

.cat {
  border: 1px solid grey;
  min-width: 200px;
  min-height: 350px;
  margin: 5px;
  padding: 5px;
  text-align: center;
}
```

```
.cat > img {
  width: 190px;
}
```

Tip   We serve the static files in the `static` folder of the same server that will serve the REST APIs. This is just for ease of development. In production, you should consider serving the static resources (HTML, CSS, JavaScript) from another server (e.g., Nginx) dedicated to serving static files. This gives you a few benefits, as follows:

- You can aggressively cache the static resources using a CDN (content delivery network).

- Your static server and API server can scale independently.

- Deployment and maintenance might be easier.

To serve the HTML file you need to install the `actix-files` crate using `cargo add actix-files` (for this project we use version 0.6.2). Next, paste following code in `src/main.rs` (Listing 5-5).

Listing 5-5. Serving the `index.html` file

```
use actix_files::{NamedFile};
use actix_web::{web, App, HttpServer, Result};

async fn index() -> Result<NamedFile> {
    Ok(NamedFile::open("./static/index.html")?)
}

#[actix_web::main]
async fn main() -> std::io::Result<()> {
    println!("Listening on port 8080");
    HttpServer::new(|| {
        App::new()
            .route("/", web::get().to(index))
    })
```

```
    .bind("127.0.0.1:8080")?
    .run()
    .await
}
```

The code is almost the same as the Hello World example, except

- the path is now / (root); and

- the handler, named index(), now returns a NamedFile from the actix-files crate.

The NamedFile::open() function opens the file in read-only mode. Because NamedFile implements Responder, we can return it directly in the handler. It's wrapped in a Result just in case the file reading failed.

Catdex

No cats yet

Figure 5-2. *Serving the index at the root address*

If you run cargo run in a terminal, a server should start on port 8080. Then you can open a browser and go to http://127.0.0.1:8080/ (since we are using the root / as our route) and see the contents of index.html being rendered (Figure 5-2).

At this point we don't see any cats. Since we are building a cat encyclopedia, we should add some cat pictures. You can update static/index.html to the following HTML (Listing 5-6).

Listing 5-6. index.html with external image and CSS

```
<!DOCTYPE html>
<html>
  <head>
    <meta charset="UTF-8" />
```

```
    <title>Catdex</title>
    <link
      rel="stylesheet"
      href="static/css/index.css"
      type="text/css"
    >
    </head>
  <body>
    <h1>Catdex</h1>
    <section class="cats">
      <article class="cat">
        <h3>British short hair</h3>
        <img src="image/british-short-hair.jpg" />
      </article>
      <article class="cat">
        <h3>Persian</h3>
        <img src="image/persian.jpg" />
      </article>
      <article class="cat">
        <h3>Ragdoll</h3>
        <img src="image/ragdoll.jpg" />
      </article>
    </section>
  </body>
</html>
```

This file now imports the following extra resources:

- image/british-short-hair.jpg

- image/persian.jpg

- image/ragdoll.jpg

You should create an image folder with mkdir image, and then put some cat images in the folder. When complete, your directory layout should look as follows:

```
.
+-- Cargo.lock
+-- Cargo.toml
+-- src
|   +-- main.rs
+-- static
|   +-- css
|   |   +-- index.css
|   +-- index.html
+-- image
|   +-- british-short-hair.jpg
|   +-- persian.jpg
|   +-- ragdoll.jpg
```

If you run the project now you'll see that the images fail to load. We'll need to create path handlers for the image paths. It's not scalable to write a custom path and handler for each individual resource as we did for the index, so instead we'll tell Actix to serve every file under the static and image folders automatically. To achieve this, you can use the actix-file::Files service, which handles static files for you with some simple configuration. You need to register this service when you create the App. Add the code in Listing 5-7 to src/main.rs.

Listing 5-7. Using the Files service to serve static files

```rust
use actix_files::{Files, NamedFile};
use actix_web::{web, App, HttpServer, Result};

async fn index() -> Result<NamedFile> {
    Ok(NamedFile::open("./static/index.html")?)
}

#[actix_web::main]
async fn main() -> std::io::Result<()> {
    println!("Listening on port 8080");
    HttpServer::new(|| {
```

```
    App::new()
        .service(
            Files::new("/static", "static")
                .show_files_listing(),
        )
        .service(
            Files::new("/image", "image")
                .show_files_listing(),
        )
        .route("/", web::get().to(index))
    })
    .bind("127.0.0.1:8080")?
    .run()
    .await
}
```

In the App factory, you can use the .service() function to attach a service to the application. The Files service will serve the files in a folder (the second parameter static or image) under a certain URL path (the first parameter /static or /image). You might notice that we also enabled .show_files_listing(). When this feature is turned on, you'll see an HTML list (Figure 5-3) of all the files under the folder if you open the /static or /image paths. This is handy for debugging, but should be turned off in production to avoid security vulnerabilities.[6]

Now if you run cargo run and visit http://localhost:8080/ in a browser, you'll see the Catdex now has images (Figure 5-4).

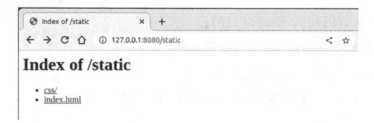

Figure 5-3.   *File listing generated by* .show_files_listing()

---

[6]https://cwe.mitre.org/data/definitions/548.html

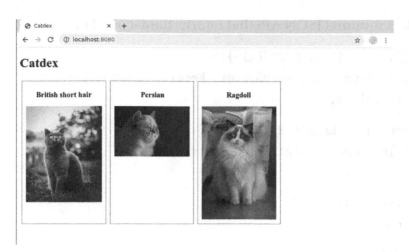

Figure 5-4. *Catdex with hard-coded images*

5.4 Converting the Cats List to a REST API

Now you have a basic web server working that serves some static HTML and images. The data is all served in HTML format, which is great for humans, but not ideal for other web services that might want to retrieve the data. Let's convert the server to provide data with a REST API.

With REST APIs we return some structural data that frontend JavaScript (or another web service that requested it) can easily process. JSON (JavaScript Object Notation) is one of the most popular options. To construct a JSON response, you can use `actix-web`'s `web::Json` helper to turn any serializable (i.e., `impl serde::Serialize`) Rust object into an HTTP response. For example, a minimal REST API endpoint that returns a hard-coded list of cats can be implemented like in Listing 5-8. Notice that because `web::Json` implements the `Responder` trait, you can simply return a `web::Json` from a handler and `actix-web` will convert it to a proper HTTP response for you. Make the following changes to expose a REST API endpoint in your web server (note you'll also need to run `cargo add serde --features derive` to add `serde` with derive macros to your project).

Listing 5-8. A minimal JSON API that returns hard-coded data

```
use actix_files::{Files, NamedFile};
use actix_web::{web, App, HttpServer, Result, Responder};
use serde::Serialize;

async fn index() -> Result<NamedFile> {
  Ok(NamedFile::open("./static/index.html")?)
}

#[derive(Serialize)]
pub struct Cat {
  pub id: i32,
  pub name: String,
  pub image_path: String,
}

async fn cats_endpoint() -> impl Responder {
  let cats = vec![
    Cat {
      id: 1,
      name: "British Short Hair".to_string(),
      image_path: "image/british-short-hair.jpg"
        .to_string(),
    },
    Cat {
      id: 2,
      name: "Persian".to_string(),
      image_path: "image/persian.jpg".to_string(),
    },
    Cat {
      id: 3,
      name: "Ragdoll".to_string(),
      image_path: "image/ragdoll.jpg".to_string(),
    },
  ];
  return web::Json(cats);
}
```

```
#[actix_web::main]
async fn main() -> std::io::Result<()> {
    println!("Listening on port 8080");
    HttpServer::new(|| {
        App::new()
            .service(
                Files::new("/static", "static")
                    .show_files_listing(),
            )
            .service(
                Files::new("/image", "image")
                    .show_files_listing(),
            )
            .service(
                web::scope("/api")
                .route("/cats", web::get().to(cats_endpoint)),
            )
            .route("/", web::get().to(index))
    })
        .bind("127.0.0.1:8080")?
        .run()
        .await
}
```

Now you can run `cargo run` to start the server. You can test the API using `curl`.[7] Note that the data you see will be the same JSON as shown here but may not all be on nice separate lines:

```
$ curl localhost:8080/api/cats
[{"id":1,"name":"British Short Hair","image_path":"image/british-
short-hair.jpg"},
{"id":2,"name":"Persian","image_path":"image/persian.jpg"},
{"id":3,"name":"Ragdoll","image_path":"image/ragdoll.jpg"}]
```

---

[7] curl might not be installed in your distribution by default. For example, for Ubuntu you can install it with `sudo apt-get install curl`.

Now we can revisit our frontend page and make the page call the API (Listing 5-9). To stay focused on the backend you'll embed plain JavaScript into your HTML response. This JSON will query the REST API you constructed. These API calls can also be made from a full-fledge frontend framework (like the yew.rs example we had in the previous chapter) where the code can be much more declarative in stye. In many cases, your REST API server might not serve any HTML at all, only exposing an endpoint returning JSON data for other services to use. You'll serve a simple page here to both show the core idea of how JavaScript can call our API, and to have a useful tool in debugging.

Listing 5-9. Making the frontend call the API

```html
<!DOCTYPE html>
<html>
<head>
  <meta charset="UTF-8" />
  <title>Catdex</title>
  <link
    rel="stylesheet"
    href="static/css/index.css"
    type="text/css"
  >
</head>
<body>
<h1>Catdex</h1>

<section class="cats" id="cats">
  <p>No cats yet</p>
</section>
<script charset="utf-8">
  document.addEventListener("DOMContentLoaded", () => {
    fetch('/api/cats')
      .then((response) => response.json())
      .then((cats) => {
        // Clear the "No cats yet"
        document.getElementById("cats").innerText = ""
```

```
    for (cat of cats) {
      const catElement = document.createElement("article")
      catElement.classList.add("cat")
      const catTitle = document.createElement("h3")
      const catLink = document.createElement("a")
      catLink.innerText = cat.name
      catLink.href = 'static/cat.html?id=${cat.id}'
      const catImage = document.createElement("img")
      catImage.src = cat.image_path

      catTitle.appendChild(catLink)
      catElement.appendChild(catTitle)
      catElement.appendChild(catImage)

      document.getElementById("cats")
        .appendChild(catElement)
    }
  })
})
</script>
</body>
</html>
```

We use the fetch() API to make the GET call, and draw the cats we received onto the page with a series document.createElement() and element.appendChild() calls. This page now looks like Figure 5-5.

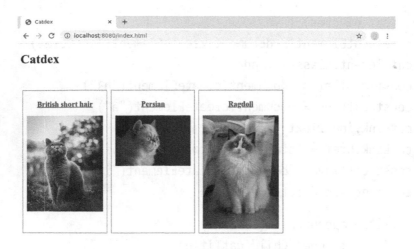

Figure 5-5. *The client-rendered index.html*

You server will now provide the cat data in JSON format when the /api/cats endpoint is called. This in turn is tested by the index.html served at the website root.

5.5 Using a Database

So far we've hard-coded the cat data into our Rust program. If the cat list never changes this is fine, but an API that always returns the same data isn't very useful. A more full-featured and interactive API would let users add, update, and remove cats, and store all that changing data somewhere. A naive way to implement this is to store the data in a mut variable. This will work fine until we need to restart the server, and then all data would be lost. The most common way to persist data past an application's lifetime is to use a database. It not only persists the data between server restarts, but also provides more efficient query ability.

In this example we are going to use PostgreSQL, a popular open-source relational database. The database runs as a separate server, and our Actix application communicates with it over TCP/IP. In theory we can write code that connects directly to the database with TCP/IP and issues raw SQL queries, but that would be very low-level and bog us down with a lot of unnecessary details. Instead, we are going to use an object-relational mapping (ORM) library to bridge between Rust code and our database. An ORM allows you to manipulate data in the database as native Rust objects (structs and enums). The ORM will convert the Rust code to raw SQL under the hood and communicate with the database. It abstracts away the database so you can work with familiar Rust syntax. It also allows you to change the SQL engine (e.g., MySQL, SQLite) without rewriting all the Rust code. The ORM we are going to use is called Diesel.[8]

Before starting to use Diesel you need to set up a PostgreSQL database. Most of the Linux distributions have it in their package repository, but they might not have the latest version. The database usually starts automatically as a background daemon and consumes disk space, so installing it on an OS you use daily might be a little awkward. To make things simple we'll use a PostgreSQL installation that's packaged as a Docker image. Docker is a container technology, which you can think of as a lightweight virtual machine. From the PostgreSQL server's perspective, the container provides an isolated OS where it can run. But it's lightweight because the container shares the host machine's OS kernel. This allows us to spin up a disposable Linux environment with PostgreSQL preinstalled. This will be easier to set up and clean up during development.

First, you'll need to install Docker. Because this process varies drastically across Linux distributions, you'll need to find the instructions for your specific OS.[9] For Debian-based Linux distributions, you can install it with `apt-get` after adding the repository.[10]

After Docker is ready, you can start a Docker container containing a PostgreSQL server with the following command (note that, depending on how you installed Docker, you may need to run this with all other Docker commands with `sudo` as root):

```
$ docker run \
  --name catdex-db \
  -e POSTGRES_PASSWORD=mypassword \
  -p 5432:5432 \
  -d \
  postgres:12.3-alpine
```

---

[8] https://diesel.rs/
[9] https://docs.docker.com/engine/install/
[10] https://docs.docker.com/engine/install/debian/

Note   You might be frustrated if you are on a platform where you need to constantly call `sudo` to use Docker. On Ubuntu you can fix this by running the following:

```
$ sudo usermod -aG docker $USER
```

You'll then need to log out and log back in with your user. You can search for post-installation steps for other platforms to remove the need for `sudo`.

This simple line of code packs a lot of information:

- `postgres:12.3-alpine` is the name of the Docker image[11] used. This is an official image provided by Docker. The "alpine" in the name suggests it's built on top of Alpine Linux, a lightweight Linux distribution.

- `-name catdex-db` creates the Docker container with a custom name so we can identify it later.

- `-e POSTGRES_PASSWORD=mypassword` passes an environment variable into the container. In this case the `POSTGRES_PASSWORD` variable will set the PostgreSQL database's default password.

- `-p 5432:5432` maps the host machine's port 5432 to the container's port 5432. 5432 is the default port used by PostgreSQL.

- `-d` runs the container in detached mode, so it will run in the background without blocking the console.

You can verify that the container has been created and started by running `docker ps`.

Before we use Rust code to interact with the database, we can use the command-line client to test the database. Install the PostgreSQL command-line client `psql` with the following command[12]:

```
sudo apt install postgresql-client
```

---

[11] `https://hub.docker.com/_/postgres`

[12] The `psql` version you get from apt might not match your PostgreSQL server version, or you may not be using a Debian-based distribution like Ubuntu. If you are experiencing any issues, please try installing the `psql` client with the matching version from `https://www.postgresql.org/download/`.

Then you can connect to the database with the following:[13]

```
psql -h localhost -p 5432 --username=postgres
```

The command will prompt you for a password, for which you can enter "mypassword." You should then be connected to the database with an interactive prompt. You can issue the command \dt to see the tables in the database (which should be empty at the moment). You can exit with either the \q command or Ctrl + D.

Once the database is up and running, we can start setting up Diesel. Diesel provides a command-line tool that you can install using the following command (see the next paragraph if you get an error):

```
cargo install diesel\_cli --no-default-features --features postgres
```

Diesel can work with different databases, like MySQL and SQLite. By default, the CLI will work with all of them, but here we use --no-default-features and --features postgres flags to tell Cargo to only install the PostgreSQL integration. You might get an error warning about the ld linker not being able to find the library pg.

This is because, during the installation process, the tool needs to compile with the PostgreSQL headers. For non-Debian-based operating systems you can get more install help at https://www.postgresql.org/download/. If you are on Debian/Ubuntu, you can install the header files with the following:

```
sudo apt-get install libpq-dev
```

We need to tell the "diesel" command-line tool about the database's URL through an environment variable. Run this command in the terminal to set it (note you'll need to rerun this command in any new terminal that you open):

```
export DATABASE_URL=postgres://postgres:mypassword@localhost
```

Then, run the command diesel setup in the catdex-api project directory. This will create a migration folder to keep the schema migration files, and a diesel.toml configuration file to tell the "diesel" tool to update the src/schema.rs file every time the schema updates.

---

[13] The username postgres is the default created by the postgres:12.3-alpine image.

Schema migration is a way to version control your database schema. In the old days, database schema changes were made by database administrators (DBAs) or developers as ad-hoc SQL commands. Making changes like this without proper version control prevents quick rollbacks or rebuilding the same database from scratch. When using schema migration, you write a SQL script to apply the schema change (up.sql) and another script to revert the change (down.sql). By using such scripts, you should be able to change and revert your database schema easily. You can also bring an old database to the latest schema by applying all the migrations it missed. A migration tool will usually determine which migration needs to be applied so you don't have to worry about figuring it out manually.

Let's create our first migration to set up our initial schema. Run this command to create a migration named create_cats:

```
diesel migration generate create_cats
```

This creates a folder in migrations/{yyyy-mm-dd-HHMMSS}_create_cats, with two files in it named up.sql and down.sql.

In up.sql, let's write the SQL code to create the cats table (Listing 5-10).

Listing 5-10. up.sql

```sql
CREATE TABLE cats (
  id SERIAL PRIMARY KEY,
  name VARCHAR NOT NULL,
  image_path VARCHAR NOT NULL
)
```

In down.sql we need to write SQL that can undo what up.sql does (Listing 5-11).

Listing 5-11. down.sql

```sql
DROP TABLE cats
```

Note that, for simplicity in our model, we are only storing the filepath to the images on disk. In a real production system you'd probably store the images directly in the database, or possibly in a different database that's more optimized for image data storage (in which case appropriate paths could be stored here). Once the migration code is written, you can run diesel migration run to apply it. This should run the up.sql file.

> **Tip**   The other two useful commands around migrations are as follows:
>
> - `diesel migration revert`: runs the `down.sql` of the most recent migration
> - `diesel migration redo`: runs the `down.sql` followed by `up.sql` of the most recent migration. After running it your database schema should be unchanged (but you might lose some data if `down.sql` drops a table!). This is useful for verifying that your `down.sql` works as intended.

Now if you connect to the database with `psql` again, and issue the command `\dt`, you should be able to see the `cats` table, along with another table labeled `__diesel_schema_migrations`, which you should ignore for now.

Since we haven't implemented the page to add new cats, let's insert some test data using `psql`. Run this SQL command in `psql`:

```
INSERT INTO cats (name, image_path)
VALUES ('Ragdoll', '/image/ragdoll.jpg');
```

Once we have some data in the database we need to define the Rust struct that represents a row of the table. Create a new file `src/models.rs` and paste the following code into it (Listing 5-12). You should also remove the `Cat` struct from `main.rs`.

Listing 5-12. Defining the ORM model

```rust
use serde::Serialize;
use diesel::Queryable;

#[derive(Queryable, Serialize)]
pub struct Cat {
    pub id: i32,
    pub name: String,
    pub image_path: String
}
```

The fields of the `Cat` model match the database schema. It also derives the `Queryable` trait so that we can use this type for SQL query results, and the `Serializable` trait which we'll need for it to be used in the HTML template. Along those lines, we add another struct in `models.rs` called `IndexTemplateData`, which is the top-level struct we'll pass in to fill out our template (it also implements `Serializable` as that's required for template input). This struct has a `Vec` of `Cats`, which will be filled out when we query the database. Thus, we can structure our data in a straightforward way as it goes from the database to our HTML template.

To use it in the `src/main.rs` file, please add the module import directive and the `use` directive at the beginning of the file. We also add the `schema.rs` that was auto-generated earlier to make it available to our main function (note that the project will still not compile until we make more changes).

```
mod model;
mod schema;
use self::model::*;
use self::schema::cats::dsl::*;
```

It might be tempting to create a database connection inside the `cats_endpoint()` handler, right before we query the database. But the server will create a new connection whenever a new client makes a request. Establishing a connection to the database has a high overhead, so it would be more efficient to keep a small pool of long-lived connections to the database, so that every time a `cats_endpoint()` handler needs to make a database query, it gets an available connection from the pool, then returns it to the pool when it's done. This not only reduces the overhead of creating connections but also reduces the stress on the database server because it has fewer connections to manage. There is a connection pool implementation in Rust called `r2d2`.[14] It works with Diesel using the `diesel::r2d2` adapter crate.

Another inefficiency regarding the database connection is that Diesel only supports synchronous I/O. If we make a synchronous call to Diesel, the thread that is running the request handler will be blocked. The thread pool will soon be depleted, and the server won't be able to serve more requests. To mitigate this problem, we can use the function `actix_web::web::block()`. This function takes a blocking function and executes it on a separate thread pool, which is different from the Actix thread pool that executes

---

[14] https://github.com/sfackler/r2d2

request handlers. The web::block() function returns a future that gets resolved when the blocking database call finishes. This way, the request handler can yield the execution to other handlers while it waits for the future to be resolved, thus increasing overall efficiency.

To add the r2d2 and diesel dependencies to the Rust project, you need to edit the Cargo.toml file as in Listing 5-13. You also need to add serde_json. You can use the cargo add command to add all of these, but given the specific versions and features, manually updating the file ensures the versions match what is included here.

Listing 5-13. Add r2d2, diesel, and serde_json to Cargo.toml

```toml
[package]
name = "catdex"
# ...

[dependencies]
actix-files = "0.6.2"
actix-web = "4.2.1"
diesel = { version = "2.0.2", features = ["postgres", "r2d2"] }
handlebars = { version = "4.3.5", features = ["dir_source"] }
r2d2 = "0.8.10"
serde = { version = "1.0.159", features = ["derive"] }
serde_json = "1.0.89"
```

We not only add the r2d2 crate, but also enable the r2d2 feature on diesel. This enables the diesel::r2d2 adapter.

Now we need to set up the connection pool in our main function, before setting up the App. Modify the main() function from Listing 5-8 to follow Listing 5-14.

Listing 5-14. Setting up r2d2 thread pool

```rust
// ...

use actix_files::{Files, NamedFile};
use actix_web::{web, App, HttpServer, HttpResponse,
    Result, error, Error};
```

```
use diesel::pg::PgConnection;
use diesel::prelude::*;
use diesel::r2d2::{self, ConnectionManager};

use std::env;
type DbPool = r2d2::Pool<ConnectionManager<PgConnection>>;

// ...
// Move "Cat" struct to "models.rs"
// ...

async fn cats_endpoint(
    pool: web::Data<DbPool>,
) -> Result<HttpResponse, Error> {
    //...
}

// ....

#[actix_web::main]
async fn main() -> std::io::Result<()> {
    // Setting up the database connection pool
    let database_url = env::var("DATABASE_URL")
        .expect("DATABASE_URL must be set");
    let manager =
        ConnectionManager::<PgConnection>::new(&database_url);
    let pool = r2d2::Pool::builder()
        .build(manager)
        .expect("Failed to create DB connection pool.");

    println!("Listening on port 8080");
    HttpServer::new(move || {
        App::new()
            .app_data(web::Data::new(pool.clone()))
            .service(
                Files::new("/static", "static")
                    .show_files_listing(),
        )
```

```
    .service(
        Files::new("/image", "image")
            .show_files_listing(),
    )
    .service(
        web::scope("/api")
            .route("/cats",
            web::get().to(cats_endpoint)),
    )
    .route("/", web::get().to(index))
})
    .bind("127.0.0.1:8080")?
    .run()
    .await
}
```

We first load the environment variable DATABASE_URL using env::var. This
database URL is then passed to a ConnectionManager's new() function. The
ConnectionManager implements the ManageConnection trait, which is how r2d2 keeps
track of which connection is still active. This connection manager is passed to an
r2d2::Pool::builder(), which actually builds the thread pool. The Pool created by
r2d2::Pool::builder() is in an Arc so it can be cloned and attached to the App using
App::data.

Note   What's the difference between App::app_data and App::data? Both
App::app_data() and App::data() are for creating states in your Actix
application. Because Actix creates a thread pool and runs one App instance per
thread, you need to decide if the state needs to be shared across threads.

If you only want local states, which means each thread get its own state and the
states work independent of each other, you can use App::data().

If you want a global state that is shared across all threads, you need to construct
a thread-safe pointer (usually an Arc) and clone() it to all threads. However, the
App::data() function will wrap the state in an Arc internally, so it will result

in an `Arc` wrapping another `Arc`. To avoid this double `Arc`, Actix allows you to construct a shared state with `web::Data::new()` and pass it using `App::app_data()`. `App::app_data()` won't wrap your shared state in an `Arc`.

There have been discussions[15] around clarifying or even simplifying the behavior of these two APIs, so it might change in the future.

The `cats` handler no longer needs to create connections itself, but instead gets a connection from the pool (Listing 5-15).

Listing 5-15. Using the connection pool in the cats endpoint handler

```
// ...

async fn cats_endpoint(
    pool: web::Data<DbPool>,
) -> Result<HttpResponse, Error> {
    let mut connection =
        pool.get().expect("Can't get db connection from pool");

    let cats_data = web::block(move || {
        cats.limit(100).load::<Cat>(&mut connection)
    })
        .await
        .map_err(error::ErrorInternalServerError)?
        .map_err(error::ErrorInternalServerError)?;
    Ok(HttpResponse::Ok().json(cats_data))
}

// ...
```

---

[15] https://github.com/actix/actix-web/issues/1454

Now, if we restart the server and call it with `curl` again, you can see that the API returns cats from the database (note we've formatted the JSON output for better readability):

```
% curl localhost:8080/api/cats
[
    {
        "id":1,
        "name":"Ragdoll",
        "image_path":"/static/image/ragdoll.jpg"
    }
]
```

If you prefer to see this API in action graphically, you can navigate to the root page at `127.0.0.1:8080`, where you'll see the single cat you added to the database displayed.

5.6 Adding Cats with a POST Command

You can now dynamically retrieve cats from the database, but there is no way to add new cats. You will next create an endpoint that can be used to handle HTTP `POST` requests to the backend. The `POST` will use a multipart request to provide the required image and data and upload it to the database.

You can start by creating the `/add_cat` endpoint that will receive the HTTP `POST`. As before, we add an `async` function handler and register it in `App`. In the handler, we need to do the following:

1. Parse the request to get the cat name and the image file.

2. Save the image file into the `static` folder.

3. Get a database connection from the connection pool.

4. Insert a new row into the database.

5. Return a proper HTTP response.

Let's start with extracting the fields from the payload. To extract information from the request in a type-safe way, we can use *extractors*. The `web::Data` parameter we had in the `index` handler is an example of an extractor. Other extractors can get information from the path, the query parameters, the JSON payload, and the `application/` `x-www-form-urlencoded` form. The multipart payload extractor is available through the `actix-multipart` crate. However, the crate provides a low-level API, which is quite cumbersome to use. We'll use a higher-level crate that is built on `actix-multipart`, called `awmp`.

To add `awmp`, simply run `cargo add awmp`, or manually add `awmp = "0.8.1"` to your `Cargo.toml`. Create a new `add_cat_endpoint` handler and add the `awmp::Parts` extractor as a parameter (Listing 5-16).

Listing 5-16. Using the `awmp::Parts` extractor

```
use std::collections::HashMap;

//...

async fn add_cat_endpoint(
    pool: web::Data<DbPool>,
    mut parts: awmp::Parts,
) -> Result<HttpResponse, Error> {
    let file_path = parts
        .files
        .take("image")
        .pop()
        .and_then(|f| f.persist_in("./image").ok())
        .unwrap_or_default();

    let text_fields: HashMap<_, _> =
        parts.texts.as_pairs().into_iter().collect();

    // TODO: Get a connection
    // TODO: Insert a row into the DB
    // TODO: Return a proper response
}
```

Because our input will contain both textual and file fields (the cat name, image path, and image file), the `Parts` extractor puts them into `files` and `texts`, respectively. From `files` we can `take()` a field named "image," which returns a `Vec<File>`. Because we know we only have one field named "image," we `pop()` the first `File`. Because `pop()`

returns an Option, we use and_then() to get the file contained in it. Awmp stores this file as a temporary file using the tempfile crate, so we can call f.persist_in() to save it permanently in the ./image folder.

Note   In this example, we directly save the user-uploaded image into the image folder, which makes it available to be retrieved immediately. But in production, this violates many security best practices. For instance:

- An attacker might be able to upload a malicious executable or script file disguised as an image.

- An attacker can also use carefully crafted filenames to place the file into a folder where they are not supposed to be.

- An attacker can also overwrite other people's images by uploading a file with the same name.

If you don't have enough security expertise, using a third-party file upload service is the easiest and most secure way. They usually provide some kind of SDK (software development kit), so you can easily integrate them into your website. If you must build it in-house, there are a few ways you can secure the website:

- Only allow certain file extensions.

- Do not trust the file extension. Detect the file type to see if they match the file extension.

- Scan the file with anti-virus software before saving.

- Sanitize the file name.

- Randomize the file name.

You can find many more attack and defense strategies on the OWASP page for "Unrestricted File Upload": https://owasp.org/www-community/vulnerabilities/Unrestricted_File_Upload.

The `texts` field contains all the text-based input fields. It has an `as_pairs()` function that returns all the fields as a `Vec` of (`key`, `value`) tuples. We can easily convert it to a `HashMap` so we can get a particular key without scanning, as follows:

```
let text_fields: HashMap<_, _> = parts
                                 .texts
                                 .as_pairs()
                                 .into_iter()
                                 .collect();
// Example of getting a key's value:
text_fields.get("name").unwrap()
```

Now that we've stored the file into the `image` folder and have all the text fields in a `HashMap`, we need to insert the row into the database. Since we are using an ORM, we need to construct a `Cat` struct and use `diesel::insert_into().values()`. But a problem quickly arises: The `Cat` struct we defined has three fields:

```
#[derive(Queryable, Serialize)]
pub struct Cat {
    pub id: i32,
    pub name: String,
    pub image_path: String
}
```

If we construct a `Cat` struct for insertion, we need to give it an `id`. But in our migration script, we declare the type of `id` to be `SERIAL`. PostgreSQL will auto-increment a `SERIAL` field whenever a new row is inserted. If we manually set `id`s, PostgreSQL will lose track of which `id` is used by the application, and this will generate conflicts. To let PostgreSQL generate the `id`, we need to define a new struct that omits the `id` field for insert. You can open the `src/models.rs` and add a new struct like in Listing 5-17 (don't forget to add the use directives during your update).

Listing 5-17. Model for inserting to cats

```
use serde::Serialize;
use diesel::{Queryable, Insertable};
use crate::schema::cats;

// ...
```

```
#[derive(Insertable, Serialize)]
#[diesel(table_name = cats)]
pub struct NewCat {
    // id will be added by the database
    pub name: String,
    pub image_path: String,
}
```

Not only is the id field omitted, but the traits we defined are also a little different. Besides the Serialize trait that's required for serialization, we also derive the Insertable trait. This tells diesel that it's a valid struct for inserting into the database. By default, diesel assumes your struct name matches the table name. But since Cats is already taken, we can only name it NewCat. Therefore, we need to annotate it with #[diesel(table_name = cats)] to specify which table it maps to.

Once you have this new struct, inserting the row into the database is as simple as in Listing 5-18.

Listing 5-18. Inserting a new cat into the database

```
async fn add_cat_endpoint(
    pool: web::Data<DbPool>,
    mut parts: Parts
) -> Result<HttpResponse, Error> {

    let file_path = // ...
    let text_fields: HashMap<_, _> = // ...

    let mut connection = pool.get()
        .expect("Can't get db connection from pool");

    let new_cat = NewCat {
        name: text_fields.get("name").unwrap().to_string(),
        image_path: file_path.to_string_lossy().to_string()
    };

    web::block(move ||
            diesel::insert_into(cats)
            .values(&new_cat)
            .execute(&mut connection)
```

```
        )
        .await
        .map_err(error::ErrorInternalServerError)?
        .map_err(error::ErrorInternalServerError)?;
    // TODO: Return a proper response
}
```

Finally, we need to respond with a proper HTTP response. We can simply respond with a 201 Created status code indicating that the new resource (i.e., the cat) was created. You also now can add the endpoint to the API service in main.

Note that depending on your system, you may need to change the temporary directory of awmp to get the project to run properly. To do this, first run mkdir tmp in your project directory, and then add the following app_data entry to your App:

```
.app_data(
    awmp::PartsConfig::default().with_temp_dir("./tmp")
)
```

The awmp crate needs a temporary directory to move temporary files as it works with them, and here we set it to be a directory within our project. At this point you should have the full add_cat endpoint ready to run, following Listing 5-19.

Listing 5-19. The complete add_cat_endpoint() handler

```
// ...

async fn add_cat_endpoint(
    pool: web::Data<DbPool>,
    mut parts: awmp::Parts,
) -> Result<HttpResponse, Error> {
    let file_path = parts
        .files
        .take("image")
        .pop()
        .and_then(|f| f.persist_in("./image").ok())
        .unwrap_or_default();

    let text_fields: HashMap<_, _> =
        parts.texts.as_pairs().into_iter().collect();
```

```rust
    let mut connection = pool.get()
        .expect("Can't get db connection from pool");

    let new_cat = NewCat {
        name: text_fields.get("name").unwrap().to_string(),
        image_path: file_path.to_string_lossy().to_string()
    };

    web::block(move ||
        diesel::insert_into(cats)
            .values(&new_cat)
            .execute(&mut connection)
    )
        .await
        .map_err(error::ErrorInternalServerError)?
        .map_err(error::ErrorInternalServerError)?;

    Ok(HttpResponse::Created().finish())
}

#[actix_web::main]
async fn main() -> std::io::Result<()> {

    // ...

    println!("Listening on port 8080");
    HttpServer::new(move || {
        App::new()
            .app_data(web::Data::new(pool.clone()))
            .app_data(
                awmp::PartsConfig::default()
                    .with_temp_dir("./tmp")
            )
            .service(
                Files::new("/static", "static")
                    .show_files_listing(),
            )
```

```
            .service(
                Files::new("/image", "image")
                    .show_files_listing(),
            )
            .service(
                web::scope("/api")
                    .route(
                        "/cats",
                        web::get().to(cats_endpoint)
                    )
                    .route(
                        "/add_cat",
                        web::post().to(add_cat_endpoint)
                    )
            )
            .route("/", web::get().to(index))
    })
        .bind("127.0.0.1:8080")?
        .run()
        .await
}
```

To test the API, first remove all images that aren't already in the database from the image directory. Then from a directory with the images, run the following curl command (while the server is running):[16]

```
curl -F "name=Persian" \
-F "image=@persian.jpg" \
localhost:8080/api/add_cat
```

This will post an image with a name to the add_cat endpoint, which saves the image in the image folder and the metadata in the database. If you navigate to the website you should now see the new cat appearing on the front page. Note this is loading the cat images.

---

[16] If you are running from a shared or network folder the code might not function properly; in this case, ensure that you are running the code on a file system mounted directly on a local disk.

5.7 API Testing

So far we've been testing our APIs manually. Automating this test process will not only help you reduce human labor, but also urge the developer to test more often and provide quick feedback. Rust comes with unit testing capability. You can unit test all your functions individually with it, and you can learn about it from the official Rust book.[17] In this book, however, we'll be focusing on the integration test, in which you spin up a real HTTP server and test it with test requests.

Actix-web provides a few helper functions to set up the test server and create test requests. A simple test that calls the /api/cats API should look like Listing 5-20.

Listing 5-20. An integration test that calls the /api/cats API, added to src/main.rs

```
// src/main.rs
// ...

fn setup_database() -> DbPool {
    let database_url = env::var("DATABASE_URL")
        .expect("DATABASE_URL must be set");
    let manager =
        ConnectionManager::<PgConnection>::new(&database_url);
    r2d2::Pool::builder()
        .build(manager)
        .expect("Failed to create DB connection pool.")
}

#[actix_web::main]
async fn main() -> std::io::Result<()> {
    let pool = setup_database();
    // ...
}
```

---

[17] https://doc.rust-lang.org/book/ch11-00-testing.html

```
#[cfg(test)]
mod tests {
    use super::*;
    use actix_web::{test, App};

    #[actix_web::test]
    async fn test_cats_endpoint_get() {
        let pool = setup_database();
        let mut app = test::init_service(
            App::new().app_data(
                web::Data::new(pool.clone())
            ).route(
                "/api/cats",
                web::get().to(cats_endpoint),
            ),
        )
        .await;
        let req = test::TestRequest::get()
            .uri("/api/cats")
            .to_request();
        let resp = test::call_service(&mut app, req).await;
        assert!(resp.status().is_success());
    }
}
```

There are a few things to focus on in this example. First, we create a test module (mod tests) and add test cases as async functions. The test case functions need to be annotated with #[actix_web::test] so they will be run in the Actix runtime. Before running the test, you need to add the actix_rt crate using the command cargo add actix_rt.

Since we are doing an integration test, which involves starting a real HTTP server that communicates to a real database (as opposed to stubbing/mocking), we can reuse the code that sets up the database and connection pool by extracting it into a function named setup_database.

To start the test server, you construct an App instance as you would do in the main() function and pass it to test::init_service(). Of course, you can omit unrelated routes to make the code more readable and easier to debug. Then you can use the test::TestRequest builder to create a test request. Here we create a GET request for /api/cats. You can make the call with test::call_service and get the response. Finally, we can check if the response is a success (i.e., status code is in the 200–299 range) with an assert!().

Tip   For a test run to not interfere with any future test runs, you need to clean the database between every test run. You could create a test PostgreSQL database and use Rust code to set up and clean up before and after each test. But since we are using Docker and it's relatively easy to create new databases, you can consider creating a fresh PostgreSQL container for every test run, and destroy it after the test finishes.

You might notice that the code that sets up the /api/cats route is duplicated in the main() function and in the test function. As your service gets more and more routes, this repetition will start making maintenance hard. Actix-web provides a way to reuse configurations using the App::configure function. You pass a configuration function to App::new().configure(). The function needs to take one parameter of the type web::ServiceConfig. The ServiceConfig struct has the same interface as App, which has the methods data(), service, route(), etc. We can create a function called api_config that sets up everything under the /api scope. This function can then be reused in the main() function and the integration test, as shown in Listing 5-21. The api_config() function can also be extracted into a separate module, so you can keep the configuration in a separate file to improve readability.

Listing 5-21. Reusing configuration using App::configure()

```
// ...

fn api_config(cfg: &mut web::ServiceConfig) {
    cfg.service(
        web::scope("/api")
            .route("/cats", web::get().to(cats_endpoint))
```

167

```rust
                .route("/add_cat", web::get().to(add_cat_endpoint)),
    );
}

#[actix_web::main]
async fn main() -> std::io::Result<()> {
    let pool = setup_database();

    println!("Listening on port 8080");
    HttpServer::new(move || {
        App::new()
            .app_data(web::Data::new(pool.clone()))
            .app_data(
                awmp::PartsConfig::default()
                .with_temp_dir("./tmp")
            )
            .configure(api_config) // Used here
            .service(
                Files::new("/static", "static")
                    .show_files_listing(),
            )
            .service(
                Files::new("/image", "image")
                    .show_files_listing(),
            )
            .route("/", web::get().to(index))
    })
        .bind("127.0.0.1:8080")?
        .run()
        .await
    }

#[cfg(test)]
mod tests {
    use super::*;
    use actix_web::{test, App};
```

```
#[actix_web::test]
async fn test_cats_endpoint_get() {
    let pool = setup_database();
    let mut app = test::init_service(
        App::new().app_data(web::Data::new(pool.clone()))
        .configure(api_config),
    )
    .await;
    let req = test::TestRequest::get()
        .uri("/api/cats")
        .to_request();
    let resp = test::call_service(&mut app, req).await;
    assert!(resp.status().is_success());
    }
}
.
```

Now you can run your tests just like with any other Rust crate by typing `cargo test` into the command line.

5.8 Building the Cat Detail API

The `cats` API is too simple for demonstrating advanced use cases like query parameters, input validation, and error handling, so we are going to rebuild the `cat` API that returns a single cat's details.

First, let's take a look at how the frontend is supposed to call the API. You might have noticed that in Listing 5-9, each cat's name is a link that points to `/cat.html?id=${cat.id}`. This page doesn't exist yet, so you need to create it in `static/cat.html` and paste the code in Listing 5-22 into it.

Listing 5-22. Single cat detail page

```html
<!DOCTYPE html>
<html>
<head>
    <meta charset="UTF-8" />
    <title>Cat</title>
</head>
<body>
<h1 id="name">Loading...</h1>
<img id="image" />
<p>
    <a href="/">Back</a>
</p>

<script charset="utf-8">
  const urlParams = new URLSearchParams(window.location.search)
  const cat_id = urlParams.get("id")
  document.addEventListener("DOMContentLoaded", () => {
    fetch('/api/cat/${cat_id}')
      .then((response) => response.json())
      .then((cat) => {
        document.getElementById("name").innerText = cat.name
        document.getElementById("image").src = cat.image_path
        document.title = cat.name
      })
  })
</script>
</body>
</html>
```

The preceding link opens the cat.html page and passes a query parameter (e.g., ?id=1). This id query parameter is extracted as an object in JavaScript by creating a new URLSearchParams(window.location.search) and then calling the .get () function on it. With the cat's ID at hand, we can call the /api/cat/${cat_id} API using fetch. The API has one path parameter for the ID, and it should return the cat's detail (including the name and the image path) in JSON format.

The most naive implementation for this API would be like that in Listing 5-23.

Listing 5-23. A naive implementation of the cat API

```rust
use serde::Deserialize;

// ...

#[derive(Deserialize)]
struct CatEndpointPath {
    id: i32,
}

async fn cat_endpoint(
    pool: web::Data<DbPool>,
    cat_id: web::Path<CatEndpointPath>,
) -> Result<HttpResponse, Error> {
    let mut connection =
        pool.get().expect("Can't get db connection from pool");

    let cat_data = web::block(move || {
        cats.filter(id.eq(cat_id.id))
            .first::<Cat>(&mut connection)
    })
        .await?.map_err(error::ErrorInternalServerError)?;
    Ok(HttpResponse::Ok().json(cat_data))
}

// ...

fn api_config(cfg: &mut web::ServiceConfig) {
    cfg.service(
        web::scope("/api")
            .route("/cats", web::get().to(cats_endpoint))
            .route("/add_cat", web::get().to(add_cat_endpoint))
            .route("/cat/{id}", web::get().to(cat_endpoint)),
    );
}
```

```
#[actix_web::main]
async fn main() -> std::io::Result<()> {
    // ...
}
```

This code extracts the `cat_id` using the `web::Path<CatEndpointPath>` extractor and tries to find it in the PostgreSQL database. If you run this after adding a new cat and then navigate to that cat's page, you'll see an image like in Figure 5-6.

Figure 5-6. *Cat detail page, rendered from data retrieved from the* `cat` *endpoint*

But there are a few issues with this implementation, as follows:

- If it fails to get a connection from the connection pool, it will `panic`! due to the `expect` and return a 500 error.

- If the ID does not exist in the database, we get a 500 Internal Server Error.

- If the ID in the path is not an integer (e.g., `/api/cat/abc`), it will return a 404 error with a message `can not parse "abc" to a i16`.

- If the ID is an integer, but is not in the correct range (e.g., negative number), we get a 400 Bad Request error.

- It's not very obvious where and why the error occurs in the source code.

500 Internal Server Error is not very informative for the frontend. The frontend only knows that something went wrong on the server side, but it can't generate a helpful error message that will help the user work around the problem. There are a few ways to do it better:

- Return a 400[18] error when the ID is invalid (e.g., not a number, out of bound).

- Return a 404 error when the ID doesn't exist in the database.

- Return a 500 error when we can't get a connection from the pool.

- Be able to customize the error message ourselves.

- Make it clear in the code where and why an error occurs.

5.9 Input Validation

Let's deal with the input validation first. We know that the cat's ID can be wrong in many ways. If it's not an integer, Actix-web's type-safe extractor will return a 404 error. This error can be customized, but we'll get back to it later. Let's first handle the case where the ID is an integer, but it's not in the sensible range.

Because our cat ID has the schema id `SERIAL PRIMARY KEY`, we know that PostgreSQL will start with 1 and increase it by 1 every time we insert a new row. Therefore, the ID can't go below 1. Also for the sake of the example, if we only allow a user to add unique cat breeds to the website, then there are only 71 standardized breeds recognized by The International Cat Association (TICA). If we keep some buffer and assume that the cat breeds might double in the future, then we will have about $71 \times 2 = 142 \approx 150$ breeds. Therefore, we can check if the cat's ID is between 1 and 150 (inclusive), and if not we can simply reject the request without even querying the database.

---

[18] There are many debates about whether a 400 or a 422 is more appropriate in this case. We'll stick with the more generic 400 error.

To validate the input parameter in a more declarative way, you can use the validator crate. Add the crates with the command `cargo add validator --features derive`. Let's then derive that onto the cat's ID, as shown in Listing 5-24.

Listing 5-24. Using `validator` on cat's ID

```
use validator::Validate;

// ...

#[derive(Deserialize, Validate)]
struct CatEndpointPath {
    #[validate(range(min = 1, max = 150))]
    id: i32,
}

async fn cat_endpoint(
    pool: web::Data<DbPool>,
    cat_id: web::Path<CatEndpointPath>,
) -> Result<HttpResponse, Error> {
    cat_id
        .validate()
        .map_err(error::ErrorBadRequest)?;

    // ... getting a connection and query from database

    Ok(HttpResponse::Ok().json(cat_data))
}
```

In this code snippet, the `web::Path` extractor now tries to extract the `CatEndpointPath` struct from the URL. The `CatEndpointPath` is marked to have a `Validate` auto-derive trait provided by the `validate` crate. This means you can call `CatEndpointPath.validate()` to validate all its fields. Each field's validation rule can be annotated on them individually. For our `id` we specify that it should be a number in the range of 1 to 150: `#[validate(range(min=1, max=150))]`. The `validator` crate also provides some common checks like whether the field is an email, IP, URL, or has a certain length.

Inside the cat_endpoint handler, we call cat_id.validate() to validate. If the validation passes, it returns an Ok<()> and we just allow the code to continue. If the validation fails, it returns an Err<ValidationError>, and we convert it to a HttpResponse::BadRequest and force it to early return with the ? operator.

Now if you start the server again with cargo run and make a call to the API with an ID outside of the range (e.g., curl -v localhost:8080/api/cat/9999 or curl -v localhost:8080/api/cat/-1),[19] you should see the 400 Bad Request response.

```
$ curl -v localhost:8080/api/cat/9999
*   Trying 127.0.0.1:8080...
* Connected to localhost (127.0.0.1) port 8080 (#0)
> GET /api/cat/9999 HTTP/1.1
> Host: localhost:8080
> User-Agent: curl/7.81.0
> Accept: */*
>
* Mark bundle as not supporting multiuse
< HTTP/1.1 400 Bad Request
< content-length: 95
< content-type: text/plain; charset=utf-8
< date: Mon, 03 Apr 2023 18:06:28 GMT
<
* Connection #0 to host localhost left intact
id: Validation error: range [{
  "max": Number(150.0),
  "min": Number(1.0),
  "value": Number(9999)
}]
```

---

[19] The '-v' option is an abbreviation of --verbose. It will make curl print extra information like HTTP status code.

5.10 Error Handling

You've just seen how invalid input for the cat_endpoint handler can cause an error, but there are many other ways that this simple endpoint can have problems. We can go through the list to see how each error is handled in kind:

- The parameter validation might fail (dealt with in previous section).

- Getting a connection from the connection pool might fail.

- Querying the cat from the database might fail because

  - web::block() might fail for unexpected reasons;

  - the Diesel ORM might fail for unexpected reasons; or

  - the Diesel query might fail because the cat doesn't exist.[20]

Each of these errors might come from different libraries (actix-web, r2d2, diesel), and you've been converting them to HTTP responses with .map_err() and ?. But it's worth taking a step back to look at how Actix-web handles errors in general.

Let's first look at the API endpoint handler's return type: Result<HttpResponse, Error>. The Error here refers to Actix-web's own actix_web::Error[21], rather than the standard library std::error::Error. An actix_web::Error contains a trait object of the trait ResponseError. The ResponseError contains metadata (e.g., status code) and helper functions to construct an HTTP response so Actix-web can easily convert a actix_web::Error into an HTTP error response.

Since most of the errors returned by our dependent libraries are not actix_web::Error, if we have to handle them with match and construct an actix_web::Error by hand, the control flow will soon be very verbose. But in our previous example we could do something like .map_err(error::ErrorBadRequest)?;. How does this work?

Actix-web provides many helper functions and implicit type conversions to help you handle errors more fluently. Error handling can get confusing and overwhelming because of all the options. To simplify things, we'll break error handling down into three main categories:

---

[20] Although we make sure the ID is within 1 to 150, we might only have 70 cats in the database, and someone might try to find a cat with ID 71.

[21] It's actually a re-export of actix_http::error::Error. It's re-exported by actix_web for convenience. actix_web::error::Error is also the same thing.

- Using the `actix_web::error` helper functions like `actix_web::error:: ErrorBadRequest`

- Using a generic error that has implemented the `ResponseError` trait

- Using a custom-built error type

Using the `actix_web::error` Helpers

The first and probably most straightforward method is to use the `actix_web::error` helpers. In the `actix_web::error` module there are helper functions for most of the commonly used HTTP status codes. For example:

- `ErrorBadRequest()`: 400

- `ErrorNotFound()`: 404

- `ErrorInternalServerError()`: 500

- `ErrorBadGateway()`: 502

These error helpers wrap any error and return an `actix_web::Error`. For example, the signature of `ErrorBadRequest` is as follows:

```
pub fn ErrorBadRequest<T>(err: T) -> Error
where
    T: Debug + Display + 'static,
```

Therefore, if we make a function call that may return a `Result<T, E>`, we can use the `.map_err()` function to convert the `E` into an `actix_web::Error`. Then, we can use the `?` operator to force the handler function to return early with the converted `actix_web::Error`.

```
cat_id
    .validate()
    .map_err(|e| error::ErrorBadRequest(e))?;
```

Or simply replace the closure with the helper function:

```
cat_id
    .validate()
    .map_err(error::ErrorBadRequest)?;
```

Note   If you are not familiar with the `.map_err()` function, its purpose is to convert the `Err` value of a `Result` from one type to another, leaving the `Ok` value unchanged. For example, if we pass a function that converts a value of type E to type F, the `.map_err()` will convert a `Result<T, E>` to `Result<T, F>`. This is useful for passing through the `Ok` value and handling the `Err`. In our example, we use it to convert the error to a type that Actix-web accepts.

Figure 5-7 visualizes the error-handling flow we have so far been using.

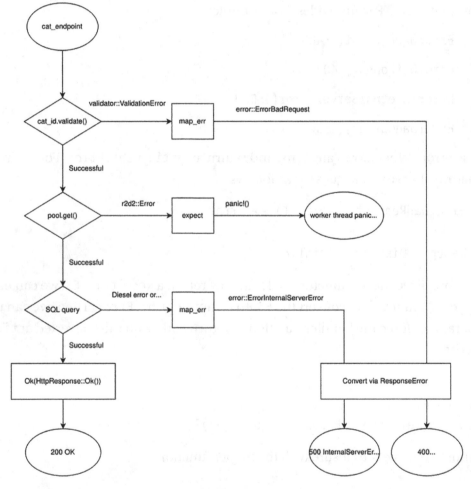

Figure 5-7. *The current error-handling flow*

Using a Generic Error That Has Implemented the ResponseError Trait

The previous method converts (or wraps) the error we got into an `actix_web::Error`. But the type definition of `Responder` only requires the error to be `Into<Error>`. And since there is an implementation of `impl<T: ResponseError + 'static> From<T> for Error`, you can return anything that implements the `ResponseError` trait.

Actix-web already implements `ResponseError` for many of the common error types you'll encounter in web services, such as the following:

- `std::io::error::Error`: when reading files

- `serde_json::error::Error`: when serialize/deserialize JSON

- `openssl::ssl::error::Error`: when making HTTPS connections

Therefore, if you have some very simple handlers that have only one error, you can just return it directly. For example, if you are serving the `index.html` by reading it in the handler with `NamedFile::open`, you can simply return `std::io::Result<T>` (i.e., `Result<T, std::io::error::Error>`), and the `io::error::Error` will be converted to an HTTP response error without writing anything extra (Listing 5-25).

Listing 5-25. Returning a `io::Result`, which implements `ResponseError`

```
use actix_files::NamedFile;
use std::io;

async fn index() -> io::Result<NamedFile> {
    Ok(NamedFile::open("./static/index.html")?)
}
```

Using a Custom-Built Error Type

The built-in implementation of `impl ResponseError for T` and `impl From <T> for Error` are helpful if you want to quickly return some error and don't want to deal with the conversion. But because many of the error types can be converted too easily, you might accidentally return some error that exposes too much detail to the user. When building an API you need to carefully choose how much detail you expose. A very detailed error is useful for debugging, but it may expose too many implementation details and give an attacker some hints on hacking your system. For example, if the application server fails to connect to the database, it might be tempting to respond with an error describing why the database connection failed, the database IP and port, or if you are really not careful, the database username and password. All these are useful pieces of information for the attacker to plan an attack based on the known vulnerabilities of the kind of database you use. Instead, you should just return a generic 500 Internal Server Error and not let the client know why. In other words, it's important to distinguish the internal error (e.g., database connection failed for a particular reason) and the user-facing error (e.g., 500 Internal Server Error).

To achieve this separation, we can implement our custom error type that implements the `ResponseError` trait. The error type can be an enum with a detailed reason that helps debugging, but the `ResponseError` implementation can convert these detailed errors into generic user-facing errors. We can also customize the error message instead of relying on the default provided by the `actix_web::error` helpers or `ResponseBuilder`.

To define our custom error, let's first create a new file called `src/errors.rs` and create an enum called `UserError`, as shown in Listing 5-26.

Listing 5-26. Custom error definition

```
#[derive(Debug)]
pub enum UserError {
    ValidationError,
    DBPoolGetError,
    NotFoundError,
    UnexpectedError,
}
```

Then, let's declare this module in `src/main.rs` and use them in our `cat_endpoint` (Listing 5-27).

Listing 5-27. Declaring and using the `UserError` in the `cat_endpoint`

```
// ...

mod errors;
use self::errors::UserError;

// ...
```

```
async fn cat_endpoint(
    pool: web::Data<DbPool>,
    cat_id: web::Path<CatEndpointPath>,
) -> Result<HttpResponse, UserError> {
    cat_id.validate().map_err(|_| UserError::ValidationError)?;
    let mut connection =
        pool.get().map_err(|_| UserError::DBPoolGetError)?;

    let query_id = cat_id.id.clone();
    let cat_data = web::block(move || {
        cats.filter(id.eq(query_id))
            .first::<Cat>(&mut connection)
    })
        .await
        .map_err(|_|UserError::UnexpectedError)?
        .map_err(|e| match e {
            diesel::result::Error::NotFound => {
                UserError::NotFoundError
            }
            _ => UserError::UnexpectedError,
        })?;
    Ok(HttpResponse::Ok().json(cat_data))
}
// ...
```

Notice that the cat_endpoint now returns the type Result<HttpResponse, UserError>. The .map_err() now converts the errors into UserError, instead of the error helper or ResponseBuilder. We also make a match in the .map_err() of the database query call, so we can isolate the special case where Diesel reports it can't find the cat (diesel::result::Error::NotFound).

The UserError has not implemented the ResponseError trait yet, so it can't be turned into an HTTP response. We can implement it in src/errors.rs, as shown in Listing 5-28. You'll also notice that we used the derive_more crate so we can auto-derive the Display trait on the UserError enum. You can add these crates by running cargo add derive_more.

Listing 5-28. Implementing ResponseError for UserError

```rust
use actix_web::http::StatusCode;
use actix_web::{error, HttpResponse};
use derive_more::Display;
use serde_json::json;

#[derive(Display, Debug)]
pub enum UserError {
    #[display(fmt = "Invalid input parameter")]
    ValidationError,
    #[display(fmt = "Internal server error")]
    DBPoolGetError,
    #[display(fmt = "Not found")]
    NotFoundError,
    #[display(fmt = "Internal server error")]
    UnexpectedError,
}

impl error::ResponseError for UserError {
    fn error_response(&self) -> HttpResponse {
        HttpResponse::build(self.status_code())
            .json(json!({ "msg": self.to_string() }))
    }
    fn status_code(&self) -> StatusCode {
        match *self {
            UserError::ValidationError => {
                StatusCode::BAD_REQUEST
            }
            UserError::DBPoolGetError => {
                StatusCode::INTERNAL_SERVER_ERROR
            }
            UserError::NotFoundError => StatusCode::NOT_FOUND,
            UserError::UnexpectedError => {
                StatusCode::INTERNAL_SERVER_ERROR
            }
        }
    }
}
```

An HTTP response has two key elements: the status code and the body. The status code is determined by the `status_code()` function. The function is a simple `match` that converts the enum variant to the appropriate status code. For the body we want to respond with a JSON object of the following format:

```
{
  "msg": "An error message"
}
```

The HTTP response is generated in the `error_response()` function using the `HttpResponse` builder. The message body is created by calling `self.to_string()`. We derive the `Display` trait on the enum and annotate each variant with `#[display(fmt="...")]` so that the `.to_string()` function will convert the enum variant to the string we specified. The JSON body is serialized using `json!()` macro from `serde_json`.

With this custom error, we can create as many internal errors as we want while converting them to something general for the user. Because the return type is `Result<HttpResponse, UserError>`, the compiler will prevent you from accidentally returning a random error that just happens to implement `ResponseError`.

Figure 5-8 visualizes the new error-handling flow after using `UserError`.

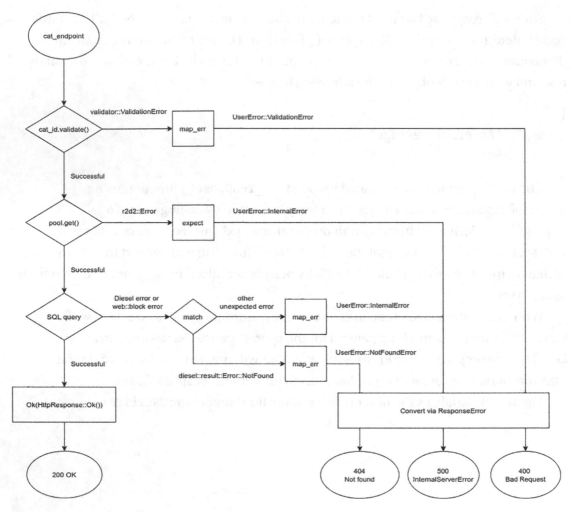

Figure 5-8. *The error-handling flow after using* `UserError`

5.11 Customizing the `web::Path` Extractor Error

We now have control over most of the errors, but we missed one case. If the ID cannot be converted to `i32`, the `web::Path` extractor will return a 404 Not Found with a default error message. But that error can also be customized through `web::PathConfig::error_handler()`. When we construct the `App` (or a `ServiceConfig`), we can define a custom error handler for `web::Path` extractors that returns custom errors. We can add it to the `api_config()` function as shown in Listing 5-29.

Listing 5-29. Custom error handler for web::Path extractor error

```
fn api_config(cfg: &mut web::ServiceConfig) {
    cfg.service(
        web::scope("/api")
            .app_data(web::PathConfig::default().error_handler(
                |_, _| UserError::ValidationError.into(),
            ))
            .route("/cats", web::get().to(cats_endpoint))
            .route("/add_cat", web::post().to(add_cat_endpoint))
            .route("/cat/{id}", web::get().to(cat_endpoint))
    );
}
```

You've thus configured a custom error handler that returns a UserError::ValidationError, which will be converted to a 400 Bad Request error thanks to our ResponseError implementation from the previous section:

```
UserError::ValidationError => {
    StatusCode::BAD_REQUEST
}
```

5.12 Logging

Good error handling helps us provide meaningful error status codes and messages to the frontend. But to really understand what happened as developers, we need to rely on logging. When the server is small and the business logic is simple, you can easily try a few requests and reproduce a bug. But when you have thousands of concurrent users, all going through different code paths, it can be hard to pinpoint exactly where the bug is. With proper logging, you can gain visibility into what happened to the requests and easily identify problems and bugs. It might also give you a view into user behavior and trends.

There is a key concept you need to understand before jumping into logging: logging facade versus logging implementation. A logging facade defines an "interface" for logging. A logging implementation adopts that "interface" and does the actual logging (e.g., writing to STDOUT; writing to a file). A logging facade gives an extra layer of abstraction so you can swap different implementations without rewriting the whole code. This is particularly useful when building libraries. A Rust library can log using a logging facade but not choose a concrete implementation. An application that uses libraries can choose an implementation, and as long as all the libraries adopt the same logging facade, they can use the same chosen implementation.

A commonly used facade is the log crate, and env_logger is a simple but effective logging implementation. The env in the name suggests that you can configure the logging level using environment variables. Actix-web also provides a Logger middleware that produces access logs using the log facade.

To enable the Logger, you .wrap() the App with the Logger middleware as shown in Listing 5-30. Don't forget to run cargo add env_logger to import the crate.

Listing 5-30. Using the Logger middleware

```
//...
use actix_web::middleware::Logger;
// ...

#[actix_web::main]
async fn main() -> std::io::Result<()> {
    env_logger::init(); // Initialize env_logger

    let pool = setup_database();

    println!("Listening on port 8080");
    HttpServer::new(move || {
        App::new()
            .wrap(Logger::default()) // Set the logger
            .app_data(web::Data::new(pool.clone()))
            .app_data(awmp::PartsConfig::default()
                .with_temp_dir("./tmp")
            )
            .configure(api_config) // Used here
            .service(
                Files::new("/static", "static")
                    .show_files_listing(),
            )
```

```
            .service(
                Files::new("/image", "image")
                    .show_files_listing(),
            )
            .route("/", web::get().to(index))
    })
        .bind("127.0.0.1:8080")?
        .run()
        .await
    }
```

The Logger middleware uses the log facade, but you need to provide a logger implementation for it to work. (For this example you'll want to check that the added version is 0.10.0.)

```
#[actix_web::main]
async fn main() -> std::io::Result<()> {
    env_logger::init();
    // ...
}
```

In the example, we use Logger::default() to get the default format. But you can also customize the log format when you initialize it.

The log facade defines the following log levels, ordered by priority:

- Error: Designates very serious errors.

- Warn: Designates hazardous situations.

- Info: Designates useful information.

- Debug: Designates lower priority information.

- Trace: Designates very low priority, often extremely verbose, information.

When you choose a log level, any log that has priority above it and includes that level will be shown. Because the env_logger's log level is configured through environment variables, we can run the server with log level set to debug in this way:

```
RUST_LOG=debug cargo run
```

When you try calling the `http://localhost:8080/api/cats` API, the `Logger` middleware should log this request (note on your system some of the specifics may be different):

```
[2022-12-19T17:52:11Z INFO  actix_server::builder]
    Starting 8 workers
[2022-12-19T17:52:11Z INFO  actix_server::server]
    Actix runtime found; starting in Actix runtime
[2022-12-19T17:52:41Z INFO actix_web::middleware::logger]
    127.0.0.1 "GET /api/cats HTTP/1.1" 200
    712 "-" "Mozilla/5.0 (X11; Linux x86_64)
    AppleWebKit/537.36 (KHTML, like Gecko)
    Chrome/107.0.0.0 Safari/537.36" 0.002274
```

You can also log custom messages. The `log` crate exposes logging macros for logging at a particular level: `error!()`, `warn!()`, `info!()`, `debug!()`, and `trace!()`. You can add logs to all the places where errors are handled (Listing 5-31). Note that we can also use this opportunity to go back and change the error type of the `cats_endpoint` and `add_cat_endpoints` functions to `UserError`.

Listing 5-31. Custom logging

```rust
//...
use log::{error, info, warn};
use actix_web::{web, App, HttpServer, HttpResponse,
    Result}; // Remove error, Error

// ...

async fn cats_endpoint(
    pool: web::Data<DbPool>,
) -> Result<HttpResponse, UserError> {
    let mut connection =
        pool.get().expect("Can't get db connection from pool");

    let cats_data = web::block(move || {
        cats.limit(100).load::<Cat>(&mut connection)
    })
```

```
        .await
        .map_err(|_| {
            error!("Blocking Thread Pool Error");
            UserError::UnexpectedError
        })?
        .map_err(|_| {
            error!("Failed to get DB connection from pool");
            UserError::DBPoolGetError
        })?;
    return Ok(HttpResponse::Ok().json(cats_data));
}

// ...

async fn cat_endpoint(
    pool: web::Data<DbPool>,
    cat_id: web::Path<CatEndpointPath>,
) -> Result<HttpResponse, UserError> {
    cat_id.validate().map_err(|_| {
        warn!("Parameter validation failed");
        UserError::ValidationError
    })?;
    let mut connection =
        pool.get().map_err(|_| {
            error!("Failed to get DB connection from pool");
            UserError::DBPoolGetError
        })?;

    let query_id = cat_id.id.clone();
    let cat_data = web::block(move || {
        cats.filter(id.eq(query_id))
            .first::<Cat>(&mut connection)
    })
        .await
        .map_err(|_|{
            error!("Blocking Thread Pool Error");
            UserError::UnexpectedError
        })?
```

```
        .map_err(|e| match e {
            diesel::result::Error::NotFound => {
                error!("Cat ID: {} not found in DB",
                        &cat_id.id);
                UserError::NotFoundError
            }
            _ => {
                error!("Unexpected error");
                UserError::UnexpectedError
            },
        })?;
    Ok(HttpResponse::Ok().json(cat_data))
}

// ...

async fn add_cat_endpoint(
    pool: web::Data<DbPool>,
    mut parts: awmp::Parts,
) -> Result<HttpResponse, UserError> {
    let file_path = parts
        .files
        .take("image")
        .pop()
        .and_then(|f| f.persist_in("./image").ok())
        .ok_or_else(|| {
            error!("Error in getting image path");
            UserError::ValidationError
        })?;
    let text_fields: HashMap<_, _> =
        parts.texts.as_pairs().into_iter().collect();

    let mut connection = pool.get()
        .map_err(|_| {
            error!("Failed to get DB connection from pool");
            UserError::DBPoolGetError
        })?;
```

```rust
    let new_cat = NewCat {
        name: text_fields.get("name").ok_or_else(|| {
            error!("Error in getting name field");
            UserError::ValidationError
        }
        )?.to_string(),
        image_path: file_path.to_string_lossy().to_string()
    };

    web::block(move ||
        diesel::insert_into(cats)
            .values(&new_cat)
            .execute(&mut connection)
    )
        .await
        .map_err(|_| {
            error!("Blocking Thread Pool Error");
            UserError::UnexpectedError
        })?
        .map_err(|_| {
            error!("Failed to get DB connection from pool");
            UserError::DBPoolGetError
        })?;

    Ok(HttpResponse::Created().finish())
}

// ...

#[actix_web::main]
async fn main() -> std::io::Result<()> {
    env_logger::init();

    let pool = setup_database();

    info!("Listening on port 8080"); // New logging line
    HttpServer::new(move || {
        App::new()
```

```
            .wrap(Logger::default())
            .app_data(web::Data::new(pool.clone()))
            .app_data(awmp::PartsConfig::default()
                .with_temp_dir("./tmp")
            )
            .configure(api_config)
            .service(
                Files::new("/static", "static")
                    .show_files_listing(),
            )
            .service(
                Files::new("/image", "image")
                    .show_files_listing(),
            )
            .route("/", web::get().to(index))
    })
        .bind("127.0.0.1:8080")?
        .run()
        .await
}
```

This makes our code longer and more verbose, but is critical to being able to debug a problem in production.

You can start the server with logging by running

```
RUST_LOG=debug cargo run
```

If you try to trigger a validation error (e.g., by calling curl localhost:8080/api/cat/-1), you should see a custom log like the following:

```
[2022-12-19T18:07:46Z INFO  catdex-api]
  Listening on port 8080
[2022-12-19T18:07:46Z INFO  actix_server::builder]
  Starting 8 workers
[2022-12-19T18:07:46Z INFO  actix_server::server]
  Actix runtime found; starting in Actix runtime
[2022-12-19T18:07:49Z WARN  catdex-api]
  Parameter validation failed
```

```
[2022-12-19T18:07:49Z DEBUG actix_web::middleware::logger]
  Error in response: ValidationError
[2022-12-19T18:07:49Z INFO  actix_web::middleware::logger]
  127.0.0.1 "GET /api/cat/-1 HTTP/1.1" 400 33 "-"
  "Mozilla/5.0 (X11; Linux x86_64) AppleWebKit/537.36
  (KHTML, like Gecko) Chrome/107.0.0.0
  Safari/537.36" 0.000380
```

With carefully planned error handling and logging, you should be able to get good visibility into how your system is behaving in production.

5.13 Enabling HTTPS

Now our API server is ready to serve the users. But we've been testing it with the HTTP protocol only. To actually serve this API out on the internet, it's important to use the HTTPS protocol, which encrypts the communication with TLS (Transport Layer Security).[22]

The first thing you need for HTTPS is a certificate for your domain name. Usually, you obtain a certificate from a certificate authority (CA). You can get a free certificate from Let's Encrypt,[23] a non-profit CA that tries to create a more secure web. But for the sake of demonstration we are going to create a self-signed certificate; i.e., we act as our own CA and sign our own certificate.

To generate the certificate (`cert.pem`) and the private key (`key.pem`),[24] you can run this commands:

```
sudo apt install openssl # Only run once

openssl req -x509 -newkey rsa:4096 \
  -keyout key.pem \
  -out cert.pem \
  -days 365 \
  -sha256 \
  -subj "/CN=localhost"
```

---

[22] Formerly SSL (Secure Sockets Layer).

[23] https://letsencrypt.org/

[24] How HTTPS works is outside of the scope for this book, but you can find many good introductions online by searching "How HTTPS works."

The openssl tool will ask you to set a password for the key.pem file. If you use this key.pem, then every time you start the Acitx-web server you need to enter the password again. To remove the password, you can run

```
openssl rsa -in key.pem -out key-no-password.pem
```

This will generate a new key file key-no-password.pem. When deploying this file to the production server, be sure to secure it with file system permissions.

Once we have the certificate and key, there are a few extra steps required for SSL:

- Install the required headers: sudo apt install libssl-dev.

- Add the openssl crate to the dependencies via cargo add openssl.

- Enable the openssl feature on actix-web via cargo add actix-web --features openssl (Listing 5-32).

Listing 5-32. Enabling the openssl feature for actix-web in Cargo.toml

```
[package]
name = "catdex-api"
# ...

[dependencies]
actix-web = { version = "4.3.1", features = ["openssl"] }
# ...
openssl = "0.10.49"
```

Finally, we can change our code so that the App builder uses .bind_openssl() instead of .bind(), shown in Listing 5-33.

Listing 5-33. Enabling SSL

```
// ...
use openssl::ssl::{SslAcceptor, SslFiletype, SslMethod};

// ...

#[actix_web::main]
async fn main() -> std::io::Result<()> {
    env_logger::init();
```

```rust
//Set up the certificate
let mut builder =
    SslAcceptor::mozilla_intermediate(SslMethod::tls())
        .unwrap();
builder
    .set_private_key_file(
        "key-no-password.pem",
        SslFiletype::PEM,
    )
    .unwrap();
builder.set_certificate_chain_file("cert.pem").unwrap();

let pool = setup_database();

info!("Listening on port 8080");
HttpServer::new(move || {
    App::new()
        .wrap(Logger::default())
        .app_data(web::Data::new(pool.clone()))
        .app_data(awmp::PartsConfig::default()
            .with_temp_dir("./tmp")
        )
        .configure(api_config) // Used here
        .service(
            Files::new("/static", "static")
                .show_files_listing(),
        )
        .service(
            Files::new("/image", "image")
                .show_files_listing(),
        )
        .route("/", web::get().to(index))
})
    .bind_openssl("127.0.0.1:8080", builder)? // Binding
    .run()
    .await
}
```

Now if you start the server with `cargo run`, you should be able to connect to the website with `https://localhost:8080` instead of `http://localhost:8080`. Your browser should show a warning because it doesn't trust our self-signed CA, but for this testing case you can inform it that you understand the risks and proceed.

5.14 Framework Alternatives

There are many server-side frameworks in Rust to choose from. We'll suggest some high-level frameworks that you might find useful. Some people want to use low-level HTTP libraries like `hyper`[25] to build web servers for better control, but they require a better understanding of the underlying technology and more code. Just like in many other areas of programming, it's usually best to start at a higher level of abstraction and only dip into a lower level when you know you need the control or performance.

If you need to build dynamic websites or powerful REST APIs, there are many options besides `Actix-web`. `Rocket`[26] is probably one of the strongest competitors. It still hasn't reached version 1.0, but continuous progress is being made. `Warp`[27] also gets a lot of attention in the community because of its unique design on composability, but the documentation and online resources are relatively scarce. There are a few others that are also relatively stable and easy to use:

- gotham[28]

- tower-web[29]

- iron[30]

- nickel[31]

- Tide[32]

---

[25] `https://hyper.rs/`

[26] `https://rocket.rs/`

[27] `https://github.com/seanmonstar/warp`

[28] `https://gotham.rs/`

[29] `https://github.com/carllerche/tower-web`

[30] `http://github.com/iron/iron`

[31] `https://nickel-org.github.io/`

[32] `https://github.com/http-rs/tide`

- rouille[33]

- Thruster[34]

For database access through ORM, you can also check out Rustorm[35] and SeaORM.[36] If you don't like using ORM and would like to work with raw SQL, you can find many client libraries for popular databases and in-memory caches:

- mysql[37] (for MySQL)

- postgres[38] (for PostgreSQL)

- mongodb[39] (for MongoDB)

- redis[40] (for Redis)

- memcache[41] (for Memcached)

If want your server to serve more advanced, full-featured web pages without relying on a frontend framework, you can rely on both static and dynamic HTML generation crates. If you are building a static website, you can use a static site generator, like Zola[42] or Cobalt.[43] You can also dynamically generate HTML on the server using various

---

[33] https://github.com/tomaka/rouille

[34] https://github.com/thruster-rs/Thruster

[35] https://github.com/ivanceras/rustorm

[36] https://www.sea-ql.org/SeaORM/

[37] https://github.com/blackbeam/rust-mysql-simple

[38] https://github.com/sfackler/rust-postgres

[39] https://github.com/mongodb/mongo-rust-driver

[40] https://github.com/mitsuhiko/redis-rs

[41] https://github.com/aisk/rust-memcache

[42] https://www.getzola.org/

[43] https://cobalt-org.github.io/

HTML templating engines. Some of web frameworks have their preference for a specific templating engine, and some keep it open (like `Actix-web`). There are many templating engines to choose from if server-side HTML generation is your goal:

- handlebars[44]

- tera[45] (Jinja2/Django-inspired syntax)

- liquid[46]

- askama[47]

- tinytemplate[48]

- maud[49]

- ructe[50]

Besides REST, there are other protocols you can use to build APIs. For example, gRPC and GraphQL are some of the popular alternatives. For gRPC, there are crates like `tonic`[51] and `grpc`.[52] For GraphQL there is `juniper`.[53] Juniper doesn't come with a web server, so it needs to be integrated into a web framework like `Actix-web`.

Although JSON is one of the most popular data representation formats, you can also use other formats like XML (`serde-xml-rs`[54]) or Protobuf (`protobuf`[55], or `prost`[56]).

---

[44] https://github.com/sunng87/handlebars-rust
[45] https://tera.netlify.app/
[46] https://github.com/cobalt-org/liquid-rust
[47] https://github.com/djc/askama
[48] https://github.com/bheisler/TinyTemplate
[49] https://maud.lambda.xyz/
[50] https://github.com/kaj/ructe
[51] https://github.com/hyperium/tonic
[52] https://github.com/stepancheg/grpc-rust
[53] https://github.com/graphql-rust/juniper
[54] https://github.com/RReverser/serde-xml-rs
[55] https://github.com/stepancheg/rust-protobuf/
[56] https://github.com/danburkert/prost

Finally, log allows us to log in many formats, but they are still for humans to consume. If we log in a machine-readable format (e.g., JSON), many existing log analysis tools can help us index and analyze the log. This is called *structured logging*. Currently, you can use the slog[57] ecosystem for structured logging. There are also efforts in introducing structured logging to log.[58]

You can find a complete list of web-related crates and get an overview of the maturity of Rust's web ecosystem at https://www.arewewebyet.org/.

5.15 Conclusion

In this chapter, you developed a server-side web application that both served static pages and provides a REST API. You integrated a database into your application to persist data between visits. You added APIs to list cats, add cats, and get more information about individual cats in the system. You added testing, input validation, error handling, logging, and HTTPS. In the next chapter, you'll remove the need for a specific server running your app and develop a serverless version in the cloud.

---

[57] https://github.com/slog-rs/slog
[58] https://github.com/rust-lang/log/issues/149

CHAPTER 6

Going Serverless with the Amazon AWS Rust SDK

In the previous chapter, you built a REST API that could serve up a static web page and interact with a database. This works fine when you deploy on your own machine and only test with low traffic. But when you need to make your site publicly accessible, managing the server becomes a headache. Traditionally, you'd have to buy physical servers and run your applications on them. You'd have to take care of every aspect of IT management, like keeping the operating system and system libraries up-to-date, making sure failed hardware was replaced, and keeping the servers powered even when there was a power outage. Unless you have a big budget and an operations team, this is not a fun job.

If you don't want to handle these troubles yourself, there are many companies that let you outsource the work and use their servers. Third-party web hosting and virtual private server (VPS) services have existed for a long time. Nowadays, you also have many Infrastructure-as-a-Service (IaaS) and Platform-as-a-Service (PaaS) providers you can choose from. They manage the servers for you and provide different levels of abstraction so you can focus on your application. Serverless computing pushes this idea to the extreme. With serverless computing, you just write the functions that handle the business logic. The hardware, OS, and the language runtime are all handled by the service provider. You can also connect them to managed databases, message queues, and file storage, which are all also fully managed by the service provider. Serverless computing is great for scaling too, letting users use anywhere from a few megabytes of memory for a few milliseconds a day to running global-scale web applications with thousands of operations per second.

In this chapter, you'll use Amazon Web Service (AWS) premier serverless platform, AWS Lambda, as the computation service. You'll also use DynamoDB, a fully managed NoSQL database from AWS. AWS provides a Rust runtime for AWS Lambda and an AWS Software Development Kit (SDK) for Rust so that you can control AWS services programmatically.

© Shing Lyu and Andrew Rzeznik 2023
S. Lyu and A. Rzeznik, *Practical Rust Projects*, https://doi.org/10.1007/978-1-4842-9331-7_6

6.1 What Are You Building?

In this chapter, you are going to rebuild the Catdex REST API in a serverless fashion, and then actually deploy it on the public internet. You'll learn to build on AWS by following these steps:

- Run Rust code as an AWS Lambda function using the Rust runtime for AWS Lambda.

- Create a REST API endpoint using the AWS Serverless Application Model (AWS SAM) and its easy-to-use templates.

- Use the `lambda_http` crate to handle API requests coming from AWS API Gateway.

- Write to DynamoDB to create a new cat using the AWS SDK for Rust.

- Read all the cats from DynamoDB.

- Upload images directly to S3, an object storage service.

- Serve the frontend from S3.

- Enable cross-origin resource sharing (CORS) so the frontend can access the API under a different domain.

6.2 What Is AWS Lambda?

AWS Lambda is a service that allows you to run code without provisioning a server. AWS manages the underlying hardware, networking, operating system, and runtime. As a developer, you only upload a piece of code, and it will run and scale automatically. A lambda function can be triggered manually (via the web console or the AWS Command Line Interface (AWS CLI)) or by events generated by other AWS services. For REST APIs, it's common to use API Gateway or Application Load Balancer to handle the request and trigger the lambda. AWS Lambda frees the developers from configuring and managing the servers, so they focus on the code. You are charged by the compute time you consume (in 100ms chunks), so if your function is sitting idle, you don't need to pay anything. Lambda can also scale automatically. If you use Lambda to power a REST API, it can automatically spin up more lambda instances when traffic is high.

AWS Lambda provides many language runtimes, like Java, Go, PowerShell, Node. js, C#, Python, and Ruby. It also provides a Runtime API so you can build your custom runtime.[1] AWS has released an experimental runtime for Rust using this runtime mechanism, so you can run Rust code on Lambda.

Note   The underlying technology that powers AWS Lambda is Firecracker VM.[2] Interestingly, Firecracker VM is written in Rust. So even if you write lambdas in other languages, your code is still powered by Rust. The project was released as an open source project by AWS. You can find ways to contribute to it by visiting its GitHub repository: `https://github.com/firecracker-microvm/firecracker`.

6.3 Registering an AWS Account

Since you are going to run your services on Amazon Web Service (AWS), you need to register an account. Visit `https://aws.amazon.com` in your browser and click the "Create an AWS Account" button. Follow the steps and sign up for an account. You might need to provide a credit card during the process.

AWS provides one year of free-tier services (usage limitations apply) when you sign up for the first time. This covers most of the services you are going to use: Lambda, DynamoDB, and S3. Therefore, you should be able to run most of the examples with minimal to no cost. But remember to clean up all the resources after you finish testing to prevent any unexpected bills.

---

[1] See `https://docs.aws.amazon.com/lambda/latest/dg/runtimes-custom.html`
[2] `https://firecracker-microvm.github.io/`

6.4 Hello World in Lambda

The first thing you are going to look at is the Hello World lambda from the AWS official Lambda Rust Runtime.[3] You are going to deploy this lambda and test it through the AWS management console and AWS CLI. First, you'll need to install Cargo Lambda,[4] which will help with packaging and testing your Lambdas. If you are on a Debian flavor of Linux (like Ubuntu) you'll first need to install Python's pip package manager using

```
sudo apt install python3-pip
```

Then, you can install Cargo Lambda using `sudo pip3 install cargo-lambda`. For other platforms, refer to the Cargo Lambda documentation for installation instructions.[5] Now you can create a Rust project that builds to a simple Lambda function by running `cargo lambda new serverless-hello-world`. When you do, a few questions will be asked. You should answer no to the first, and simply hit Enter for the second without making any selection.

```
$ cargo lambda new serverless-hello-world
> Is this function an HTTP function? No
> AWS Event type that this function receives
```

Now a project will be generated with a basic `src/main.rs`. You can replace it with the basic hello world code found in Listing 6-1.

Listing 6-1. Hello serverless world

```rust
use lambda_runtime::{run, service_fn, Error, LambdaEvent};
use serde::{Deserialize, Serialize};

#[derive(Deserialize)]
struct Request {
    first_name: String,
}
```

---

[3] https://github.com/awslabs/aws-lambda-rust-runtime/
[4] https://www.cargo-lambda.info/
[5] https://www.cargo-lambda.info/guide/installation.html

```rust
#[derive(Serialize)]
struct Response {
    message: String,
}

async fn function_handler(
    event: LambdaEvent<Request>
) -> Result<Response, Error> {
    let name = event.payload.first_name;

    let response = Response {
        message: format!(
            "Hello, {}",
            if name == "" {"Serverless World"} else {&name}
        ),
    };

    Ok(response)
}

#[tokio::main]
async fn main() -> Result<(), Error> {
    tracing_subscriber::fmt()
        .with_max_level(tracing::Level::INFO)
        .with_target(false)
        .without_time()
        .init();

    run(service_fn(function_handler)).await
}
```

In the main function, you can see you set up a tracing_subscriber for logging. The log generated by the lambda will be collected in AWS CloudWatch, AWS's logging and metrics service. Then, you use the run and service_fn functions to set up your handler, in this case function_handler. That means when an event triggers the lambda, it will call the function_handler() function and pass the event.

Handling events and returning responses is the core operation of a Lambda handler function. A lambda can handle different types of events from different sources, like API Gateway, SQS, S3, or a DynamoDB stream. Each event has its own structure, so you'll have to write your code accordingly. In this example, you are going to define a simple event format using struct Request, which contains a single field called first_name. The struct implements the Deserialize trait from Rust's serde crate. Similarly, you'll define a Response as the lambda's output format and implement Serialize on it so that it can be converted to JSON.

Figure 6-1. *Lambda console*

The function_handler function is very straightforward; it generates a response using first_name if it's not the empty string, or the default "Serverless World" otherwise. This is used as the text in the response message "Hello, <text>!"

At this point, you are ready to deploy your Lambda function, and there are a few different options to do so. To do the minimal amount of additional setup on this first example, we'll create a zip archive of the lambda function and then upload it directly to the AWS console. Run the following command to create the archive:

```
cargo lambda build --release --arm64 --output-format zip
```

After this finishes, you can find the archive at target/lambda/serverless-hello-world/bootstrap.zip.

To test the lambda, you need to do the following:

1. Visit the AWS Management Console `https://aws.amazon.com/console/` from your browser. Log in with your credentials.

2. In "Find Services," find "Lambda" and click on the result.

3. In the Lambda console (Figure 6-1), click "Create function."

4. In the function creation page, select "Author from scratch." Set the "Function name" as "hello-world." Select "Custom runtime – Provide your own bootstrap on Amazon Linux 2" in the "Runtime" field. You should also select `arm64` for the platform. Then click "Create function."

5. Once you are redirected to the `hello-world` function's page, scroll down to the "Function code" section and click "Actions." From a dropdown you should be able to select "upload," which will let you upload the `rust.zip` file you created previously.

To test this lambda, you can click on the "Test" button on the lambda page (Figure 6-2). If it's the first time you are testing it, AWS console will prompt you to create a test event (Figure 6-3). You can give it an event name called "test" and add a test event body like so:

```
{
  "first_name": "Ferris"
}
```

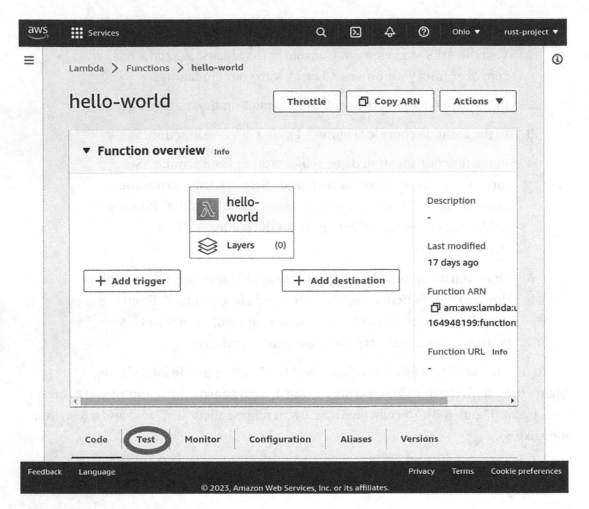

Figure 6-2. *The Test button*

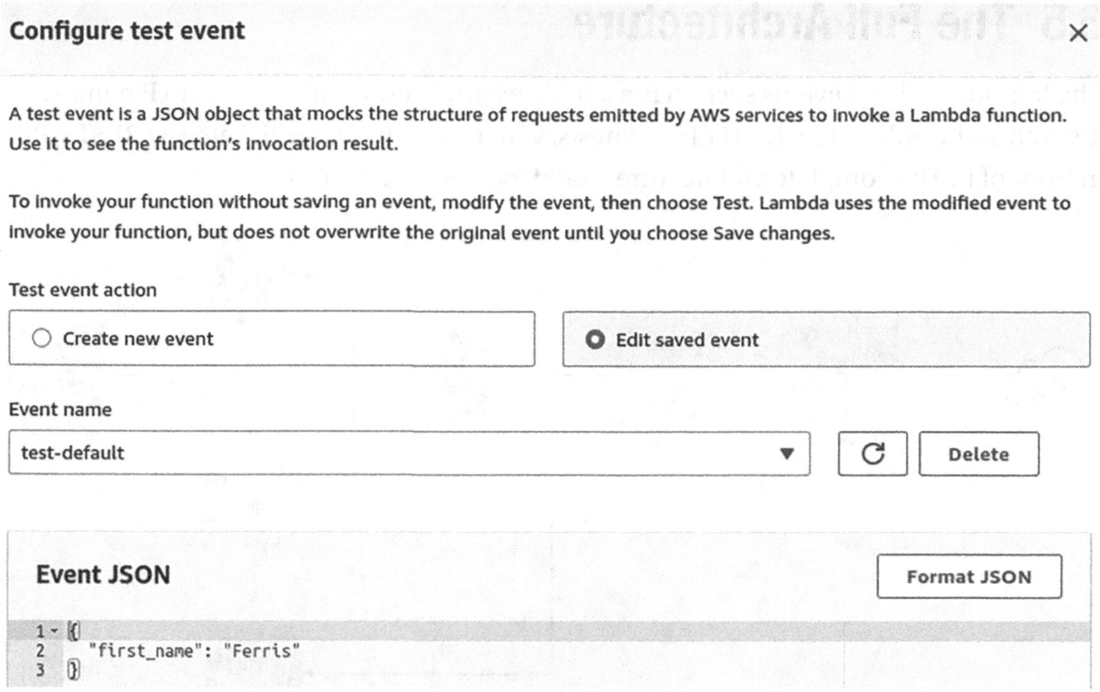

Configure test event   ✕

A test event is a JSON object that mocks the structure of requests emitted by AWS services to invoke a Lambda function. Use it to see the function's invocation result.

To invoke your function without saving an event, modify the event, then choose Test. Lambda uses the modified event to invoke your function, but does not overwrite the original event until you choose Save changes.

Test event action

○ Create new event	● Edit saved event

Event name

test-default	▼	C	Delete

Event JSON   Format JSON

```
1 ▾ {
2      "first_name": "Ferris"
3   }
```

Figure 6-3. *Creating a test event*

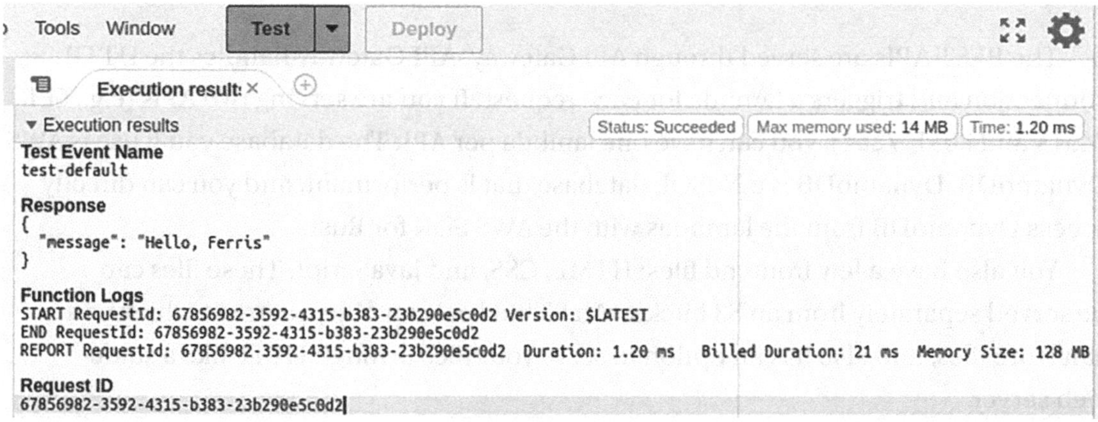

⟩   Tools   Window   **Test** ▼   Deploy   ⤢ ⚙

▤ /   Execution result: ✕   ⊕

▾ Execution results   Status: Succeeded | Max memory used: 14 MB | Time: 1.20 ms

Test Event Name
test-default

Response
```
{
  "message": "Hello, Ferris"
}
```

Function Logs
START RequestId: 67856982-3592-4315-b383-23b290e5c0d2 Version: $LATEST
END RequestId: 67856982-3592-4315-b383-23b290e5c0d2
REPORT RequestId: 67856982-3592-4315-b383-23b290e5c0d2 Duration: 1.20 ms   Billed Duration: 21 ms Memory Size: 128 MB

Request ID
67856982-3592-4315-b383-23b290e5c0d2

Figure 6-4. *Test output*

Then click "Save." Now the dropdown menu will show a test event named "test." If you click "Test" again, the test event will be sent to the lambda, and you should see an output and some logs, as shown in Figure 6-4.

6.5 The Full Architecture

The lambda in the previous section is a simple example and can't serve HTTP requests just yet. To be able to receive HTTP requests, you need to put an API Gateway REST API in front of it. The complete architecture would look like Figure 6-5.

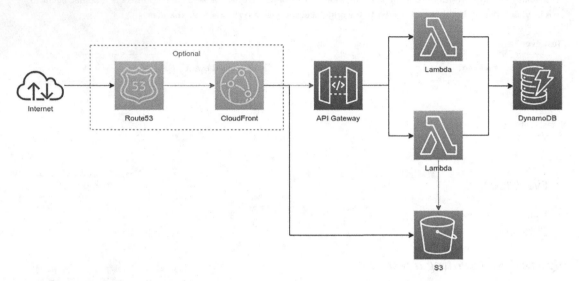

Figure 6-5. *A simple REST API architecture*

The REST APIs are served through API Gateway. API Gateway handles the HTTP connection and triggers a lambda for each request. If you are serving two APIs (e.g., `GET` `/cats` and `POST` `/cat`), you can have one lambda per API. The database you'll use is AWS DynamoDB. DynamoDB is a NoSQL database that is performant, and you can directly access DynamoDB from the lambdas with the AWS SDK for Rust.

You also have a few frontend files: HTML, CSS, and JavaScript. These files can be served separately from an S3 bucket. An S3 bucket is an object store in which you can store files, and also has an option to serve your files through HTTP like a static web server.

The URLs exposed by API Gateway and S3 static file hosting are auto-generated by AWS, so you can't really customize them. You can, however, add a CloudFront CDN and add a custom domain name through Route53, a managed DNS service. This way you have full control over what domain name the API and static files use. But this is beyond the scope of this book and not related to Rust, so we'll skip adding them here. You can consult the official AWS documentation if you are interested in setting this up. We'll focus on setting up the rest of the architecture.

6.6 Using the AWS Serverless Application Model (AWS SAM)

Configuring all these resources through the web console is not an easy task. It's hard to keep track of what is actually deployed in production. It's also hard to re-create the whole stack from scratch if you destroy it by accident. Infrastructure-as-code (abbreviated as IaC) is a way to solve this problem. You define your infrastructure and the configuration through code, and the IaC tool of your choice will configure everything according to your code. If you make any change to the definition, the change can be reflected with a quick deployment. Thus, you can version control your infrastructure like code, and fixing or re-creating the whole stack is just a simple deployment away.

In this chapter you are going to use the AWS Serverless Application Model to define your infrastructure, or AWS SAM for short. AWS SAM not only manages the infrastructure (using an extension of AWS CloudFormation under the hood), but also helps you manage the whole lifecycle of the application, from testing and packaging the lambda code to logging.

You are going to use the template-in template as the basis of the new serverless catdex. To create a project with an AWS SAM template, you first need to install the AWS SAM CLI. Follow the instructions on the documentation to install the latest AWS SAM CLI for your operating system: https://docs.aws.amazon.com/serverless-application-model/latest/developerguide/serverless-sam-cli-install.html.

For Linux, you need to download the ZIP file for the CLI using the link in the documentation. Then, unzip the ZIP file and execute the installation script:

```
$ unzip aws-sam-cli-linux-x86_64.zip -d sam-installation
$ sudo ./sam-installation/install
```

To verify the installation, run the following:

```
$ sam --version
SAM CLI, version 1.76.0 # You should see the version number
```

6.7 Setting Up AWS SAM CLI Credentials

The SAM CLI needs you to set AWS credentials so it can manage AWS resources on your behalf. You can follow the step-by-step instructions to set it up:

https://docs.aws.amazon.com/serverless-application-model/latest/developerguide/prerequisites.html

In short, you need to do the following:

1. Create a new IAM user with programmatic access. Attach the AdministratorAccess policy[6] to it.

2. Copy the newly created user's access key and secret access key.

3. Install the AWS CLI V2 (if you haven't already) to configure credentials.

4. Set the access key and secret access key using aws configure.

6.8 Creating the Catdex Serverless Project

To create a project, you can run the same Cargo Lambda command as before, with a new project name: **catdex-serverless**. This time you should answer that you are creating an HTTP function, and that you'll be creating an Amazon API Gateway REST API. You can see the output in Listing 6-2.

Listing 6-2. cargo lambda output

```
$ cargo lambda new catdex-serverless
> Is this function an HTTP function? y
> Which service is this function receiving events from? Amazon Api Gateway
REST Api
```

---

[6] It's a bad idea to give your IAM user administrator access in production. You should grant permission based on the principle of least privilege. But for demonstration purpose it's easier to give full access.

You now should have a project with an example HTTP lambda function handler included. Cargo Lambda is great for setting up the basic project that contains the lambda function, but it doesn't directly set up the supporting architecture we just described. Our first step in setting up our infrastructure is to create a `template.yaml` file, the AWS SAM template, which will be where we define all of the various pieces of our serverless architecture. The AWS SAM template is an extension to CloudFormation, which is an AWS service that lets you model, provision, and manage AWS and third-party resources by treating infrastructure as code. The `template.yaml` file contains infrastructure-as-code definitions for the services like API Gateway and AWS Lambda, and should be located in the `catdex-serverless` project as shown here:

```
.
+-- template.yaml
+-- Cargo.toml
+-- src
|   +-- main.rs
```

Now you can fill out the `template.yaml` file with the code from Listing 6-3.[7] This AWS SAM template file defines the infrastructure using the AWS SAM specification.[8] The AWS SAM template is an extension of AWS CloudFormation templates, with some additional components that provide a higher-level abstraction over lower-level CloudFormation components.

Listing 6-3. The `template.yaml` from the template

```
# template.yaml
AWSTemplateFormatVersion: '2010-09-09'

Transform: AWS::Serverless-2016-10-31
Description: >
  catdex-serverless

  Sample SAM Template for catdex-serverless
```

---

[7] Some comments are removed to improve the readability.

[8] https://docs.aws.amazon.com/serverless-application-model/latest/developerguide/sam-specification.html

```yaml
Globals:
  Function:
    Timeout: 3

Resources:
  CatTable:
    Type: AWS::Serverless::SimpleTable
    Properties:
      PrimaryKey:
        Name: cat
        Type: String

  PostCatFunction:
    Type: AWS::Serverless::Function
    Properties:
      CodeUri: target/lambda/catdex-serverless/
      Handler: bootstrap
      Runtime: provided.al2
      Architectures: ["arm64"]
      Events:
        HelloWorld:
          Type: Api
          Properties:
            Path: /cat
            Method: post
      Environment:
        Variables:
          TABLE_NAME: !Ref CatTable
      Policies:
        - DynamoDBWritePolicy:
            TableName: !Ref CatTable

Outputs:
  PostApi:
    Description: "API Gateway endpoint URL for Prod stage
      for Post function"
```

```
  Value: !Sub "https://${ServerlessRestApi}.execute-api.
    ${AWS::Region}.${AWS::URLSuffix}/Prod/"
PostCatFunction:
  Description: "Post Lambda Function ARN
  Value: !GetAtt PostCatFunction.Arn
CatTable:
  Description: "DynamoDB table name"
  Value: !GetAtt CatTable.Arn
```

Note   CloudFormation is an infrastructure-as-code service. It allows you to declare the AWS resources (i.e., your infrastructure) you need in a JSON or YAML format template. CloudFormation will create, update, or delete the resources on your behalf to match the declared template. This allows you to manage complex infrastructure without the need to click hundreds of buttons on the AWS console. You can also utilize coding best practices like version control and code review on your infrastructure configuration.

The template.yaml consists of three sections: Globals, Resources, and Outputs. The Globals section defines shared configurations that apply to all resources. In this template, all AWS Lambda functions are configured to have a default timeout of three seconds. The Resources section defines the AWS services to be created and their configurations. The Outputs section allows you to print out custom information when the SAM deployment finishes. This is useful when you want to print out randomly assigned information like the REST API URL, the resource ID, or Amazon Resource Names (ARN), so you can find them in the AWS console.

Let's take a closer look at the resources defined in the Resources section: CatTable and PostCatFunction. CatTable is an AWS::Serverless::SimpleTable—an Amazon DynamoDB table. You could use Amazon Relational Database Service (RDS) to run a PostgreSQL database so you would be able to reuse the same code from the previous chapter. However, to show how the AWS SDK works, you are going to use DynamoDB, a NoSQL database provided by AWS. The SimpleTable type is an abstraction over DynamoDB, provided by SAM, which hides the low-level configuration. It defines a single primary key called cat for the table. This will be the primary database where we keep track of which cats have been loaded into the system. In many systems you'd usually use a UUID, timestamp, or some other primary key that can ensure uniqueness in the database. In our case this would be a bit of overengineering and take away from the basics we want to display, so we just make the key the cat's name.

The `PostCatFunction` is a `AWS::Serverless::Function`, which is also a SAM-provided abstraction over an AWS Lambda function. It has a `CodeUri` that points to the Rust binary output path `target/lambda/catdex-serverless`, which means it runs the Rust code provided in the template. The runtime is a custom runtime on Amazon Linux 2 (`provided.al2`) on `arm64` hardware. The Rust runtime is built on the custom runtime feature of AWS Lambda. You can also see an `Events` section, which defines the API endpoint that should trigger this lambda function. SAM creates an implicit Amazon API Gateway to receive HTTP Post calls and trigger the lambda function.

The Rust code, which will be explained shortly, needs to write to the DynamoDB table defined earlier. But the table name is generated at runtime and is not known before you deploy, so to avoid hard-coding the table name, you can pass it to the lambda function as an environment variable. You can then read the table name from the environment variable using Rust code.

Access to AWS resources like the DynamoDB table is controlled by AWS Identity and Access Management (IAM). By default, the lambda function doesn't have permission to access the DynamoDB table. To grant it permission to write to the DynamoDB table, you can attach a `DynamoDBWritePolicy` to the lambda function. This is a pre-defined policy with write permission to the DynamoDB table you specify, so you don't have to write the low-level IAM policy document yourself.

Once you've added the template file to your project, you can use the AWS SAM CLI to do a guided deploy (after you've built the project). Enact the following steps, noting that you'll likely want to have your AWS Region set to somewhere close to where you're located. You also should hit "Enter" to any prompt that doesn't have any entries afterward (all except the request to save arguments to a configuration file) in order to select the default response (Figure 6-6).

```
arzeznik@arzeznik-mint-21:/media/sf_book/final_tests/catdex-serverless$ sam deploy --guided

Configuring SAM deploy
======================

        Looking for config file [samconfig.toml] :  Found
        Reading default arguments  :  Success

        Setting default arguments for 'sam deploy'
        ==========================================
        Stack Name [sam-app]:
        AWS Region [us-east-2]:
        #Shows you resources changes to be deployed and require a 'Y' to initiate deploy
        Confirm changes before deploy [y/N]:
        #SAM needs permission to be able to create roles to connect to the resources in your template
        Allow SAM CLI IAM role creation [Y/n]:
        #Preserves the state of previously provisioned resources when an operation fails
        Disable rollback [y/N]:
        PostCatFunction may not have authorization defined, Is this okay? [y/N]: y
        Save arguments to configuration file [Y/n]: y
        SAM configuration file [samconfig.toml]:
        SAM configuration environment [default]:
```

Figure 6-6. *Guided deployment using the AWS SAM CLI*

After finishing these steps you should have a `samconfig.toml` file created that will let you rerun deployments without re-answering all of the preceding questions. Your file should look something like the following. This will allow you to just run `sam deploy` in the future without the `--guided` flag, making deployment updates much easier.

```
version = 0.1
[default]
[default.deploy]
[default.deploy.parameters]
stack_name = "sam-app"
s3_bucket = "<your auto-generates S3 bucket name>"
s3_prefix = "sam-app"
region = "us-east-2"
capabilities = "CAPABILITY_IAM"
image_repositories = []
```

Running the command should also give you the ARN of the Post lambda function (Figure 6-7).

```
CloudFormation outputs from deployed stack
-----------------------------------------------------------------------------------
Outputs
-----------------------------------------------------------------------------------
Key                 CatTable
Description         DynamoDB table name
Value              arn:aws:dynamodb:us-east-2:003164948199:table/sam-app-CatTable-1XWOW9OORL732

Key                 PostApi
Description         API Gateway endpoint URL for Prod stage for Post function
Value              https://3m5ezvf2ui.execute-api.us-east-2.amazonaws.com/Prod/

Key                 PostCatFunction
Description         Post Lambda Function ARN
Value              arn:aws:lambda:us-east-2:003164948199:function:sam-app-PostCatFunction-SpBjt2nLOlpa
-----------------------------------------------------------------------------------
```

Successfully created/updated stack - sam-app in us-east-2

Figure 6-7. *Output after deploying with the AWS SAM CLI*

Before you move on, it's a good idea to test the deployed lambda function environment. In the previous section we tested the lambda function using the AWS Console. Here we'll show another testing option using the AWS CLI. Note the ARN for the lambda function is listed in the output of sam deploy, and we can use this to run a lambda from the CLI like so, using the Value for the name of the preceding lambda function output:

```
$ aws lambda invoke \
--cli-binary-format raw-in-base64-out \
--payload '{"httpMethod": "POST"}' \
--function-name arn:aws:lambda:us-east-2:003164948199:function:
    ↪ sam-app-PostCatFunction-SpBjt2nLOlpa \
output.json
{
    "StatusCode": 200,
    "ExecutedVersion": "$LATEST"
}
```

The CLI invokes the lambda function with an empty HTTP POST request. Since our Hello World code isn't doing anything with the request, this should succeed and return a response. The response is saved in the output.json file. If everything is set up properly, you should see a response like the following (though it will be formatted all on one line with no white space):

```
{
  "statusCode":200,
  "headers":{
    "content-type":"text/html"
  },
  "multiValueHeaders":{
    "content-type":["text/html"]
  },
  "body":"Hello AWS Lambda HTTP request",
  "isBase64Encoded":false
}
```

At this point you have your basic infrastructure configuration, along with a test that deployment works, and you can call your lambda function. Now you can dive into the specific details of your lambda function.

6.9 Building the Upload API

You're now ready to start customizing your lambda function to allow uploading cat images to DynamoDB. You'll start by moving the src/mains.rs to src/bin/lambda/post-cat.rs, in preparation for multiple lambdas. Instead of main.rs you should have a lib.rs in the src folder. After we update the project structure you will build the POST /cat API to create a new cat and upload a new image.

After moving files, your project structure should look as follows:

```
.
+-- template.yaml
+-- Cargo.toml
+-- src
|-- |-- bin
```

```
|-- |-- |-- lambda
|-- |-- |-- + -- post-cat.rs
|-- +-- lib.rs
```

You'll also need to update `Cargo.toml` to add the binary to your project:

```
[[bin]]
name = "post-cat"
path = "src/bin/lambda/post-cat.rs"
```

Before we move any further actually changing the code, you'll need to pull in the AWS SDK for DynamoDB along with the `serde` crate. You can run the following:

```
cargo add aws_sdk_dynamodb serde
```

Then, ensure that the version being used is 0.24.0. Currently the AWS SDK for Rust is in developer beta, and could still see major changes before being fully released. For this reason, you'll want to be sure you are using the same version as the examples here. You'll also want to pull in the aws-config crate using `cargo add aws-config`, and ensure you have version 0.54.1 in your `Cargo.toml` file. You'll also need to change a single line in `template.yaml`, changing the `CodeUri` of the `PostCatFunction` from `arget/lambda/catdex-serverless` to `target/lambda/post-cat`. You'll be able to put additional lambda functions in the project in the future by following the same structure and keeping shared code in the `src/lib.rs` module.

With the new dependencies in place, you can jump into `post-cat.rs`:

```rust
use aws_sdk_dynamodb as dynamodb;
use aws_sdk_dynamodb::model::AttributeValue;
use lambda_http::{http::StatusCode, run, service_fn,
    Body, Error, Request, RequestExt, Response};
use serde::Deserialize;

#[derive(Deserialize)]
struct RequestBody {
    name: String,
}

async fn function_handler(
    request: Request,
    client: &dynamodb::Client,
```

```rust
    table_name: &str,
) -> Result<Response<Body>, Error> {
    let body: RequestBody = match request.payload() {
        Ok(Some(body)) => body,
        _ => {
            return Ok(Response::builder()
                .status(StatusCode::BAD_REQUEST)
                .body("Invalid payload".into())
                .expect("Failed to render response"))
        }
    };

    let dynamo_request = client
        .put_item()
        .table_name(table_name)
        .item("cat", AttributeValue::S(body.name.clone()));
    dynamo_request.send().await?;

    let resp = Response::builder()
        .status(StatusCode::OK)
        .header("content-type", "text/html")
        .body(format!("Added cat {}", body.name).into())
        .map_err(Box::new)?;
    Ok(resp)
}

#[tokio::main]
async fn main() -> Result<(), Error> {
    tracing_subscriber::fmt()
        .with_max_level(tracing::Level::INFO)
        .with_target(false)
        .without_time()
        .init();

    let config = aws_config::load_from_env().await;
    let client = dynamodb::Client::new(&config);
    let table_name = std::env::var("TABLE_NAME")?.to_string();
```

```
    run(service_fn(|request| {
        function_handler(request, &client, &table_name)
    }))
    .await
}
```

The new function handler and accompanying main do a few things for now:

1. Extract the request body (i.e., payload) to get the cat's name.

2. Create a PutItemRequest, which will create the new cat in the database after it's provided the cat's name and send is called on the request object.

3. Call client.put_item() to create the DynamoDB item.

In the example in the previous chapter, you uploaded the cat's image through the API. However, API Gateway has a payload size limit of 10 MB, so the image needs to be smaller than that. To overcome that, we're going to use the S3 pre-signed URL, which we'll discuss shortly. For now this example doesn't contain the file upload part. Notice that the function_handler() function now takes an event (the first parameter) of the type Request; this is provided by the lambda_http crate. You can call request.payload() to get the request body. You expect the body to have the following form:

```
{
  "name": "Persian"
}
```

So you define a RequestBody struct, which derives the serde::Deserialize trait, to tell Rust how to deserialize it. When you call request.payload(), if the return value is a Some(RequestBody), you can assign it to a variable body.

Next, you use the passed-in DynamoDB client and prepare the PutItemInput. The PutItemInput expects the table name and a new item as a key-value pair, the key being a String and the value being an AttributeValue. Therefore, you use the name specified in body for the new cat's name. For every place that might fail (e.g., parsing payload, calling put_item()), you use match to handle the errors and return an appropriate HTTP response, or simply bubble them up with ? or unwrap.

Note how we've also added a few things to the main function. We grab the name of the DynamoDB table from the TABLE_NAME environment variable. This environment variable is actually set up in the Lambda execution environment by the AWS SAM template. We can specify different environment variables that give each lambda function in our architecture knowledge about other components without having to hard-code the names of those components. This is one of the nice benefits that makes lambda functions really easy to work with; the permissions can easily be kept separate from the code.

Note also we've actually pulled the AWS credentials from the environment also and created the DynamoDB client outside the handler function. This allows the client to avoid having to reconnect for every run of the handler function; if the lambda is "warm" and ran recently, it will still have its code loaded and ready to go for another request. When lambdas have not run for a while they need to start "cold," which means retrieving and loading the initial code. Without going into too many details of about low-level performance, it can be useful to maintain connections or slow-to-initialize structures outside of the handler function and pass the function and the parameters in as a closure.

With this code updated, you can build and update the lambda with the following pair of commands:

```
$ cargo lambda build --release --arm64
$ sam deploy
```

At this point, there are two ways you can test your deployed lambda. First, you can again directly use the AWS CLI to invoke the lambda with a properly formatted payload (remembering to update the function name to the ARN returned at the end of sam deploy):

```
$ aws lambda invoke \
--cli-binary-format raw-in-base64-out \
--payload '{"httpMethod": "POST",
  "body":"{\"name\":\"catsay\"}",
  "headers": {"content-type": "application/json"}}' \
--function-name arn:aws:lambda:us-east-2:003164948199:function:
  sam-app-PostCatFunction-SpBjt2nLOlpa \
output.json
```

This directly invokes the lambda with an HTTP payload. This isn't how your users will be invoking the lambda, however; they will be making POST requests against an HTTP endpoint on the web. The PostApi CloudFormaton output from sam deploy has a value that provides an API Gateway endpoint URL that is accessible on the web.

Note how in the `template.yaml` file you created you specified the path for the POST function as /cat; this means that your POST API is accessible by adding /cat to the end of the API Gateway URL. With this information, you can run a `curl` from the command line to test your HTTP POST API (remember to use your own URL here):

```
$ curl \
--header "Content-type: application/json" \
--request POST \
--data '{"name": "meow"}' \
https://3m5ezvf2ui.execute-api.us-east-2.amazonaws.com/Prod/cat
```

If you set up everything correctly, you should see Added cat meow in your terminal.

6.10 Building the /cats API

You've deployed a simple lambda function behind an API Gateway that receives POST requests and adds the cat names to a DynamoDB table. While you can add cats to the database, you can't read out the current list of cats. This section will walk you through the GET API that will let you do just that, by adding a second lambda to your project.

First, you'll need to create a new file at src/bin/lambda/get-cats.rs. This is where the code for your new lambda will be added. Then, you'll need to update your Cargo. toml file to include the new binary:

```
[[bin]]
name = "get-cats"
path = "src/bin/lambda/get-cats.rs"
```

Then, you need to update the `template.yaml` to add the new lambda function into your architecture (Listing 6-4).

Listing 6-4. Template updates for get cats API

```
# ...

Resources:
  # ...

  GetCatsFunction:
    Type: AWS::Serverless::Function
```

```yaml
    Properties:
      CodeUri: target/lambda/get-cats/
      Handler: bootstrap
      Runtime: provided.al2
      Architectures: [ "arm64" ]
      Events:
        GetCats:
          Type: Api
          Properties:
            Path: /cats
            Method: get
      Environment:
        Variables:
          TABLE_NAME: !Ref CatTable
      Policies:
        - DynamoDBReadPolicy:
            TableName: !Ref CatTable
Outputs:
  # ...
  GetCatsFunction:
    Description: "Get Cats Lambda Function ARN"
    Value: !GetAtt GetCatsFunction.Arn
  # ...
```

Compared to the previous lambda function, here we need to add DynamoDB read permissions. We change the path to /cats and the method to cats, but otherwise this new lambda function is similar to the previous. Once you've made the Cargo.toml and template.yaml changes, you can finally write the code for src/bin/lambda/get-cats.rs Listing 6-5. You should run cargo add serde_json to add the newly required dependency, and when copying the code duplicate the main function and then only focus on the updated function_handler function.

Listing 6-5. Get cats Lambda function

```rust
use aws_sdk_dynamodb as dynamodb;
use lambda_http::{http::StatusCode, run, service_fn, Body,
    Error, Request, Response};
use serde::Serialize;

#[derive(Serialize)]
struct ResponseBody<'a> {
    cats: Vec<&'a String>,
}

async fn function_handler(
    _request: Request,
    client: &dynamodb::Client,
    table_name: &str,
) -> Result<Response<Body>, Error> {
    let scan_output = client
        .scan()
        .table_name(table_name)
        .send()
        .await;

    let scan_output = scan_output?;

    let response_body = ResponseBody {
        cats: scan_output
            .items()
            .unwrap_or_default()
            .into_iter()
            .map(|val| val.get("cat").unwrap().as_s().unwrap())
            .collect(),
    };
```

```
    let resp = Response::builder()
        .status(StatusCode::OK)
        .header("content-type", "text/html")
        .body(serde_json::to_string(&response_body)
            .unwrap()
            .into()
        )
        .map_err(Box::new)?;
    Ok(resp)
}

// .. async fn main ...
```

The setup of the handler is similar to the POST handler. In this case, a custom ResponseBody is used to hold the list of cats.[9] The request received by the handler is not actually used, and instead a scan is directly initiated with the DynamoDB client to retrieve the full list of cats from the table.

Note   DynamoDB supports two major ways for querying data: query and scan. When you query, you need to specify the partition key so DynamoDB can directly find the item. Scan, on the other hand, needs to scan through the whole table. You can specify filtering criteria to further refine the result.

Scan is significantly slower than query, but it's useful for situations when you don't know the partition key in advance. If you already know the partition key you are trying to find, always use query over scan.

---

[9] We've made maybe a slight over-optimization by annotating lifetimes on the ResponseBody. While this is strictly not necessary and you could write the code with just String and clone, if this was returning a large list it could have appreciable memory savings, which in turn would directly translate into cost savings. There's a balance between performance and usability in code, but since this book is about learning, we thought it would be good to give you a gentle introduction to a place you can create more performant code

After the scan, a transformation on the returned items iterator takes place, which allows for the construction of a ResponseBody. This response is then returned to the client that called the lambda. We use unwrap here as we know that cat is the primary key and will never be empty, but for more general systems you should always be properly checking and handling any errors. When this is complete we are able to return a simple list of cats as shown here:

```
[
 {
   "cats": ["Persian", "Ragdoll"]
 }
]
```

The Serialize method on the ResponseBody struct allows for it to be converted to a String using serde_json.

To test the new API, you can run the same build and deploy commands as previously, and then use curl to make the HTTP GET request:

```
$ cargo lambda build --release --arm64
$ sam deploy
$ curl --header "Content-type: application/json" \
--request GET \
https://3m5ezvf2ui.execute-api.us-east-2.amazonaws.com/Prod/cats
```

You can now go ahead and use the curl example from the previous section to add additional cats to the database, which you'll retrieve with the get-cats response.

6.11 Uploading the Image Using S3 Pre-signed URL

We've so far only added cat names to our database. We could try to directly upload images also by encoding them into our POST requests, but API Gateway has a 10 MB request size limit, so you can't upload image files larger than that. This would work for many images, but it would be a pain if an image were slightly too large and then rejected. To overcome this limitation, you can use an S3 pre-signed PUT URL. You can use the AWS API to upload a file to S3, but since the S3 bucket is private by default, you need to provide valid credentials so AWS can verify your identity and check if you have the proper access to the bucket. However, you'll be adding a nice frontend to the project to upload cats, and there is no secure way to store the AWS credentials on the frontend page. A pre-signed URL solves this problem. A pre-signed URL allows anyone to upload files to the pre-defined S3 location within a limited time, without the need to provide AWS credentials. When creating the pre-signed URL, you provide AWS credentials, so the user of the URL will get the same permissions as the credentials used to sign it. The pre-signed URL generation takes place in the backend (i.e., in the lambda function), so the credentials are never exposed to the frontend.

In this use case, you can let the frontend call the POST /cat endpoint to create the cat in the DynamoDB. Then, the POST /cat API needs to generate a pre-signed URL and return it to the frontend. The frontend uses this pre-signed URL to upload the cat image directly to S3. Figure 6-8 shows a sequence diagram for this flow. Since this is a demo, the image will then be served directly through the S3 built-in server. But in production, you might want to upload the file to a separate bucket and sanitize the image before putting it into the bucket that serves the static files. Also, while you'll get this working with the frontend by the end of this project, you can test all of this manually (like the previous sections) by using curl with the returned pre-signed URL. It's always good to test components by themselves before connecting them together, and here we'll test the S3 functionality before we get it working on the frontend.

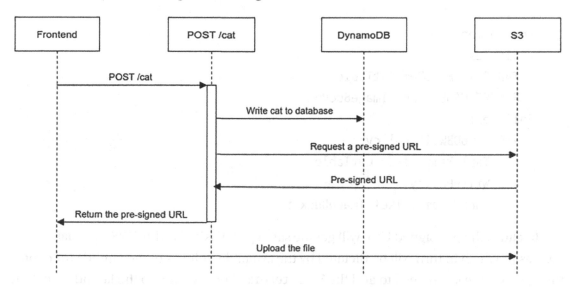

Figure 6-8. Sequence diagram for adding a new cat using the pre-signed URL

This approach has a few advantages over uploading through API Gateway and Lambda. First, S3 allows you to upload files up to 5 GB.[10] Second, you prevent bandwidth from going through API Gateway, and you also saved processing time and memory usage in the lambda, potentially saving some costs (as comparatively speaking direct uploads to S3 can be very cheap).

To be able to generate a pre-signed URL, you need to first add the bucket to `template.yaml` along with permissions to the POST lambda function:

```yaml
Resources
  CatTable:
  # ...
  ImageBucket:
    Type: AWS::S3::Bucket
    Properties:
      AccessControl: Private

PostCatFunction:
Type: AWS::Serverless::Function
Properties:
  # ...
  Environment:
  Variables:
    TABLE_NAME: !Ref CatTable
    BUCKET_NAME: !Ref ImageBucket
  Policies:
    - DynamoDBWritePolicy:
        TableName: !Ref CatTable
    - S3WritePolicy:
        BucketName: !Ref ImageBucket
```

Because the pre-signed URL will get the same permission as the AWS role that creates it (which in turn will be dictated by the available policies of the lambda function that generates it), you need to add the S3WritePolicy permission to the lambda function

---

[10] If you use the multipart upload the limit can be increased to 5 TB.

policies for the POST Cat function. You also will need to add a bucket to store the images, and an environment variable to the lambda function to pass in the bucket name. As a final step before working with the code, you'll need to add the AWS S3 crate with

```
cargo add aws_sdk_s3
```

With these permissions, environment variables, and dependencies added, let's add some code to src/bin/lambda/post-cat.rs so you can generate the pre-signed URL (Listing 6-6).

Listing 6-6. Presigned URL generation

```rust
use aws_sdk_dynamodb as dynamodb;
use aws_sdk_dynamodb::model::AttributeValue;
use aws_sdk_s3 as s3;
use aws_sdk_s3::presigning::config::PresigningConfig;
use lambda_http::{http::StatusCode, run, service_fn, Body, Error
    ↪ ,
    Request, RequestExt, Response};
use serde::{Deserialize, Serialize};
use std::time::Duration;

#[derive(Deserialize)]
struct RequestBody {
  name: String,
}

#[derive(Serialize)]
struct ResponseBody {
  upload_url: String,
}

async fn function_handler(
  request: Request,
  dynamo_client: &dynamodb::Client,
  s3_client: &s3::Client,
  table_name: &str,
  bucket_name: &str,
```

```rust
) -> Result<Response<Body>, Error> {
  let body: RequestBody = match request.payload() {
    Ok(Some(body)) => body,
    _ => {
      return Ok(Response::builder()
        .status(StatusCode::BAD_REQUEST)
        .body("Invalid payload".into())
        .expect("Failed to render response"))
    }
  };

  let presigned_request = s3_client
    .put_object()
    .bucket(bucket_name)
    .key(&body.name)
    .presigned(
      PresigningConfig::expires_in(Duration::from_secs(60))?
    )
    .await?;
  let response_body = ResponseBody {
    upload_url: presigned_request.uri().to_string(),
  };

  let dynamo_request = dynamo_client
    .put_item()
    .table_name(table_name)
    .item("cat", AttributeValue::S(body.name.clone()));
  dynamo_request.send().await?;

  let resp = Response::builder()
    .status(StatusCode::OK)
    .header("content-type", "text/html")
    .body(serde_json::to_string(&response_body)?.into())
    .map_err(Box::new)?;
  Ok(resp)
}
```

```rust
#[tokio::main]
async fn main() -> Result<(), Error> {
  tracing_subscriber::fmt()
    .with_max_level(tracing::Level::INFO)
    .with_target(false)
    .without_time()
    .init();

  let config = aws_config::load_from_env().await;
  let dynamo_client = dynamodb::Client::new(&config);
  let s3_client = s3::Client::new(&config);
  let table_name = std::env::var("TABLE_NAME")?.to_string();
  let bucket_name = std::env::var("BUCKET_NAME")?.to_string();

  run(service_fn(|request| {
    function_handler(
        request,
        &dynamo_client,
        &s3_client,
        &table_name,
        &bucket_name,
    )
  }))
  .await
}
```

The first thing that needs to be done is to add the S3 clients, similar to how the Dynamo clients were set up. We rename the previous client variable to dynamo_client in order to make the code more clear, and then pass both clients into the function handler closure, along with the DynamoDB table name and S3 bucket name.

The handler function still receives the POST request, but before putting it into the DynamoDB table, it generates an S3 pre-signed URL request. This URL is valid to upload a file to a specific bucket and key for 60 seconds from creation, after which it becomes invalid. The DynamoDB write then is performed, and the upload URL is returned in the final response.

You can deploy to AWS with the usual combination of commands:

```
cargo lambda build --release --arm64
sam deploy
```

If you call the API with `curl`, you should receive the pre-signed URL in the response body:

```
$ curl \
--header "Content-type: application/json" \
--request POST \
--data '{"name": "Persian"}' \
https://3m5ezvf2ui.execute-api.us-east-2.amazonaws.com/Prod/cat
{
  "upload_url":"<Response URL here>"
}
```

You can use this URL to upload the file like so:

```
$ curl -X PUT -H "Content-Type: image/jpeg" -T persian.jpg \
    "https://sam-app-imagebucket-4wa7ymmzide3.s3.us-east-2.amazonaws.com/
    Persian?x-id=PutObject&X-Amz-Algorithm=AWS4-HMAC-SHA256&
    X-Amz-credentials=...&X-Amz-Date=20200819T095109Z&X-Amz-Expires=3600&
    X-Amz-Security-Token=...&X-Amz-Signature=...&X-Amz-SignedHeaders=host"
```

This uploads a file named `persian.jpg` to the local machine. A few fields like `X-Amz-credentials` and `X-Amx-Security-Token` are omitted because they change every time you generate a new URL.

Note   There are many different ways to interact with and test AWS services. We started using the AWS Console, then switched to the AWS CLI, and then finally have been running tests through public-facing APIs using `curl`. We'll soon see how we can use a frontend to test the code. If you are having trouble with something, you should remember all of these tools and use them to test your systems. AWS has great documentation and strong APIs for both building and debugging systems in the cloud. We suggest you take some time to explore these even when you aren't stuck, as they can prove quite insightful on how to build web systems at scale.

6.12 Adding the Frontend

You've written a pair of lambda functions, one posting cats, and one for getting the full list of cats. Now, with the API ready, you can serve HTML, JavaScript, and CSS on AWS. You can upload the files to an S3 bucket and enable ""static website hosting" on that S3 bucket. This can be done manually, but that involves using the AWS Console to change a large set of various settings in sometimes different places. Having a single script that can set everything makes it easier to iterate, and provides a single record of all setup changes made for the frontend. To automate this process, you will write a few helper programs locally that use the AWS SDK for Rust to automatically deploy all the necessary files to a new bucket.

To start with, you'll need a place to save the frontend code, so you should create a folder using the following command executed from the main project directory:

```
mkdir -p client/dist
```

This is a relatively common location and format in which to store client code in a project. Then, create the following files in it:

- index.html: the cats overview page (Listing 6-7).

- css/index.css: CSS stylesheet for index.html (Listing 6-8).

- add.html: the add new cat form (Listing 6-9).

Note that in the added listings (Listing 6-7 and Listing 6-8) you'll need to update the URL to point to the correct URL you have for your project.

Listing 6-7. Index file

```html
<!DOCTYPE html>
<html>
<head>
  <meta charset="UTF-8" />
  <title>Catdex</title>
  <link rel="stylesheet" href="css/index.css" type="text/css">
</head>
<body>
<h1>Catdex</h1>
<p>
  <a href="/add.html">Add a new cat</a>
</p>

<section class="cats" id="cats">
  <p>No cats yet</p>
</section>
<script charset="utf-8">
  document.addEventListener("DOMContentLoaded", () => {
    fetch('<INSERT URL>')
      .then((response) => response.json())
      .then((cats) => {
        document.getElementById("cats").innerText = ""
        for (cat of cats.cats) {
          const catElement = document.createElement("article")
          catElement.classList.add("cat")
          const catTitle = document.createElement("h3")
          const catLink = document.createElement("a")
          catLink.innerText = cat
          const catImage = document.createElement("img")
          catImage.src = `images/${cat}`

          catTitle.appendChild(catLink)
          catElement.appendChild(catTitle)
          catElement.appendChild(catImage)
```

```
        document.getElementById("cats").appendChild(catElement)
      }
    })
  })
</script>
</body>
</html>
```

Listing 6-8. CSS file

```css
.cats {
  display: flex;
}

.cat {
  border: 1px solid grey;
  min-width: 200px;
  min-height: 350px;
  margin: 5px;
  padding: 5px;
  text-align: center;
}

.cat > img {
  width: 190px;
}
```

Listing 6-9. Add cat HTML page

```html
<!DOCTYPE html>
<html>
<head>
  <meta charset="UTF-8" />
  <title>Catdex</title>
  <link rel="stylesheet" href="css/index.css" type="text/css">
</head>
<body>
```

```html
<script>
  async function submitForm(e) {
    e.preventDefault()

    const cat_name = document.getElementById('name').value

    const cat_post_response = await fetch('<INSERT URL>', {
      method: 'POST',
      mode: 'cors',
      headers: {
        'Content-Type': 'application/json'
      },
      body: JSON.stringify({ name: cat_name })
    })

    const image_upload_url = (await cat_post_response.json()).upload_url

    const image = document.getElementById("image").files[0]

    const image_upload_response = await fetch(image_upload_url,
    {
      method: 'PUT',
      body: image,
    })

    if (image_upload_response.status === 200) {
      alert("Success")
    } else {
      alert("Failed")
    }
    return false
  }
</script>
<h1>Add a new cat</h1>

<form onsubmit="return submitForm(event)">
  <label for="name">Name:</label>
  <input type="text" name="name" id="name" value="" />
```

```
<label for="image">Image:</label>
<input type="file" name="image" id="image" value="" />
<button type="submit">Submit</button>
</form>

</body>
</html>
```

The index.html and index.css are similar to the ones in previous chapters. The add.html has a slightly different logic than before. Instead of just calling the POST /cat API, you also make a second PUT call to update the image. Be sure you updated the URL endpoints in both .html files with the appropriate locations based on the output of running sam deploy.

You have a few options to deploy the website. You can follow the online directions and manually upload the files and set the permissions via the AWS console,[11] but that can be slow, prone to errors, and frustrating to iterate if you want to perform repeated operations. You could also use another website deployment manager, but that would be adding another large dependency for a rather simple task. Instead, you can use the AWS SDK for Rust to write a small executable that will deploy your website. This is a good excuse to get more practice with the SDK, and will also let you rapidly iterate and re-deploy your website if needed.

The first step is to create a simple program that will upload the files and set the appropriate policies for our S3 bucket. Add the following to your Cargo.toml file:

```
[[bin]]
name = "create-bucket"
path = "src/bin/create-bucket.rs"
```

This program will create a new bucket. This bucket should have a unique name, since it will be publicly accessible on the internet; the file uses "catdex-frontend" but you can set any name as desired. You should also set the region appropriately for your location.

---

[11] https://docs.aws.amazon.com/AmazonS3/latest/userguide/
HostingWebsiteOnS3Setup.html

After you've created the bucket, you'll need to upload the website files and set proper permissions. For this we add one more file, which is detailed in Listing 6-10 and can be placed in bin/put-website.rs.

Listing 6-10. Frontend setup code

```rust
use aws_sdk_s3 as s3;
use aws_sdk_s3::model::{
  IndexDocument, WebsiteConfiguration,
};
use aws_sdk_s3::types::ByteStream;
use std::path::Path;

#[tokio::main]
async fn main() {
  let config = aws_config::load_from_env().await;
  let s3_client = s3::Client::new(&config);

  let body = ByteStream::from_path(
    Path::new("../../client/dist/index.html")
  )
    .await
    .unwrap();
  s3_client
    .put_object()
    .body(body)
    .bucket("catdex-frontend")
    .key("index.html")
    .content_type("text/html")
    .send()
    .await
    .unwrap();

  let body = ByteStream::from_path(
    Path::new("../../client/dist/add.html")
  )
    .await
    .unwrap();
```

```rust
s3_client
  .put_object()
  .body(body)
  .bucket("catdex-frontend")
  .key("add.html")
  .content_type("text/html")
  .send()
  .await
  .unwrap();

let body = ByteStream::from_path(
  Path::new("../../client/dist/css/index.css")
)
  .await
  .unwrap();
s3_client
  .put_object()
  .body(body)
  .bucket("catdex-frontend")
  .key("css/index.css")
  .content_type("text/css")
  .send()
  .await
  .unwrap();

let cfg = WebsiteConfiguration::builder()
  .index_document(
      IndexDocument::builder()
        .suffix("index.html").build()
  )
  .build();
s3_client
  .put_bucket_website()
  .bucket("catdex-frontend")
  .website_configuration(cfg)
  .send()
```

```
    .await
    .unwrap();

  s3_client
    .put_bucket_policy()
    .bucket("catdex-frontend")
    .policy(include_str!("../../bucket_policy.json"))
    .send()
    .await
    .unwrap();
}
```

This file uses your local AWS credentials (which you set when you ran aws configure) to perform various operations on the ImageBucket specified in the AWS SAM CLI template, which is where we will also host our website. It starts with three put operations, one for each of the three content files for the website.[12] After uploading all of the files, you can set the bucket website configuration and set the policy to make the bucket publicly accessible. To set this policy, you'll need to create one more file, bucket_policy.json, at the root directory of the project.

Listing 6-11. Bucket policy configuration

```
{
    "Version": "2012-10-17",
    "Statement": [
      {
        "Sid": "PublicReadGetObject",
        "Effect": "Allow",
        "Principal": "*",
        "Action": [
          "s3:GetObject"
        ],
```

---

[12] Once you added more files you'd probably want to automatically read all the files in the directory and iterate over them instead of hardcoding them as here, but to keep things simple we'll just copy the operation for now.

```
    "Resource": [
      "arn:aws:s3:::catdex-frontend/*"
    ]
  }
  ]
}
```

However, if you open the website now, you'll notice that the API calls are failing. This is because of the same-origin policy. Under that policy, the web page cannot access APIs under a different origin, which is the combination of URI scheme, hostname, and port. Because the web page is served under `http://catdex-frontend.s3-website. us-east-2.amazonaws.com/index.html`, but the API is under `https://abc0123def. execute-api.eu-central-1.amazonaws.com/`, the same-origin policy will block the API call. The same-origin policy is a security feature that can block many kinds of attacks.

Since you control both the frontend and the backend APIs, you can use cross-origin resource sharing (CORS) to overcome this restriction. With CORS enabled on the backend API, it can grant access to the frontend serving from a different origin.

To enable CORS, first you need to update the globals in the `template.yaml`:

```
Globals:
  Function:
    Timeout: 3
  Api:
    Cors:
      AllowMethods: "'GET,POST'"
      AllowHeaders: "'content-type'"
      AllowOrigin: "'*'"
```

Second, both the APIs need to respond with an `Access-Control-Allow-Origin` header. This header specifies the origin that is allowed to access it. For simplicity, you specify `Access-Control-Allow-Origin: *`, which allows every origin. This is of course not very secure. If you are running production workloads, always explicitly specify the exact host.

To add this header to the API, you can tweak the `src/bin/lambda/get-cats.rs` and `src/bin/lambda/post-cat.rs` like in Listing 6-12, to add additional headers in the response.

Listing 6-12. CORS updates to response headers

```
// ...
let resp = Response::builder()
        .status(StatusCode::OK)
        .header("content-type", "text/html")
        .header("Access-Control-Allow-Origin", "*")
        .header("Access-Control-Allow-Headers", "Content-Type")
        .header("Access-Control-Allow-Methods", "GET")
        .body(serde_json::to_string(&response_body).unwrap()
            .into()
        )
        .map_err(Box::new)?;
    Ok(resp)

// ...
```

Finally, there is a small issue with the default CORS setting set by sam deploy. It allows PUT requests from https://*.amazonaws.com, but the frontend is served using HTTP, not HTTPS. Therefore, you need to re-configure the CORS setting using the AWS SDK. You can add these settings to your put-website.rs (Listing 6-13).

Listing 6-13. CORS udpates to website upload code

```
let cors_rule_1 = CorsRule::builder()
  .allowed_headers("*")
  .allowed_methods("PUT")
  .allowed_methods("POST")
  .allowed_origins("http://*.amazonaws.com")
  .max_age_seconds(0)
  .build();

let cors_rule_2 = CorsRule::builder()
  .allowed_headers("*")
  .allowed_methods("GET")
  .allowed_origins("*")
  .build();
```

```
let cfg = CorsConfiguration::builder()
  .cors_rules(cors_rule_1)
  .cors_rules(cors_rule_2)
  .build();

s3_client
  .put_bucket_cors()
  .bucket(BUCKET)
  .cors_configuration(cfg)
  .send()
  .await
  .unwrap();
```

You can build and re-deploy your full project now:

```
$ cargo lambda build --release --arm64
$ sam deploy
$ cargo run --bin put-website
```

Now you should be able to go to the catdex website from any public computer, display cats, and add additional cats.

6.13 A Note on Security

Before we close out this section, it's worth having a quick discussion about best security practices. Just like when learning most subjects for the first time, we skimmed over a few points to be able to stay on topic and make progress learning some cool new technologies. We didn't want to get bogged down in the details of properly setting up best security practices in a cloud environment, and a few times we explicitly stated we were going to ignore best practices to get something working. This is fine for learning, but if you are going to learn or work in the cloud space, you should be taking security seriously and spend the time to learn best practices for any infrastructure you are setting up. There are a huge number of resources available in other books and online. Ignoring security could result in getting hacked, losing critical data, or ending up with a massive unexpected bill. We don't want to scare you away from developing in the cloud, but we do want to make it clear that you should make all of your security choices consciously when you work with online systems.

6.14 Next Steps

With that out of the way, let's review what we've covered and some next steps you can take on your serverless journey.

In total, we showed how to combine a couple of lambda functions, a DynamoDB database table, and an S3 bucket to create a fully functioning website served on the public internet. You could add more features to the frontend, even serving up the single-page app we saw in Chapter 4. You could add additional lambda functions on the backend, for example to be able to delete a cat that may have been added by mistake. You can also spend time on the DevOps side of things, combining the multi-step deployment processes and scripts we created into a single unified deployment script, which could then be run in a CI/CD environment. You could even look into a whole different framework to replace some of the DevOps code you wrote, so you can focus your time primarily on the features of your web service.

The AWS SDK for Rust is currently in developer preview, which means it may change in the future. Hopefully you've seen it's power both in Lambda functions and run locally to set up infrastructure as code. These applications only scratch the surface of the vast coverage of this SDK, and the over 200 AWS services it supports. You could try extending this service to use AWS CloudFront like mentioned earlier, or even try creating a more traditional server and SQL database web model from the previous chapter with EC2 and RDB. There's a lot of great material to read out there, and Rust is just starting to break into these spaces, making them a great combination to learn together. And since many users have seen better performance and lower costs in the cloud using Rust, its usage is only likely to grow in the future.

6.15 Conclusion

In this chapter, you created a serverless catdex application. You started with a simple Hello World lambda that you created, manually uploaded, and ran using `cargo lambda` and the AWS console. You then set up the AWS SAM CLI to easily create multiple AWS services with infrastructure-as-code. You created a simple lambda with the AWS SAM CLI, then extended your project to multiple lambdas that write to and read from AWS DynamoDB. You then added an S3 bucket to your project, which you used to generate pre-signed URLs and store images. As a final step, you created a static web page that was served from AWS S3 and interacted with DynamoDB using AWS lambdas. Now that you've spent three chapters working with Rust-based web technologies, it's time for a change. In the next chapter, you'll work on creating a simple desktop game in Rust.

CHAPTER 7

Building a Game

Video games have come a long way from their early implementations. *Super Mario Bros.* for NES ran on an 8-bit CPU with a 1.79 MHz clock rate. The game itself is roughly 31 kilobytes. Nowadays, you can easily get a gaming PC with an 8-core central processing unit (CPU) running at 3–5 GHz, and games that are 50–70 gigabytes. That is thousands of times more computing power and millions of times more storage space. Games are growing more and more complex as well, so the life of a game programmer is becoming tougher than before.

Rust is a great potential candidate for building games. Its low-level memory safety guarantee and exceptional performance make it ideal for building robust and performant game engines and games. At the same time, its high-level syntax allows you to write your game logic in a clean and modular way.

Although the ecosystem is still very young, there are already some beautiful games built in Rust. There are also a few game engines, which we'll discuss in the last section. We'll be using the Bevy game engine to demonstrate how to build a game in Rust. The project is still under active deployment, so the code and documentation change rapidly. We'll be using the current stable version, 0.9.1.

7.1 What Are We Building?

Back in the days when flash games were still a thing, there was a very simple but highly addictive game from Japan called *Pikachu Volleyball*. The game featured two Pikachus (a *Pokémon* character) playing beach volleyball. You could either play against the computer or compete with others using the same keyboard. We are going for nostalgia by recreating (a subset of) this game.

© Shing Lyu and Andrew Rzeznik 2023
S. Lyu and A. Rzeznik, *Practical Rust Projects*, https://doi.org/10.1007/978-1-4842-9331-7_7

The game will have the following features:

- It will be a 2D game, with one player (a cat) on the left and one player on the right.

- WASD keys control the movement of the left player, and the arrow keys control the right player

- A ball will be fed from the middle, and each player has to bounce the ball back to their opponent using their head and body.

- The ball will bounce and fall under the influence of gravity.

- You score when the ball touches the ground on your opponent's side.

- There will be music and sound effects.

7.2 Bevy and the Entity Component System Pattern

Bevy is a game engine built on the entity component system (ECS) pattern. ECS is an architectural pattern in game-engine design. The core idea of ECS is to promote composition over inheritance, while also optimizing the order in which memory is accessed for performance. To give an example, imagine a role-playing game (RPG). In the game we have a player, some monsters, and some destructible trees. The player and monsters can move and attack, and we also need to keep track of their location and health. When a monster touches the player we need to reduce the health of the player, so we need to track collisions as well.

First, we have entities. Entities are objects in the game like the player, the monsters, and the trees. Implementing all the aspects of the entities in one piece of code would quickly become unmanageable. Instead, we separate each aspect into components, and we can attach components onto entities, composing the game objects using a collection of components. For example, we can create the following components:

- Attack: attack power and range

- Transform: keep track of location, orientation, and scale

- Collision: detect collisions

- Health: keep track of the health and death

Then our entities can be composed as follows:

- Player: Attack + Transform + Collision + Health

- Monster: Attack + Transform + Collision + Health

- Tree: Transform + Collision[1]

Finally, to make the game move, we implement systems to update each component. One system is responsible for one aspect of the game. For example, we can have systems like the following:

- Movement: move the entities and update their transform. For example, the monsters will move by themselves.

- Input: Takes user input and updates the player's location and performs attacks.

- Collision: Checks for collision and stop the entities from crossing each other; may also incur damage.

- Attack: When an attack happens, reduce the health of the victim based on the attacker's attack power. For trees, destroy it when being attacked.

Systems can be based on single components, or more often will deal with an interaction between components. For example, the collision system would need to look at entities' transform components to determine when components collide, and may also need access to each entity's health component to handle any damage from the collision.

Using this architecture, we can make our code cleaner and more structured, helping us to build very complicated games. Creating a new novel entity often is as simple as giving it a quick combination of components that already handle the required behavior. If new behavior is desired, a new component can be created for the entity and then be reused in the future when other new entities use that same behavior. Just like in any form of programming, this leads to having to make decisions about how specialized or generic your components will be. For simple projects, specialized components and some duplication is OK, but as your project grows it's easier to use common components and simply change how they are combined.

---

[1] We could give health to the tree, but to keep it simple we just assume the trees are destroyed with one blow.

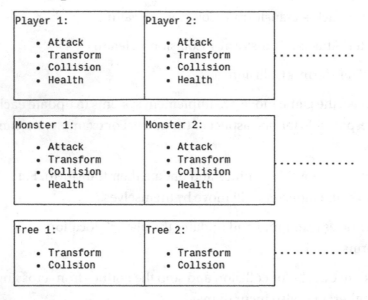

Figure 7-1. *Object oriented–style game design with encapsulation of state*

While entity component systems have the benefit of making the composition of base components very easy, they also can have very large performance benefits. You could take a composition-oriented approach in Rust without using an entity component system by creating a new struct for each entity type in the game, and implementing traits on those structs corresponding to the capabilities of the underlying entities. You could then store these entities and operate on them. You likely would have to write a little more boilerplate to wire up each entity type (or use some macros), but you still could create a simple composition-based system. Each individual entity, however, like a player or a monster, would likely take up a lot of space in memory because they would store all information together in a single struct, and look much like encapsulated objects in an object-oriented paradigm (Figure 7-1). Now, imagine iterating over all of these objects just to calculate collisions; you'd care about the size and position of each object, but all the other information, like health, sprite rendering, and so on, would not be used. Modern processers are very fast at sequentially accessing memory, and the extra components in any entity just take up space in between the data you care about. The problem is even worse if your entities contain pointers to other data, like Box or Vec, since that data is held somewhere else in the heap and will break the sequential access pattern.

Entity Component System

Transform	Transform	Transform	Transform	
• Id (Player 1)	• Id (Player 2)	• Id (Monster 1)	• Id (Tree 1)	· · · · · · · · · · · ·

Collision	Collision	Collision	Collision	
• Id (Player 1)	• Id (Player 2)	• Id (Monster 1)	• Id (Tree 1)	· · · · · · · · · · · ·

Health	Health	Health	
• Id (Player 1)	• Id (Player 2)	• Id (Monster 1)	· · · · · · · · · · · ·

Figure 7-2. *Entity component design with efficient memory access*

Many game developers realized over time that when iterating over entities in a game, they only cared about a small subset of that entity's components, like the transform and size, when calculating collisions, and that if they could pack together only the things that usually were used together, modern processers would have an easier time rapidly loading all of the data. This is where an entity component system shines. Internally, most entity component systems have the equivalent of a single Vec for each component type, so for example a Vec<Transform> or Vec<Collision> (Figure 7-2). Since Vec stores its elements sequentially in memory, all instances of a specific type of component can be accessed efficiently without other data getting in the way. Each component has an id to make clear which entity that component belongs to, but otherwise holds only the component-relevant information. They tend to be designed to not hold pointers to other data either, so that all the data for that component is immediately available in adjacent memory and not somewhere else on the heap. In this example, collisions can rapidly be calculated by iterating over the Vec<Transform> and Vec<Hitbox> component lists without having to fetch other memory. Different systems can be created that work on different subsets of components separately, and the overall result is a program architecture finely tuned to run extremely fast on modern processor architectures.

Now that you have some basic knowledge of entity component systems, it's time to get started writing your game.

7.3 Creating a Bevy Project

Before we write any Bevy code we have to install a few dependencies. Bevy relies on a few system libraries for things like sound, font rendering, XML parsing, etc. Therefore, we need to install these system dependencies first. On ubuntu[2] we can run the following command to install them all:

```
$ sudo apt install g++ \
  pkg-config \
  libx11-dev \
  libasound2-dev \
  libudev-dev
```

Then we can create a project and add Bevy:

```
$ cargo new cat_volleyball
$ cd cat_volleyball
$ cargo add bevy
```

You Cargo.toml file should look something like Listing 7-1.

Listing 7-1. Cargo.toml for Bevy project

```
[package]
name = "cat_volleyball"
# ...

[dependencies]
bevy = "0.10.1"
```

Now you can update your main.rs to match Listing 7-2. If you run the project with cargo run you should see an empty window pop up. This is the standard skeleton for a Bevy project, and if you run the app you should see a black blank window pop up as in Figure 7-3.

---

[2]You can find instructions for other platforms here: https://bevyengine.org/learn/book/getting-started/setup/#install-os-dependencies.

Listing 7-2. Example of a simple Bevy skeleton project

```
use bevy::prelude::*;

fn main() {
  App::new()
    .add_plugins(DefaultPlugins)
    .run();
}
```

Your `src/main.rs` (Listing 7-2) file might look like it does not contain much (a blank window is not much to look at), with only the plugin group `DefaultPlugins` being added. However, this default group contains many important plugins that are responsible for creating this window and performing various actions in the main game, and in many other frameworks getting to this point can take a lot more work. The components include logging, time tracking, transforms (location, orientation, and scale), windows, user input, and debugging. You can look at the Bevy source code to see the full details of the default list of plugins.[3]

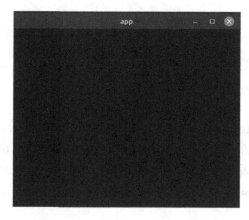

Figure 7-3. *Application with default plugins*

We will define our game using a combination of components and systems. Each component is a struct that can contain some information, while a system is a function that will be run on some subset of the components. The specific subset that is used for

---

[3] https://docs.rs/bevy/latest/bevy/struct.DefaultPlugins.html

any system is determined by a query/queries that are defined in the arguments to the system function. These queries pull in only the components needed by this system. We'll start adding systems after we make some initial customizations.

7.4 See the World Through a Camera

Although the game engine will create a virtual world for us, it doesn't know which part of the world to display on the screen. Therefore, we need to create a camera that tells the engine which part of the engine should be displayed and from which angle.

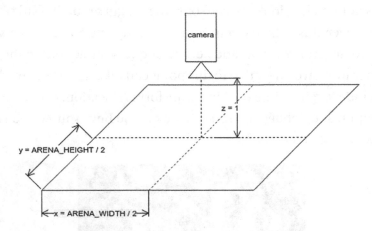

Figure 7-4. *Camera location*

Coordinates in our game will be given in pixels, and the play arena will be in the xy plane, from (0,0) to (200,200).[4] Since we are creating a 2D game the default orientation of the camera is acceptable, we just need to decide where to center it along with the window size. We set `ARENA_WIDTH: f32 = 200.0` and `ARENA_HEIGHT: f32 = 200.0`.[5]

---

[4] Feel free to adjust any of the game parameters as you desire; a big part of making a good game is tweaking the various features to find the perfect combination of fun and difficulty.

[5] Notice Bevy (and many other game engines) use single precision floating point numbers, which are represented by `f32` in Rust. Generally games don't need full double floating point precision, and the savings in memory can be major, which is why single precision floating point arithmetic is used.

The camera itself is centered at the middle of the arena at unit height above the canvas, (ARENA_WIDTH/2.0,ARENA_HEIGHT/2.0, 1.0), with its viewing window sized to fit the full arena (Figure 7-4). We can put the command to spawn a camera in a setup function that will hold all the initial setup code for our game.

The setup function will spawn a camera bundle, the first entity we are adding to our app. Bevy uses bundles as a simple way of creating common entities with all their appropriate components. You can also directly create entities from a tuple of base components or mixtures of base components and bundles, which we'll do in the next section. To instruct Bevy to call the setup function at loading time, we add it to the app using the add_startup_system method (Listing 7-3). To confirm that our camera is working properly, we can change the camera color using the insert_resource method on our app. In the example code in Listing 7-3 we've left the color as black (red, green, and blue values all at 0.0), but you can change these values and re-run the app to see the background reflect the new color.

Notice how when spawning the camera we provided the Transform component explicitly to the Camera2dBundle, while leaving all other components at their defaults. This is a common pattern in Bevy, and lets us avoid specifying every detail for every component of an entity, instead only specifying components that differ from some common default.

Listing 7-3. Initializing the camera

```
use bevy::prelude::*;

const ARENA_WIDTH: f32 = 200.0;
const ARENA_HEIGHT: f32 = 200.0;

fn setup(mut commands: Commands,) {
  commands.spawn(Camera2dBundle {
    transform: Transform::from_xyz(
      ARENA_WIDTH/2.0,
      ARENA_HEIGHT/2.0,1.0),
    ..default()
  });
}
```

```
fn main() {
  App::new()
    // set the global default
    .add_plugins(DefaultPlugins.set(WindowPlugin {
      primary_window: Some(Window {
          title: "Cat Volleyball".into(),
          resolution: (ARENA_WIDTH, ARENA_HEIGHT).into(),
          ..default()
      }),
      ..default()
    }))
    .insert_resource(ClearColor(Color::rgb(0.0, 0.0, 0.0)))
    .add_startup_system(setup)
    .run();
}
```

7.5 Adding the Cats

Next, we are going to add some moving parts to the game, starting with the cats
representing the players. Start off by creating a top-level folder titled assets, which is
the default directory used by Bevy to store game assets like sprites, sounds, textures, and
other game data. Inside this folder you can create another textures folder in which to
save the cat-sprite.png file, which contains our player cat sprite (Figure 7-5).

Figure 7-5. *cat-sprite.png*

Listing 7-4. Initializing the camera

```
// ...

const PLAYER_HEIGHT: f32 = 32.0;
const PLAYER_WIDTH: f32 = 22.0;

// ...
#[derive(Copy, Clone)]
enum Side {
  Left,
  Right,
}

#[derive(Component)]
struct Player {
  side: Side,
}

fn initialize_player(
  commands: &mut Commands,
  cat_sprite: Handle<Image>,
  side: Side,
  x: f32,
  y: f32,
) {
  commands.spawn((
    Player { side },
    SpriteBundle {
      texture: cat_sprite,
      transform: Transform::from_xyz(x, y, 0.0),
      ..default()
    },
  ));
}

fn setup(mut commands: Commands,
  asset_server: Res<AssetServer>) {

//...
```

```
let cat_sprite = asset_server.load("textures/cat-sprite.png");
initialize_player(
  &mut commands,
  cat_sprite.clone(),
  Side::Left,
  PLAYER_WIDTH / 2.0,
  PLAYER_HEIGHT / 2.0,
);
initialize_player(
  &mut commands,
  cat_sprite.clone(),
  Side::Right,
  ARENA_WIDTH - PLAYER_WIDTH / 2.0,
  PLAYER_HEIGHT / 2.0,
);
}

// ...
```

You can see the code for initializing the players in Listing 7-4. We'll start by defining our own new component, a Player, which will contain a single field Side. This field lets you differentiate between the two players. We want to initialize one left and one right player, so we write an initialization function and then call that function in the setup function we wrote previously. In the initialization function we spawn a player as a tuple containing a Player component and a SpriteBundle, which just like the previous camera bundle is actually a set of multiple other components. We can use most of the default components in the SpriteBundle, but we need to provide the specific player sprite along with a custom transformation for the player's starting location.

We need to think a bit about exactly where we should place our new players. We place the players on each side of the arena, as in Figure 7-6 and Figure 7-7. If we locate the two players at (0.0, 0.0) and (ARENA_WIDTH, 0.0), you'll see that they are centered exactly on the corners of the arena, and only a quarter of each player is visible. We'll need to do some math to follow the diagrams and offset the centers of the players so the full sprites appear in each corner. Shifting by half each player's width and height gives us the correct coordinate pair (PLAYER_WIDTH/2.0, PLAYER_HEIGHT/2.0) and (ARENA_WIDTH - PLAYER_WIDTH/2.0, PLAYER_HEIGHT/2.0) for the left and right players, respectively.

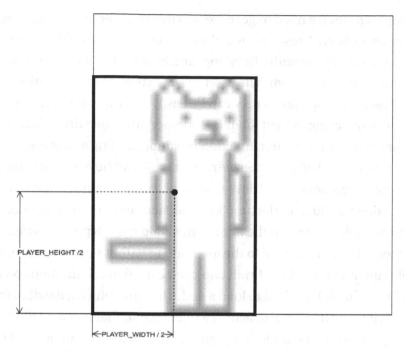

Figure 7-6. *Left player location*

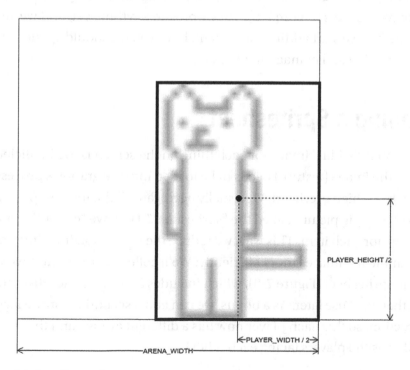

Figure 7-7. *Right player location*

To load single sprites we need to get access to the asset server. The asset server is one of many resources in Bevy. A resource is a global location that provides access to some information or service for the entire Bevy app, and in addition to using premade Bevy resources you can create your own. The asset server acts as a single location in which to store loaded assets like sprites so they can be easily retrieved and used by multiple components without having to load them into memory multiple times. You can add the asset server to your setup system function by simply adding a new argument to the function: `asset_server: Res<AssetServer>`. Generally, all Bevy system functions work in this way; various arguments to retrieve resources, entities, components, and other features can be directly added to the function interface, and Bevy will connect the code automatically internally. Note that the argument added has a type of `Res<AssetServer>`. The `Res` wrapper acts as a reference to the asset server without passing the entire resource in; it implements the `Deref` trait and can be used to call methods on the asset server. We call the `.load()` method to load a sprite file and return a `Handle<Image>` to the loaded sprite. The `Handle` also acts as a reference so that it can be easily cloned without creating a clone of the underlying sprite. These handles can be used to initialize the `SpriteBundle` component with the sprites used for each player.

At this point you should be able to run your program and see the cats for each player in the bottom two corners (Figure 7-8). They won't do anything yet, and we've still got a ways to go. Before we start adding movement, however, we should spend a little time making sprite loading and management easier.

7.6 Loading a Spritesheet

Usually, using an individual image for each thing on the screen is too inefficient for a game because the image (texture) needs to be loaded into the graphics processing unit (GPU), which has a high overhead. We usually aggregate all the images (or some of the related ones) into a big picture called the "spritesheet." Then we "cut out" a small section of the big image for each item. This way, we reduce the overall loading time and allow the GPU to handle the images more efficiently. We'll collect all the sprites we want to use in a single spritesheet (Figure 7-9), which includes a mirror cat for the right player and the ball that we'll use later. As a bonus, we can add a second cat sprite facing in the opposite direction, so that each player now has a different avatar (and the volleyball game actually has the players facing each other).

We need to go back and refactor our player display code to load and handle the spritesheet; the changes are shown in Listing 7-5.

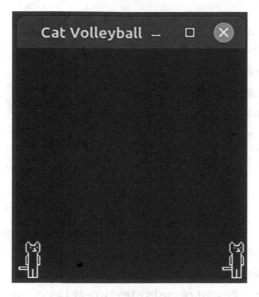

Figure 7-8. *Player cats in the arena; note that the sizing may be different in your application, as the window might be larger*

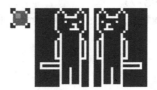

Figure 7-9. *Updated spritesheet.png*

Listing 7-5. Code to load a spritesheet

```
// ...

fn initialize_player(
  commands: &mut Commands,
  atlas: Handle<TextureAtlas>,
  cat_sprite: usize,
  side: Side,
  x: f32,
```

```
  y: f32,
) {
  commands.spawn((
    Player { side },
    SpriteSheetBundle {
      sprite: TextureAtlasSprite::new(cat_sprite),
      texture_atlas: atlas,
      transform: Transform::from_xyz(x, y, 0.0),
      ..default()
    },
  ));
}

fn setup(
  mut commands: Commands,
  asset_server: Res<AssetServer>,
  mut texture_atlases: ResMut<Assets<TextureAtlas>>,
) {
  let spritesheet = asset_server.load(
    "textures/spritesheet.png");
  let mut sprite_atlas = TextureAtlas::new_empty(
   spritesheet,
   Vec2::new(58.0, 34.0));

  let left_cat_corner = Vec2::new(11.0, 1.0);
  let right_cat_corner = Vec2::new(35.0, 1.0);
  let cat_size = Vec2::new(22.0, 32.0);

  let left_cat_index = sprite_atlas.add_texture(
    Rect::from_corners(
      left_cat_corner,
      left_cat_corner + cat_size,
    )
  );
  let right_cat_index = sprite_atlas.add_texture(
    Rect::from_corners(
      right_cat_corner,
```

```
    right_cat_corner + cat_size,
  )
);

let texture_atlas_handle = texture_atlases.add(sprite_atlas);

commands.spawn(Camera2dBundle {
  transform: Transform::from_xyz(
    ARENA_WIDTH/2.0,
    ARENA_HEIGHT/2.0,1.0),
  ..default()
});

initialize_player(
  &mut commands,
  texture_atlas_handle.clone(),
  left_cat_index,
  Side::Left,
  PLAYER_WIDTH / 2.0,
  PLAYER_HEIGHT / 2.0,
);
initialize_player(
  &mut commands,
  texture_atlas_handle,
  right_cat_index,
  Side::Right,
  ARENA_WIDTH - PLAYER_WIDTH / 2.0,
  PLAYER_HEIGHT / 2.0,
);
}

// ...
```

We update the code to initialize each player to take a handle to a TextureAtlas
instead of to an Image, and also add an index into that atlas for the desired texture in
the atlas. We replace the SpriteBundle with a SpriteSheetBundle that takes the atlas,
along with a texture atlas sprite from the index. Otherwise the player initialization stays
the same.

In the setup function, we update the arguments to provide a mutable reference to the TextureAtlas assets. The TextureAtlas is a single location where we can store all texture atlases in the whole program. We load our spritesheet just like any other image into the asset server and then create a new texture atlas from this image with its total size. To get individual sprites from the atlas we generate the coordinates of rectangles encompassing each sprite (these rectangles are defined by the upper left and lower right points in pixels on the spritesheet). Note that for images the (0,0) coordinate is in the top left. After we've added the textures and received the indices for these textures in the atlas, we add the new atlas to our larger atlas collection and are left with a handle to the asset that can be passed to the player initializers. As a bonus, we now have the cat player on the right side facing their opponent (Figure 7-10).

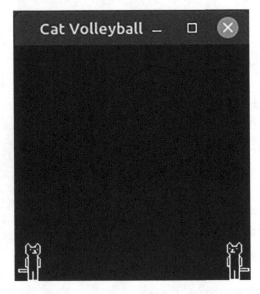

Figure 7-10. *Cats with the correct position, from a spritesheet*

Note we could have continued using individual images loaded as sprites and it probably wouldn't have had a large effect on our game's performance, but for larger games a single spritesheet can have huge advantages. This approach also shows how entity component systems can generally be very flexible; we switched out a few of our player's visual components by choosing a different bundle, but otherwise the game remains the same. Moving forward, we can refer to sprites using a texture atlas combined with an index into that atlas.

7.7 Moving the Cats

The cats are now rendered nicely, but they are static. We want to control them with a keyboard.

The first step is to determine which inputs we want available to each player. We want the left player to use the A and D keys, while the right player uses the left and right arrows. We can implement two methods on the Side enum (Listing 7-6) to return the keys that correspond to left and right movement, based on the current side. Bevy represents these key presses with a KeyCode enum, and we'll assign the keys we want for control. In a larger application we might want to load these from a config file to allow easy key-binding customization in-game, but for us hardcoding them here is fine.

While we are adding methods to the Side enum we'll also provide a range method. Each cat player will be limited to their own side, much like on a real volleyball court. We'll code in the permissible range for a player based on their side into this method; when processing players, we can call range to ensure a player hasn't strayed out of their play zone.

Listing 7-6. Implementing side methods

```
impl Side {
  // Get keycode for move left
  fn go_left_key(&self) -> KeyCode {
    match self {
      Side::Left => KeyCode::A,
      Side::Right => KeyCode::Left,
    }
  }

  // Get keycode for move right
  fn go_right_key(&self) -> KeyCode {
    match self {
      Side::Left => KeyCode::D,
      Side::Right => KeyCode::Right,
    }
  }
}
```

```
  // Determine the permissible range of the cat
  fn range(&self) -> (f32, f32) {
    match self {
      Side::Left => (
        PLAYER_WIDTH / 2.0,
        ARENA_WIDTH / 2.0 - PLAYER_WIDTH / 2.0
      ),
      Side::Right => (
        ARENA_WIDTH / 2.0 + PLAYER_WIDTH / 2.0,
        ARENA_WIDTH - PLAYER_WIDTH / 2.0,
      ),
    }
  }
}
```

At this point, you're ready to create your first non-startup system. You can follow Listing 7-7 to write the player function that will define the player system. First, let's take a look at the arguments we're providing to the function, which again will be auto-filled by the Bevy framework whenever this function is called:

- keyboard_input: Res<Input<Keyboard>>: Provides a reference to the keyboard input resource. This can be used to determine which keys are currently pressed.

- time: Res<Time>: Provides a reference to the time resource. Since our player system function can be called with different amounts of time between steps, we'll use this resource to determine the time since last step, which will help us ensure player movement is smooth.

- mut query: Query<(&mut Player, &mut Transform)>: A Query that can be iterated over to provide each entity that contains both a Player and a Transform, providing mutable references to both.

It's worth taking a little more time digging into the elegance of the Query type here. We want to write a system that moves our players; to move a player we need to get some information from that player (what side it's on and therefore where it can move and which inputs it reacts to) and then modify that player's transform. By putting a shared reference to Player and a mutable reference to Transform in the query, Bevy will give us an iterator that iterates over every entity with both of these components. We can ignore all the other components that a player entity has, just focusing on the transform. This is extremely composable and extensible; the player system will operate on any entity that has this pair of components.

Listing 7-7. The player system

```
const PLAYER_SPEED: f32 = 60.0;

fn player(
  keyboard_input: Res<Input<KeyCode>>,
  time: Res<Time>,
  mut query: Query<(&Player, &mut Transform)>,
) {
  for (player, mut transform) in query.iter_mut() {
    let left = if keyboard_input.pressed(
        player.side.go_left_key())
    {
      -1.0f32
    } else {
      0.0
    };
    let right = if keyboard_input.pressed(
        player.side.go_right_key())
    {
      1.0f32
    } else {
      0.0
    };
    let direction = left + right;
    let offset = direction * PLAYER_SPEED
      * time.raw_delta_seconds();

    // Apply movement deltas
    transform.translation.x += offset;
    let (left_limit, right_limit) = player.side.range();
    transform.translation.x = transform.translation.x.clamp(
```

```
        left_limit, right_limit);
    }
}

// ...

fn main() {
  App::new()
    // ... Other systems and setup
    .add_system(player)
    .run();
}
```

In the actual player function, the first bit of code determines whether there is a request for the player to move left or right. You can query the Input resource to see if any of the pressed buttons match that player's buttons for moving left or right. We use two variables, left and right, and set them to -1.0 and 1.0 respectively if the appropriate button is pressed, or zero if not. This lets us calculate the total direction by simply adding them, with the final direction variable then being 0.0 if neither or both of the buttons are pressed.

Next, you'll need to determine the player's total movement during this timestep. To let the players move smoothly, you can set a fixed speed in PLAYER_SPEED. The time difference between two executions of the system can be read from time.raw_delta_ seconds(). (The raw addition lets us directly get the seconds as an f32 instead of as an intermediate representation as a Rust Duration type.) The final formula for movement is then just the distance moved times the direction (which may be 0.0, meaning no move occurred), giving us the following:

$$offset = movement\ direction \times player\ speed \times time\ delta$$

which corresponds to the following code line:

```
let offset = direction * PLAYER_SPEED * time.raw_delta_seconds();
```

Once the movement offset is calculated, we can update the player's X position:

$$x_{after} = x_{before} + offset$$

We can get the current position (x_{before}) using transform.translation.x. So, the final position is simply transform.translation.x + offset.

However, if we don't restrict the range of `transform.translation.x`, the players can move out of the window and into each other's field. Therefore, we have to limit the `transform.translation.x` value to only half of the arena. The left player's range will be `[0, arena_width / 2]`, and the right player will be `[arena_width / 2, arena_width]`. We've already coded these limits to be returned as a method from the `Side` enum, including handling the adjustments for each player's width. The simplest way to enforce this is to retrieve the limits and then feed them into the `clamp` function. This function takes a value and, if it's outside the given minimum and maximum, "clamps" it to be either the minimum or maximum value. This is a simple way to ensure that each player cannot move out of their designated area, and can be tested by trying to move the cats around (Figure 7-11).

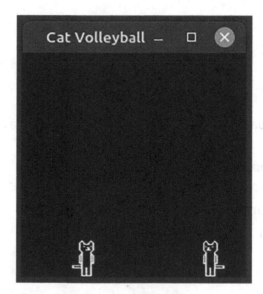

Figure 7-11. *Moving the cat players with keyboard*

7.8 Creating the Ball

Since we have the players ready, let's bring the ball into the game (we won't add a net since we've already got plenty of other code we still need to write). Adding a `Ball` component is as straightforward as adding the `Player`. We just add the struct, annotate it with `#[derive(Component)]`, and add velocity and radius fields to the struct (we'll be using these later for the ball's movement). The rest of the code in Listing 7-8 follows closely what we did for initializing a player. A new initialization function is created that spawns an entity as a tuple of a `Ball` and a `SpriteSheetBundle`, using a passed-in atlas and index to generate the sprite, and putting the ball at the center of the arena (`ARENA/WIDTH/2.0, ARENA_HEIGHT/2.0`). The initialization function is called in the wider setup function, with the sprite selected from the appropriate location in our loaded spritesheet. After running this new code we can see the ball in the arena (Figure 7-12).

Listing 7-8. Create the ball component and initialize it

```
const BALL_VELOCITY_X: f32 = 30.0;
const BALL_VELOCITY_Y: f32 = 0.0;
const BALL_RADIUS: f32 = 4.0;

#[derive(Component)]
pub struct Ball {
  pub velocity: Vec2,
  pub radius: f32,
}

/// Initializes one ball in the middle-ish of the arena.
fn initialize_ball(
  commands: &mut Commands,
  asset_server: &Res<AssetServer>,
  atlas: Handle<TextureAtlas>,
  ball_sprite: usize,
) {
  commands.spawn((
    Ball {
      velocity: Vec2::new(BALL_VELOCITY_X, BALL_VELOCITY_Y),
      radius: BALL_RADIUS,
    },
    SpriteSheetBundle {
      sprite: TextureAtlasSprite::new(ball_sprite),
      texture_atlas: atlas,
      transform: Transform::from_xyz(
        ARENA_WIDTH / 2.0,
```

```
        ARENA_HEIGHT / 2.0, 0.0),
      ..default()
    },
  ));
}

fn setup(
  // ...
) {
  // ... setup cat indicies

  let ball_corner = Vec2::new(1.0, 1.0);
  let ball_size = Vec2::new(8.0, 8.0);
// create texture atlas handle.

  let ball_index =
    sprite_atlas.add_texture(Rect::from_corners(
        ball_corner,
        ball_corner + ball_size
    ));

  // ... init camera ...
  initialize_ball(
    &mut commands,
    &asset_server,
    texture_atlas_handle.clone(),
    ball_index,
  );
  // ... init players ...
}
```

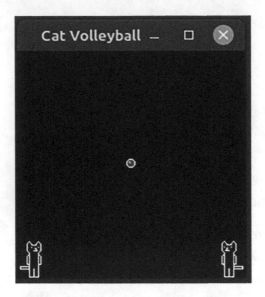

Figure 7-12. *Ball added to the arena*

7.9 Can't Defy Gravity

Notice how in the previous section we had the ball with an initial velocity moving to the right, based on (BALL_VELOCITY_X, BALL_VELOCITY_Y). We now need to implement a new system that will move the ball. If we were to directly copy our code for player movement, the ball would just drift to the right until it went off the screen. Instead, we need to simulate gravity, slowly accelerating the ball downward while simultaneously maintaining its rightward velocity. The code in Listing 7-9 implements the move_ball system, which does exactly this.

Listing 7-9. Ball movement system

```
pub const GRAVITY_ACCELERATION: f32 = -40.0;

fn move_ball(
    time: Res<Time>,
    mut query: Query<(&mut Ball, &mut Transform)>
) {
    for (mut ball, mut transform) in query.iter_mut() {
        // Apply movement deltas
```

```
    transform.translation.x += ball.velocity.x
        * time.raw_delta_seconds();
    transform.translation.y += (ball.velocity.y
        + time.raw_delta_seconds()
        * GRAVITY_ACCELERATION / 2.0)
        * time.raw_delta_seconds();
    ball.velocity.y += time.raw_delta_seconds()
        * GRAVITY_ACCELERATION;
    }
}
// ...

fn main() {
    App::new()
        // ...
        .add_system(move_ball)
        // ...
}
```

This system takes the resource Res<Time> and a query that returns entities with Ball and Transform components. Since there is no acceleration in the *x* direction, we can directly write the new *x* position as the old position plus the velocity times the time:

```
x = x + velocity * time_difference
```

For the *y* position, based on the definition of acceleration,

$$x(t) = \frac{d}{dx} v(t)$$
$$v(t) = \frac{d}{dx} y(t)$$

it might be tempting to write the following:

```
velocity = velocity + acceleration * time_difference
y = y + velocity * time_difference
```

However, this approach (known as Euler integration) introduces some error that is dependent on the time difference, and it is noticeable when the time difference is not steady. If the frame rate is different, the trajectory of the ball will also be slightly different. To fix the issue, we use a different algorithm called *velocity Verlet integration*:

```
y = y + (velocity + time_difference * acceleration / 2) * time_difference
velocity = velocity + acceleration * time_difference
```

After translating this to the code in Listing 7-9, we get a much more accurate simulation of a falling ball. We just need to add the new move_ball system to our Bevy app, and the velocity and position will be updated on each frame.

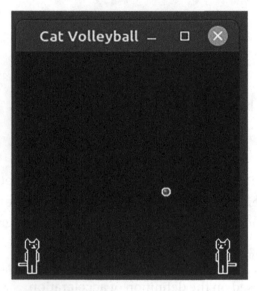

Figure 7-13. *Ball moving due to gravity*

Now, if we run cargo run, the ball shoots to the right and falls in a beautiful curve (Figure 7-13).

7.10 Making the Ball Bounce

The ball now drops naturally, but it fell through the floor and the cat players. To make the game playable, we need to implement a bounce system that makes the ball bounce when it hits the boundary of the window or the player. This is as simple as adding another system to the game (Listing 7-10), though this system will be the most complicated one we've implemented thus far. Note that the bounce function has a pair of queries as parameters—one for the ball and one for the players. This lets us query both components simultaneously, since we'll need both a ball and a player to determine if they collide.

Before you can get started with this section, you'll need to add the rand crate (we'll use this crate to add a little bit of randomness to the bounces):

```
$ cargo add rand
```

Then, you can add the bounce system skeleton.

Listing 7-10. Bounce system skeleton

```rust
use rand::Rng;

// ... Imports and other systems

fn bounce(
  mut ball_query: Query<(&mut Ball, &Transform)>,
  player_query: Query<(&Player, &Transform)>,
) {
  for (mut ball, ball_transform) in ball_query.iter_mut() {
    let ball_x = ball_transform.translation.x;
    let ball_y = ball_transform.translation.y;

    if ball_y <= ball.radius && ball.velocity.y < 0.0 {
      ball.velocity.y = -ball.velocity.y;
    } else if
      ball_y >= (ARENA_HEIGHT - ball.radius) && ball.velocity.y > 0.0
    {
      ball.velocity.y = -ball.velocity.y;
    } else if ball_x <= ball.radius && ball.velocity.x < 0.0 {
      ball.velocity.x = -ball.velocity.x;
    } else if
      ball_x >= (ARENA_WIDTH - ball.radius) && ball.velocity.x > 0.0
    {
      ball.velocity.x = -ball.velocity.x;
    }
```

```
      // ... additional collision detection
   }
}

// ... other systems and setup

fn main() {
  App::new()
    // ...
    .add_system(bounce)
    // ...
}
```

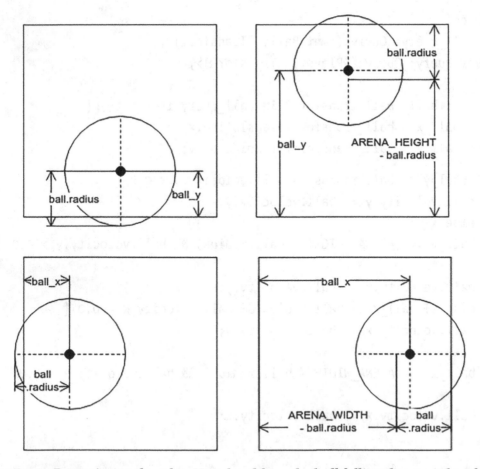

Figure 7-14. *Bouncing at the edge. You should see the ball falling down and to the right when your program starts (it's rather hard to show something moving in a book)*

First, let us handle the bouncing around the edge of the window. In each frame, we track the location of the ball; if the ball has gone outside of any edge, and its velocity is making the ball going out even further,[6] then we'll invert the velocity on that axis. For example, if the ball goes outside of the right edge, and its x velocity is +10 pixel/sec (i.e., moving toward the right), then it will flip the x velocity to -10 pixel/sec (i.e., moving toward the left). Generalize this idea to the four edges, and we get Listing 7-11. The four cases in Listing 7-10 are illustrated in Figure 7-14.

Listing 7-11. Bouncing the ball at the edge

```
use rand::Rng;
// ...
fn point_in_rect(
  x: f32, // ball's x and y location
  y: f32,
  left: f32, // the player box's boundary
  bottom: f32,
  right: f32,
  top: f32,
) -> bool {
  x >= left && x <= right && y >= bottom && y <= top
}

fn bounce(
  mut ball_query: Query<(&mut Ball, &Transform)>,
  player_query: Query<(&Player, &Transform)>,
) {
  for (mut ball, ball_transform) in ball_query.iter_mut() {

  // ... Previous edge collision code ...

    for (player, player_trans) in player_query.iter() {
      let player_x = player_trans.translation.x;
      let player_y = player_trans.translation.y;
```

---

[6] This is required because sometimes the ball already bounced, but it's still outside of the window in the next frame. In this case, the ball will be trapped at the edge because the velocity keeps inverting.

```
if point_in_rect(
  ball_x,
  ball_y,
  player_x - PLAYER_WIDTH / 2.0 - ball.radius,
  player_y - PLAYER_HEIGHT / 2.0 - ball.radius,
  player_x + PLAYER_WIDTH / 2.0 + ball.radius,
  player_y + PLAYER_HEIGHT / 2.0 + ball.radius,
) {
  if ball.velocity.y < 0.0 {
    // Only bounce when ball is falling
    ball.velocity.y = -ball.velocity.y;

    let mut rng = rand::thread_rng();
    match player.side {
      Side::Left => {
        ball.velocity.x = ball.velocity.x.abs()
          * rng.gen_range(0.6..1.4)
      }
      Side::Right => {
        ball.velocity.x = -ball.velocity.x.abs()
          * rng.gen_range(0.6..1.4)
      }
    }
  }
}
// ...
```

We also need to make the ball bounce when it hits the players. Otherwise, it passes
through the players as if they are thin air. We don't need to define the contour of the
player and do a real physical collision simulation. We can simplify this by imagining the
player to be a rectangular box, and if the ball's location falls within this box, we assume
that the ball collides with the player (Figure 7-15). We can put this collision logic in a
helper function to simplify the main collision code (Listing 7-11).

When the ball collides, we don't calculate the direction it should bounce back according to physics. Instead, we invert the y-axis velocity, so the falling ball now bounces upward. For the x-axis, we force the ball to fly toward the opponent. So for the left player, the ball will go right when hit, and vice versa. We do this by first taking the absolute value of the current velocity and then giving it the correct sign. To give the game some playability, we randomly speed up or slow down the ball in the x-axis on collision, so the ball's trajectory is unpredictable, using the rand crate. We use these rules to make the calculation simple but keep the game interesting.

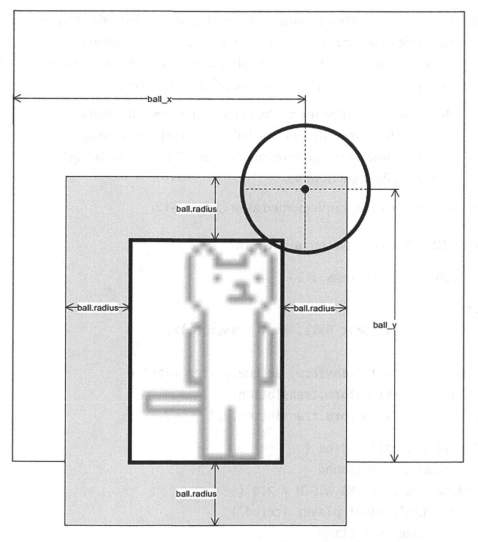

Figure 7-15. Collision detection between a player and the ball

7.11 Keeping Score

The game is now fully playable, but we have to keep score with paper and pen. To make the game track the score for us, just as you guessed, we will simply spin up another system.

Our algorithm should look like the following:

1.   If the ball touches the bottom boundary (i.e., the ball's center is less then one radius above the ground), it's a goal.

2.   We check the ball's *x* coordinate to see if it's on the left side or the right side of the arena. If it's on the right side, the left player gets a point, and vice versa (the ball landing on the right side means the right player failed to return it, so the left player scores).

3.   Reposition the ball to the center of the arena. Reset the ball's *y*-axis velocity to zero. Reverse the ball's *x*-axis velocity to make the ball shoot toward the point-earner's side; this is for simulating the change of the right of serve.

This code can be easily implemented as in Listing 7-12.

Listing 7-12. The score system algorithm

```
// ... imports and systems ...

fn scoring(
  mut query: Query<(&mut Ball, &mut Transform)>,
) {
  for (mut ball, mut transform) in query.iter_mut() {
    let ball_x = transform.translation.x;
    let ball_y = transform.translation.y;

    if ball_y < ball.radius {
      // touched the ground
      if ball_x <= ARENA_WIDTH / 2.0 {
        println!("Right player scored");
        // Change direction
        ball.velocity.x = ball.velocity.x.abs();
      } else {
```

```
    println!("Left player scored");
    // Change direction
    ball.velocity.x = -ball.velocity.x.abs();
}
// reset the ball to the middle
transform.translation.x = ARENA_WIDTH / 2.0;
transform.translation.y = ARENA_HEIGHT / 2.0;

ball.velocity.y = 0.0; // reset to free drop
    }
  }
}

// ... setup ...

fn main() {
  App::new()
    // ...
    .add_system(scoring)
    // ...
    .run();
}
```

In Listing 7-12, we only print who scored, but we can't expect the gamer to look at the log file of the game. So, we are going to show the score directly on the screen using a text resource.

First, we need to create a resource data struct to hold the score, as follows:

```
#[derive(Resource)]
struct Score {
    left: usize,
    right: usize,
}
```

Then, in we can store our data in the Score struct instead of printing it to the log (Listing 7-13). Note we've added a ResMut<Score> to the function's arguments, which will give us a mutable reference to the single Score resource the Bevy engine automatically creates. We increment the score by one every time they score and limit the number to 999, so the text won't overflow the screen.

Listing 7-13. Keeping the score in ScoreBoard

```
fn scoring(
  mut query: Query<(&mut Ball, &mut Transform)>,
  mut score: ResMut<Score>,
) {
  for (mut ball, mut transform) in query.iter_mut() {
      let ball_x = transform.translation.x;
      let ball_y = transform.translation.y;

      if ball_y < ball.radius {
          // touched the ground
          if ball_x <= ARENA_WIDTH / 2.0 {
              score.right += 1;
              // Change direction
              ball.velocity.x = ball.velocity.x.abs();
          } else {
              score.left += 1;
              // Change direction
              ball.velocity.x = -ball.velocity.x.abs();
          }
          // reset the ball to the middle
          transform.translation.x = ARENA_WIDTH / 2.0;
          transform.translation.y = ARENA_HEIGHT / 2.0;

          ball.velocity.y = 0.0; // reset to free drop
      }
  }
}
```

Now that we have the score ready, we can show it on the screen with two ScoreBoard entities. We first create a ScoreBoard component struct with a Side field to differentiate between the two players. Then we add an initialize_scoreboard() function as in Listing 7-14, similar to how we initialize the balls and players. The initialization function creates an entity that contains a Scoreboard component along with the set of components in TextBundle. We can set the font size, color, and the font itself by setting the text style, and we do so by loading the font file fonts/square.ttf into the asset server.[7] We allow the initialization function to provide the horizontal position, but fix the vertical position for all scoreboards to be at the same height. Note that for text elements the position is given in pixels from the top-left pixel on the screen; these pixels do not correspond to our coordinate system for the ball and the players. With the initialize function created, we can call it twice to create a separate scoreboard for each player's score.

Listing 7-14. Initializing the UiText entities

```rust
// ... other constants ...
pub const SCORE_FONT_SIZE: f32 = 20.0;

#[derive(Component)]
struct ScoreBoard {
  side: Side
}

fn initialize_scoreboard(
  commands: &mut Commands,
  asset_server: &Res<AssetServer>,
  side: Side,
  x: f32,
) {
  commands.spawn((
    ScoreBoard { side },
    TextBundle::from_sections([
        TextSection::from_style(TextStyle {
          font_size: SCORE_FONT_SIZE,
          color: Color::WHITE,
          font: asset_server.load("fonts/square.ttf"),
    })])
      .with_style(Style {
        position_type: PositionType::Absolute,
        position: UiRect {
```

---

[7] Bevy does not contain any default fonts, so we need to be sure to specify a font here that we've loaded.

```
        top: Val::Px(25.0),
        left: Val::Px(x),
        ..default()
      },
      ..default()
    })
    .with_text_alignment(match side {
      Side::Left => TextAlignment::Left,
      Side::Right => TextAlignment::Right,
    }),
  ));
}

// ... other systems ...

fn setup(
  mut commands: Commands,
  asset_server: Res<AssetServer>,
  mut texture_atlases: ResMut<Assets<TextureAtlas>>,
) {
    // ...

  initialize_scoreboard(
    &mut commands,
    &asset_server,
    Side::Left, ARENA_WIDTH / 2.0 - 25.0
  );
  initialize_scoreboard(
    &mut commands,
    &asset_server,
    Side::Right,
    ARENA_WIDTH / 2.0 + 25.0
  );
}
```

```
fn main() {
  App::new()
      // ...
      .insert_resource(Score { left: 0, right: 0 })
      // ...
      .run();
}
```

You have initialized your scoreboard now, but you also need to handle updating the scoreboard and calculating the score. This involves creating a new system function `score_display` that will update the scoreboard based on each player's current score (Listing 7-15).

We first implement the `scoring` system function by taking in a query on any balls with transforms, along with a reference to the `Score` resource. If the ball hits the floor (equivalent to the ball y position's being less than the ball's radius) we determine what half of the arena the ball is in, and give a point to the player on the other side. We then set the ball's x velocity to point toward the player who just won the point, representing the other player's getting the right to serve. The ball is then reset to the center of the arena, and the velocity set to zero.

We add a second system `score_display` that updates the scoreboard with the current score. It works by querying over all entities with both text and scoreboards, and then pulls the correct score to update the text based off the scoreboard's `Side` field.

When this is all completed and the two new systems are added and running, the score-board will look like Figure 7-16.

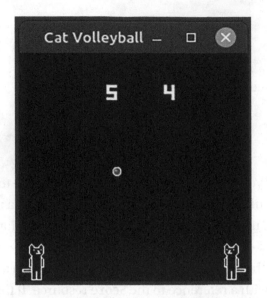

Figure 7-16. *Showing the score. Note that the score value may not be centered, especially if your app shows up in a larger window than the play area*

Listing 7-15. Update the score on the UI in the WinnerSystem

```
// ...

fn scoring(
  mut query: Query<(&mut Ball, &mut Transform)>,
  mut score: ResMut<Score>,
) {
  for (mut ball, mut transform) in query.iter_mut() {
    let ball_x = transform.translation.x;
    let ball_y = transform.translation.y;

    if ball_y < ball.radius {
      // touched the ground
      if ball_x <= ARENA_WIDTH / 2.0 {
        score.right += 1;
        // Change direction
        ball.velocity.x = ball.velocity.x.abs();
      } else {
        score.left += 1;
```

```rust
        // Change direction
        ball.velocity.x = -ball.velocity.x.abs();
      }
      // reset the ball to the middle
      transform.translation.x = ARENA_WIDTH / 2.0;
      transform.translation.y = ARENA_HEIGHT / 2.0;

      ball.velocity.y = 0.0; // reset to free drop
    }
  }
}

fn score_display(
  score: Res<Score>,
  mut query: Query<(&mut Text, &ScoreBoard)>
) {
  for (mut text, scoreboard) in query.iter_mut() {
    text.sections[0].value = match scoreboard.side {
      Side::Left => score.left.to_string(),
      Side::Right => score.right.to_string(),
    };
  }
}

// ...

fn main() {
  App::new()
    // ...
    .add_system(scoring)
    .add_system(score_display)
    .run();
}
```

7.12 Let There Be Music

Now we have a complete game, but it doesn't feel complete without sound effects and background music. To be able to play music in the game, we need to first add an audio resource and update a few places in the code to be able to load our desired sound clips (Listing 7-16). The audio system in Bevy is very simple, but it can do everything we need for our basic game.

Listing 7-16. Loading the AudioBundle

```
#[derive(Component)]
pub struct Ball {
  pub velocity: Vec2,
  pub radius: f32,
  pub bounce: Handle<AudioSource>, // Audio source for bouncing
  pub score: Handle<AudioSource>, // Audio source for scoring
}

// ...

fn initialize_ball(
  // ...
) {
  let bounce_audio = asset_server.load("audio/bounce.ogg");
  let score_audio = asset_server.load("audio/score.ogg");
  commands.spawn((
    Ball {
      velocity: Vec2::new(BALL_VELOCITY_X, BALL_VELOCITY_Y),
      radius: BALL_RADIUS,
      bounce: bounce_audio,
      score: score_audio,
    },
    // ...
  ));
}

// ...
```

```
fn setup(
  mut commands: Commands,
  asset_server: Res<AssetServer>,
  mut texture_atlases: ResMut<Assets<TextureAtlas>>,
  audio: Res<Audio>, // Added audio subsystem
) {
  audio.play_with_settings(
    asset_server.load(
      "audio/Computer_Music_All-Stars_-_Albatross_v2.ogg"
    ),
    PlaybackSettings::LOOP.with_volume(0.25),
  );
  // ...
}
```

You will add two new fields to the Ball, a bounce and score, which are both handles to an AudioSource. These are initialized by loading sound files into the asset server and then passing the handles, and will be used for ball sound effects. We can also load the background music file in the main setup function, and then play it on loop to give our game some general ambiance.

Listing 7-17. Audio module for loading the background music

```
fn bounce(
  mut ball_query: Query<(&mut Ball, &Transform)>,
  player_query: Query<(&Player, &Transform)>,
  audio: Res<Audio>, // Audio resource added
) {
  for (mut ball, ball_trans) in ball_query.iter_mut() {
    let ball_x = ball_trans.translation.x;
    let ball_y = ball_trans.translation.y;

    if ball_y >= (ARENA_HEIGHT - ball.radius)
      && ball.velocity.y > 0.0
    {
      audio.play(ball.bounce.clone()); // bounce sound added
      ball.velocity.y = -ball.velocity.y;
```

```rust
        } else if ball_x <= ball.radius && ball.velocity.x < 0.0 {
          audio.play(ball.bounce.clone()); // bounce sound added
          ball.velocity.x = -ball.velocity.x;
        } else if ball_x >= (ARENA_WIDTH - ball.radius)
          && ball.velocity.x > 0.0
        {
          audio.play(ball.bounce.clone()); // bounce sound added
          ball.velocity.x = -ball.velocity.x;
        }
        for (player, player_trans) in player_query.iter() {
          let player_x = player_trans.translation.x;
          let player_y = player_trans.translation.y;

          if point_in_rect(
            // ...
          ) {
            if ball.velocity.y < 0.0 {
              audio.play(ball.bounce.clone());
              // ... remaining bouncing on player code ...
            }
          }
        }
      }
    }
}

fn scoring(
  mut query: Query<(&mut Ball, &mut Transform)>,
  mut score: ResMut<Score>,
  audio: Res<Audio>, // Audio resource added
) {
  for (mut ball, mut transform) in query.iter_mut() {
    let ball_x = transform.translation.x;
    let ball_y = transform.translation.y;
```

```
    if ball_y < ball.radius {
        audio.play(ball.score.clone()); // play scoring sound
        // ... remaining code for touching the ground ...
    }
  }
}
```

The final step is to update our bouncing and scoring code to actually play the sounds we've loaded for the ball (Listing 7-17). We need to update both the bounce and scoring systems. In both of them we add a new Res<Audio> argument to get a reference to the audio resource. For bounce we need to play the ball's bounce sound for hitting the sides and top of the arena (but not the floor, as that will be handled by scoring). While we're at it, we should also remove the code that makes the ball bounce on the floor, so that we can avoid possible data races between the bouncing and the scoring systems. We also add a bounce sound when the ball hits the player. Finally, in the scoring function, you also need to add an audio.play whenever a player scores (equivalent to the ball touching the bottom floor).

Finally, we have a working game! We learned how to render players and the ball on the screen using the spritesheet. Then we added keyboard control to let us control the players. We added a few systems to handle simple physics like gravity and bouncing. We keep the score using the Score resource and display the score using some ScoreBoardss. Lastly, we add the background music and sound effect to the game to spice it up.

7.13 Alternatives

In terms of a full-fledged game engine, Bevy has become the clear leader, but there are many other options out there for Rust-based game development. Other games engines exist such as Piston and ggez. However, the development of Piston is less active than Bevy at the moment, and ggez took a different path and focused only on 2D games. These game engines are still relatively young comparing to commercial ones like Unity and Unreal engine, and there have been many other relatively popular Rust game engines that have come and gone (such as Amethyst, whose developers moved to work on Bevy). These frameworks are also not as mature as commonly used graphics libraries like SDL2 and OpenGL.

If you want to use a more established engine you can choose to use Rust bindings for existing libraries. As Michael Fairley, the author of the Rust game "A Snake's Tale," demonstrated in his blog post,[8] you can build a game using Rust bindings to libraries like SDL2 and OpenGL. The Unity and Godot engines both have very good Rust bindings available (in particular Godot-Rust). You can also choose crates for doing math, image, and font rendering and combine them with these engine wrappers to make a game. You'll need more experience to put these things together, but if you're an experienced game developer who is familiar with these libraries in other languages (e.g., C/C++), this might be an easy way to get up to speed.

Note   You'll find that the Rust community loves to track the progress of a certain area using the "Are we X yet" sites. This is a tradition from the Mozilla community, which many Rustaceans are also involved in. Whenever there is a big project or a certain goal that people want to track progress, someone will build an "Are we X yet" site to track it. You can find a list of all the "are we yet" sites at `https://wiki.mozilla.org/Areweyet`.

The game ecosystem in Rust is still in its early stages but shows a lot of promise. As in many other fields of Rust, there is an "Are we game yet" page that tracks the progress of the game development ecosystem: `http://arewegameyet.com/`. On this website, you'll find many useful crates that can help you fulfill your game development needs. You'll also find a list of games built with Rust. If you are unsure about which game engine to choose, maybe it's a good idea to look at the existing games and figure out which libraries they used.

7.14 Conclusion

In this chapter you built a simple game with Rust and Bevy. You learned about the Entity Component System and how this architecture is used in game development. You created a simple game by setting up a screen, camera, and characters. You added physics and collision handling to let the characters and ball move. You then extended the game to add music and score keeping. In the next chapter, you'll leave the virtual world and develop some code that interacts with physical devices.

---

[8] https://michaelfairley.com/blog/i-made-a-game-in-rust/

CHAPTER 8

Physical Computing in Rust

Up until now, all the programs you have written have only existed in the virtual world. However, a big part of the physical world we live in is controlled by software. Traffic lights, self-driving cars, airplanes, and even rockets and satellites are just a few examples. Much of this software has to be built and executed in a drastically different environment than the usual desktop environment. It usually has to run on relatively weaker CPUs with less available memory. It might sometimes need to run without an operating system, or on specialized embedded operating systems.

Traditionally, these applications are written in C or C++ for maximum performance and low-level control of memory. Many of the embedded platforms are so limited that garbage collection is not feasible. But this is where Rust shines. Rust can provide performance and low-level control like C or C++, but also guarantees a higher level of safety. A Rust program can be compiled to run on many different central processing unit (CPU) architectures, like Intel, ARM, RISC-V, and MIPS. It also supports various mainstream operating systems and can even run without an operating system.

8.1 What Are You Building?

In this chapter, you'll be focusing on using Rust on a Raspberry Pi. A Raspberry Pi is an inexpensive computer with a credit card–size footprint created to make computer education more accessible. It has a few key important features that help us demonstrate the points for this chapter:

- It has general-purpose input/output (GPIO) pins. You can use it to interact with physical circuits like LEDs and buttons.

© Shing Lyu and Andrew Rzeznik 2023
S. Lyu and A. Rzeznik, *Practical Rust Projects*, https://doi.org/10.1007/978-1-4842-9331-7_8

- It's powerful enough to run a full Debian-based operating system (Raspberry Pi OS), so you can learn physical computing and cross-compilation without going deep into bare-metal programming. But if you are feeling adventurous, you can try writing your own mini Rust operating system for it.

- It has an ARM CPU. You can demonstrate how to compile and cross-compile code for an ARM platform.

To begin with, you'll install a full operating system on the Raspberry Pi. Then you'll install the complete Rust toolchain on it. You'll build two electrical circuits on a breadboard, one for output and one for input, and use Rust to interact with them as follows:

- Output: The first circuit will allow us to generate output to the physical world with light. You'll create a simple LED circuit connected to a GPIO output pin. You can write a Rust program to turn the LED on and off and blink it at a fixed interval.

- Input: You can take input from the physical world as well. You'll add a push button to the circuit. The Rust program can detect button clicks and then toggle the LED on and off.

These two examples will help us gain an understanding of how Rust code interacts with the physical world. However, you are compiling them on the Raspberry Pi itself. In many of the embedded applications, the target platform (i.e., the Raspberry Pi or similar board) is not powerful enough to compile the code. You can instead compile on another, more powerful computer, but it might have a CPU architecture and OS that is different from the target platform. This method of compiling is called cross-compilation. You'll set up a cross-compilation toolchain and cross-compile the previous example with it. Finally, to give you a sneak peek into how the GPIO pin works, you'll use lower-level APIs to control them. You'll be able to get a sense of how the high-level GPIO libraries work.

8.2 Physical Computing on Raspberry Pi

Physical computing can be a big change for those used to web or desktop projects. A lot more effort is spent on setting up a testing environment and tool chain, and ensuring that you won't drive yourself crazy later because you don't know if it's your code or the hardware that's having a problem. We'll take some time first setting up the Raspberry Pi 4 hardware and OS before we jump in to writing code for it. Taking a little extra effort now will save a lot of pain down the road.

Getting to Know Your Raspberry Pi

You'll be using a Raspberry Pi 4 Model B board for this chapter. But a Raspberry Pi 3 should also work.

A Raspberry Pi board is a miniature computer. It has all the necessary components of any other computer: CPU, memory, Wi-Fi, Bluetooth, HDMI output, USB, etc.

The Raspberry Pi 4 uses an ARM CPU, while most of the mainstream personal computers (PCs) use the x86 architecture with CPUs from Intel or AMD.[1] ARM CPUs are more common in mobile, embedded, and Internet of Things (IoT) devices due to their lower power consumption. Since Rust is a language that compiles to machine code, it is important that you compile for the correct CPU architecture; otherwise, the binary won't run.

The Raspberry Pi features many peripherals. It has an SD card reader so you can load the program and an operating system onto an SD card. It has a USB-C power input so it can run on a phone charger or even a portable power bank. For video output, you can use its micro-HDMI output to connect to an HDMI monitor. To control the device, you can use a USB mouse and keyboard. Finally, you can see two rows of metal pins (on the top left edge of Figure 8-1). These are GPIO (general-purpose input/output) pins, which you'll use to interact with external electrical components like LEDs and push buttons.

Figure 8-1. *A Raspberry Pi 4 Model B*

---

[1] Although, Apple's M1 and M2 chips are ARM-based and are slowly eating away the market share.

Installing Raspberry Pi OS Using Raspberry Pi Imager

In the first example, you are going to learn how to compile and run a Rust program directly on a Raspberry Pi via an operating system. There are many operating systems available for the Raspberry Pi. You need to install an operating system image onto the SD card and let the Raspberry Pi boot from the image. The official Raspberry Pi operating system is called Raspberry Pi OS. Raspberry Pi OS is a Debian-based operating system that has a friendly desktop environment and has many useful software packages pre-installed, like the Firefox browser, text editor, calculator, and also programming environments.

The easiest way to install Raspberry Pi OS is to use an installer called Raspberry Pi Imager. It provides a step-by-step wizard to guide you through the installation process. Here are the steps:

- Head to the Raspberry Pi Imager download page at `https://www.raspberrypi.com/software/` (Figure 8-2) and follow the installation instructions. For example, on a Ubuntu x86 PC, run `sudo apt install rpi-imager`.

- Plug an SD card (at least 8 GB, formatted to the FAT format) into your PC.

- Start the Raspberry Pi Imager with root permission and follow the instructions on the screen to install Raspberry Pi OS on the SD card (Figure 8-3).

- Plug the SD card into the Raspberry Pi.

Figure 8-2. *The Raspberry Pi OS and Raspberry Pi Imager download page*

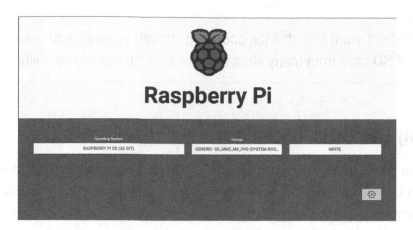

Figure 8-3. *The Raspberry Pi Imager installation process*

- Connect your Raspberry Pi to a keyboard, a mouse, and an HDMI monitor.

- Connect your Raspberry Pi to a 5V/3A USB-C power source (usually a phone charger). This will turn the Raspberry Pi on.

- Once the Raspberry Pi has booted, you should see a desktop like Figure 8-4.

Figure 8-4. *Raspberry Pi OS desktop environment*

Tip   If you don't want to install the operating system yourself, you can also buy a pre-installed SD card from many electronics or educational stores online.

Installing the Rust Toolchain

As you did for the Linux desktop, you can install the Rust compiler and cargo on the Raspberry Pi OS with `rustup`. Open a terminal on your Raspberry Pi OS and run the following command, copied from the Rust official installation page at `https://www.rust-lang.org/tools/install`:

```
curl https://sh.rustup.rs -sSf | sh
```

This installs the Rust toolchain[2] on the Raspberry Pi. One big difference you might notice is that `rustup` detects the ARM CPU and suggests a different target architecture, `armv7-unknown-linux-gnueabihf` (Figure 8-5). You want `rustc` to compile the Rust code into the ARM assembly so that the binary can run on the Raspberry Pi. Therefore, you'll take `rustup`'s suggestion and install the toolchain for ARM. Once it's installed, don't forget to add the `cargo` folder to the `PATH` environment variable so the `cargo` command will work.

```
Current installation options:


   default host triple: armv7-unknown-linux-gnueabihf
     default toolchain: stable
               profile: default
  modify PATH variable: yes

1) Proceed with installation (default)
2) Customize installation
3) Cancel installation
>
```

Figure 8-5.   *Rustup suggests installing the ARM target*

---

[2] The code in this chapter was tested on Rust 1.63.0.

Understanding the GPIO Pins

Once you have set the stage for the Raspberry Pi, you are going to look at two rows of metal pins that occupy one side of the circuit board. These pins are called GPIO (general-purpose input/output) pins. These GPIO pins are used for communicating with the outside world. When a pin is acting as an output, you can control it with software to let it output either 3.3 volts (written as "3V3") or 0 volts. When a pin works as an input, it can detect whether the pin has a high (3V3) or low (0V) voltage.

Not all pins are used as input/output pins. Some pins have special purposes, like consistently providing 5V power or working as a ground (constant 0V). Figure 8-6 shows the layout of the pins. You can also find an interactive pin layout at `https://pinout.xyz/`.

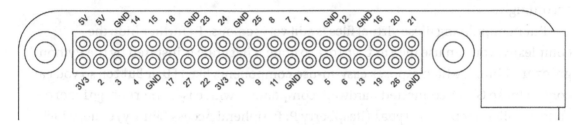

Figure 8-6. *Raspberry Pi 3 B+ GPIO layout (BCM numbering)*

There are a few different kinds of pins:

- 5V: 5V power supply

- 3V3: 3.3V power supply

- GND: ground

- Number: For the GPIO pin, the number is the Broadcom SOC channel (BCM) number. This is the pin number used to identify the pin in the example code.[3]

---

[3] You might find the number confusing because they seem random. BCM is the internal numbering of pins in the Broadcom-brand CPU used by the Raspberry Pi. Some Raspberry Pi GPIO libraries also support "board" numbering, which is the sequential left to right, bottom to top numbering from 1 to 40.

Some of the pins can also be configured to communicate using particular protocols, like Pulse-Width Modulation (PWM), Serial Peripheral Interface (SPI), Inter-Integrated Circuit (I²C), or Serial (UART), which are out of scope for this book.

On a very high level, these GPIO pins are controlled by hardware registers. Registers are components in the chip that act like computer memory. You can read or write bits to them. To set the mode (input, output, or special protocol) of a pin, you can write a specific bit pattern to some register. These registers are exposed as memory addresses (/dev/gpiomem), so you can change their value as if you are writing to a particular memory location. But direct manipulation of memory is too low-level for most use cases, so there are a few abstractions on top of it. In Raspberry Pi OS, these registers are exposed as device files (/sys/class/gpio/*⁴). You can read from these virtual files to get the register's value. If you write to these files like regular files, the register will be set accordingly.

But manipulating these virtual files is still very tedious. To further hide the complexity, you can use the `rust_gpiozero` crate. That crate is inspired by the Python `gpiozero` library, which exposes easy-to-use components like `LED` or `Button` so you can control these GPIO-connected hardware components with ease. The `rust_gpiozero` crate is built on top of the `rppal` (Raspberry Pi Peripheral Access Library) crate, which allows low-level access to various peripherals like the GPIO pins.

Building an LED Circuit

First, you will use a Raspberry Pi to light up a light-emitting diode (LED) (Figure 8-7). An LED is a small electronic component that will emit light when electrical current flows through it. The "D" in LED stands for *diode*, which means it only allows the electrical current to flow in one direction. The LED has two metal legs. The positive leg is called the *anode*, which is usually the longer leg of the two. The negative leg is called the *cathode*. You should provide a high voltage to the anode, say 3.3V, and ground the cathode. This creates a current flowing from the anode to the cathode so the LED lights up.

Although Raspberry Pi doesn't provide a very high voltage or current, the current might still be too high for the LED and might break it. To protect against such a scenario, you can add a resistor (Figure 8-8) to the circuit. A resistor creates resistance to the current, effectively limiting the current that goes through the LED.

---

⁴They are provided by Sysfs, a Linux virtual file system.

It's pretty hard to connect free-floating LEDs and resistors without soldering. But soldered components are hard to break apart and re-arrange. To make it easier to experiment with circuits, you can use a breadboard (Figure 8-8). A breadboard is a plastic board with tiny holes that LEDs, wires, and other electronic parts can plug into. Inside the holes are rows of metal pieces that act as temporary wires. A breadboard is perfect for prototyping because you can easily plug in electronic parts and form a circuit. You can unplug them if you make any mistakes. You use jumper wires to connect the circuits. A jumper wire is a pre-cut wire with a rigid plastic and metal head on each end. The head makes it easy to plug the wire into the breadboard and makes them more durable than raw, unprotected wires.

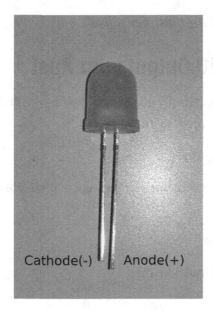

Figure 8-7. *An LED*

Let's connect a circuit according to Figure 8-9. A photo of the circuit is shown in Figure 8-10. In this circuit, the electric current goes from GPIO pin 2 to the anode leg of the LED (connected through the breadboard) and comes out of the cathode leg. The current then goes through the current-limiting resistor to the ground rail (the column on the breadboard that is marked blue with a "-" logo), and finally goes to the ground GPIO pin. You can turn the LED on and off by setting GPIO pin 2 to high (3V3) or low (0V) with Rust.

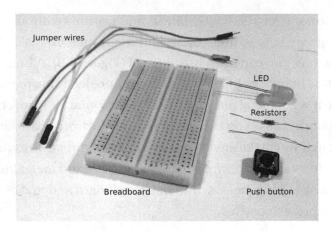

Figure 8-8. *A breadboard and jumper wires*

Controlling the GPIO Output with Rust

To start using `rust_gpiozero`, simply go to your Raspberry Pi desktop, open the terminal, and create a new project by running

```
$ cargo new physical-computing
```

Then switch to the project directory by typing `cd physical-computing` and add the `rust_gpiozero` crate:

```
$ cargo add rust_gpiozero
```

Your `Cargo.toml` should look like this:

```
# ...
[dependencies]
rust_gpiozero= "0.1"
```

Now that you have the project and dependency ready, open `src/main.rs` and write the following code:

```
// src/main.rs
use rust_gpiozero::*;

fn main() {
    let led = LED::new(2);

    led.on();
}
```

You can compile and run this code on the Raspberry Pi by running `cargo run`. The compilation might take longer because the Raspberry Pi ARM CPU might not be as powerful as the one in your PC. If your circuit is connected correctly, you should see the LED light up.

Tip   If your LED is not lighting up, don't panic. Try to swap the direction of the LED, and it will probably work.

In the preceding code example, you initiate an LED struct with pin number 2. The pin number indicates pin number 2 in Figure 8-6, to which the LED circuit is connected. During initiation, `rust_gpiozero` will set the GPIO pin in output mode automatically. Then, when you call `led.on()`, it will set the correct bit in the register and make the GPIO pin go high (3.3V), which turns the LED on. As you might have guessed, the way to turn off this LED is as simple as changing the code to `led.off()` and running `cargo run` again.

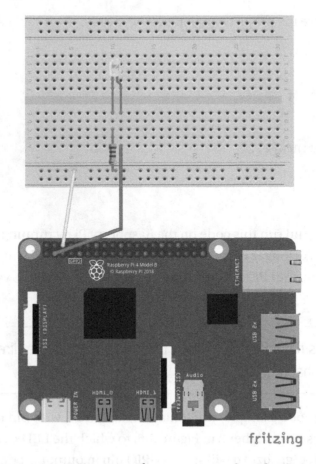

Figure 8-9. *The LED circuit diagram (image created with Fritzing)*

Figure 8-10. *The LED circuit*

If you wish to flash the LED, you can use a `loop` and add a one-second pause between `led.on()` and `led.off()`. The pause can be easily achieved with the `sleep()` function provided by the standard library.

```rust
// src/main.rs
use rust_gpiozero::*;
use std::thread::sleep;
use std::time::Duration;

fn main() {
    let led = LED::new(2);

    loop{
        println!("on");
        led.on();

        sleep(Duration::from_secs(1));
```

```
    println!("off");
    led.off();

    sleep(Duration::from_secs(1));
  }
}
```

To make things even simpler, rust_gpiozero already implemented flashing. You can replace the loop with the LED::blink() function:

```
// src/main.rs
use rust_gpiozero::*;

fn main() {
    let mut led = LED::new(2);

    led.blink(1.0, 1.0);

    led.wait(); // Prevents the program from exiting
}
```

The LED::blink() function takes two parameters: the on_time and off_time. The on_time is how many seconds the LED should stay on; the off_time is how many seconds to pause before the LED turns on again. You also have to call the LED::wait() function to prevent the program from exiting right after the LED::blink() call.

Reading Button Clicks

You have learned how to control a light signal output with Rust. Let's take a look at how you can accept physical inputs. You can configure the GPIO pin to use the input mode and receive inputs from a physical button.

When a GPIO input pin is configured to input mode, it triggers the code if the voltage reaches the desired level. However, the GPIO input pin by itself does not ensure the voltage stays at either 0V or 3V3. It is in a *floating* state where its voltage is floating between 0V and 3V3, which makes it prone to false triggering. To tackle this problem, the Raspberry Pi has internal resistors that can be configured to keep the GPIO pin at 0V or 3V3. These are the resistors tagged "Pull-down resistor" and "Pull-up resistor" in Figures 8-11 and 8-12. Note that the actual internal physical layout of the GPIO pin circuits is more complicated than these figures. Both resistors actually are present for each GPIO pin, and enable (connected) or disabled (disconnected) based on how the pins are set up in software. The provided diagrams only show the setup of a GPIO pin with one of these two resistors enabled. When you enable the pull-down resistor, it will connect the pin to the ground, thus pulling the voltage down to 0V. When you enable the pull-up resistor, it will connect the pin to an internal 3V3 voltage source and pull the voltage up to 3V3.

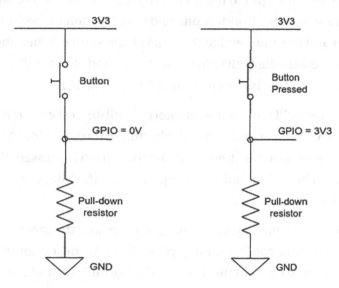

Figure 8-11. *Input pin with an internal pull-down resistor*

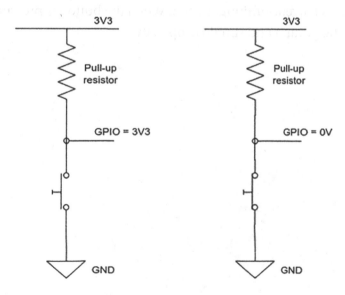

Figure 8-12. *Input pin with an internal pull-up resistor*

You can imagine a button as two pieces of metal that stay separate in their natural state, so no current flows through when the button is not pressed. When you press the button, the two pieces of metal touch and short-circuit, allowing current to flow through. Since the GPIO input pin can detect voltage change, you can use the GPIO pins to detect a button press in two different ways, as follows:

1. Configure the GPIO pin to use an internal pull-down resistor so its voltage stays at 0V. Connect one end of the button to the GPIO input pin and the other end to the 3V3 voltage source. When the button is pressed, the GPIO pin is short-circuited with the 3V3 source, so its voltage is drawn up to 3V3 (Figure 8-11).

2. Configure the GPIO pin to use an internal pull-up resistor, so it stays at 3V3. Connect one end of the button to the GPIO input pin and the other end to the ground. When the button is pressed, the GPIO pin is short-circuited with the ground, so its voltage is drawn down to 0V (Figure 8-12).

In both cases, the GPIO pin detects a voltage change and triggers the code. You'll be using the pull-up resistor configuration (option 2) for the next example. You can add some circuits on top of the LED circuit, as shown in Figure 8-13, and the photo is shown in Figure 8-14. You attach one end of the button to GPIO pin 4, which is configured to have a pull-up resistor that keeps it at 3V3. The other end of the button is connected to the ground through a current-limiting resistor. When the button is pressed, GPIO pin 4 is short-circuited to the ground and should drop to 0V.

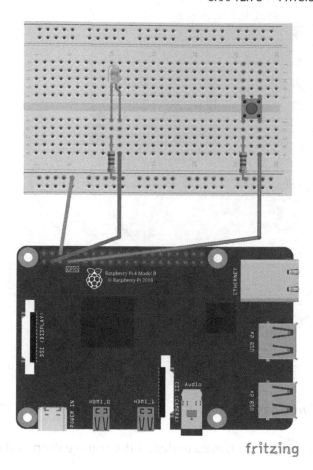

Figure 8-13. *The button circuit diagram (image created with Fritzing)*

Figure 8-14. *The button circuit*

Then, you can rewrite `src/main.rs` to detect the voltage drop and toggle the LED, as follows:

```
// src/main.rs
use rust_gpiozero::*;

fn main() {
    let mut led = LED::new(2);
    let mut button = Button::new(4);

    loop{
        println!("wait for button");
        button.wait_for_press(None);
        // Make the led switch on
        println!("button pressed!");
        led.toggle();
    }
}
```

The code initializes an LED struct and a Button struct. The Button::new() function configures the specified pin to use a pull-up resistor. If you wish to use a pull-down resistor instead, use Button::new_with_pulldown(). In the loop, button.wait_for_press() blocks the program indefinitely until the button is pressed. You can optionally set a timeout by replacing the None parameter with a Some(f32), where the f32 number is the timeout in seconds. When the button is clicked, the function will return and proceed to the next line, led.toggle(), which does what its name suggests: toggles the LEDs on or off.

As mentioned before, there are two pieces of metal in the button. When you press the button, ideally the two pieces of metal touch each other immediately and stay touching until you let go. But in reality, the metal pieces might vibrate and bounce off each other after they make contact for a fraction of a second. So, there might be a very short period of time when the metal pieces touch and bounce off repeatedly until they finally settle in the touched position. Since the loop runs very fast, the bounce might trigger the button.wait_for_press() function multiple times, so the LED will flicker and might not reach the final state you want it to. To counter this issue, you can *debounce* the circuit by ignoring all the subsequent button-press events after the first press event for a short period of time. This can be implemented like so:

```rust
// src/main.rs
use rust_gpiozero::*;
use std::time::{Duration, Instant};

fn main() {
    let mut led = LED::new(2);
    let mut button = Button::new(4);

    let mut last_clicked = Instant::now();
    loop{
        button.wait_for_press(None);

        if last_clicked.elapsed() < Duration::new(1, 0) {
            continue
        }

        led.toggle();
        last_clicked = Instant::now()
    }
}
```

The last_clicked timestamp keeps track of when the button was last clicked. When the button.wait_for_press() function returns, you first check last_clicked.elapsed(), which is the time elapsed since the button was last clicked. If the elapsed time is less then a second (Duration::new(1, 0)[5]), this press event is considered to be a bounce and is ignored. If one second already passed, the LED is toggled and the last_clicked timestamp is updated. With this debounce setup, the LED no longer flickers. If you think one second is too long, you can reduce the debounce time to make the button more responsive.

8.3 Cross-Compiling to Raspberry Pi

You might notice that the Rust program compiles relatively slowly on your Raspberry Pi. This is because the Raspberry Pi CPU is not as powerful as most mainstream desktop CPUs. But Raspberry Pi's CPU is already quite powerful in the embedded world, where many of most commonly used chips can't even run a full operating system. For some applications, especially mass-produced products that only to handle a few buttons, a speaker, or a few numbers on a simple display, you can expect much weaker (but more energy-efficient) CPUs or even microcontrollers. For example, things like coffee makers, alarm clocks, or even audio-playing greeting cards do not require much compute, and can be made a lot cheaper by using far weaker microchips. These devices are designed to run on very limited hardware resources and may run on batteries, so it's not possible to load all the source code onto them and compile them on the device itself. This is when you need to use cross-compilation. Cross-compilation means you compile the source code on a different machine (the host) than the one running the application (the target). For example, you can compile the code on a powerful Intel-x86-based Linux desktop, and run the binary on the Raspberry Pi target with an ARM CPU. In this case, the compiler itself is running on an x86 architecture CPU, but it generates machine code (in binary format) for an ARM architecture CPU.

To set up the cross-compilation environment, you need to move back to the Linux PC. You need to install the compiler toolchain on the x86 Linux PC for the Raspberry Pi 4 Model B, which itself runs on an ARM Cortex-A72 CPU. You can add a compile target with rustup:

```
rustup target add armv7-unknown-linux-gnueabihf
```

---

[5]Duration::new() takes two arguments: the first is the seconds, and the second is the additional nanoseconds. Therefore, (1, 0) means 1 second + 0 nanosecond = 1 second.

Note   You might be wondering why you install the `armv7` target while the ARM Cortex-A72 CPU is advertised as ARMv8 architecture? This is because the ARM Cortex-A72 CPU supports both 32-bit mode and 64-bit mode. By default, the Raspberry Pi OS is built on 32-bit Linux. Therefore, the CPU will run in 32-bit mode, which only supports ARMv7-compatible features. If you run `cat /proc/cpuinfo`, it will also report itself as an ARMv7 CPU.

There is a 64-bit version of the Raspberry Pi OS, but we'll keep using the 32-bit one for backward compatibility since you may have an older Raspberry Pi model.

You also need a linker. You might not be aware of the linker if you work on an x86-based Linux system. Most of the time, the linker is already installed when you install other programs. Usually, the linker comes packaged with a C compiler, so you can easily install gcc (GNU Compiler Collection) to get the ARM linker, as follows:

```
$ sudo apt-get install gcc-10-multilib-arm-linux-gnueabihf
```

Before you compile, you also need to let `cargo` know where to look for the linker. You can open the configuration file `~/.cargo/config` (create one if it doesn't exist yet) and add the following setting:

```
# ~/.cargo/config
[target.armv7-unknown-linux-gnueabihf]
linker = "arm-linux-gnueabihf-gcc-10"
```

This tells the compiler to use the linker provided by `arm-linux-gnueabihf-gcc-10` when compiling for the target `armv7-unknown-linux-gnueabihf`. Now, let's create a new project with `cargo new blink-cross-compile`. You can open the `src/main.rs` file and copy the code for blinking an LED into it. Also don't forget to add the `rust_gpiozero` dependency to the `Cargo.toml` file.

To compile the Rust project to a specific target, use the `--target` argument like so:

```
cargo build --target=armv7-unknown-linux-gnueabihf
```

This will produce a binary in `target/armv7-unknown-linux-gnueabihf/debug/` named `blink-cross-compile`. Notice that the binary is placed in the `target/armv7-unknown-linux-gnueabihf/debug/` folder, not the default `target/debug` folder. If you try to execute this binary on the x86 Linux system, you'll get the following error message:

```
$ ./blink-cross-compile
bash: ./blink-cross-compile: cannot execute binary file: Exec format error
```

This is because this binary is cross-compiled for an ARM CPU. You can verify this by examining the file with the Unix `file` command:

```
$ file ./blink-cross-compile
./blink-cross-compile: ELF 32-bit LSB shared object, ARM, EABI5 version
1 (SYSV),
  dynamically linked, interpreter /lib/ld-, for GNU/Linux 3.2.0,
  BuildID[sha1]=43d4fc4e17539883185e15c3d442986f2fb2f03d, not stripped
```

Copy this binary onto the Raspberry Pi SD card (for example, in the home directory) and boot up the Raspberry Pi OS. Once the Raspberry Pi is booted, open a terminal and cd to the location of the binary and execute it. You should see the LED blinking just like before.

8.4 How Does the GPIO Code Work?

The `rust_gpiozero` crate abstracts away most of the complexity of setting up the GPIO pins. But you might wonder how it works at a lower level.

As mentioned in Section 8.2, the GPIO registers are exposed by two different interfaces: `/dev/gpiomem` and `Sysfs`. Let's first take a look at how Sysfs works.

Sysfs exposes the GPIO registers as virtual files. To turn on an LED, you can write a simple shell script using the Sysfs virtual files:

```
# led-on.sh
echo "2" > /sys/class/gpio/export
echo "out" > /sys/class/gpio/gpio2/direction

echo "1" > /sys/class/gpio/gpio2/value
```

First, you need to write the pin number to the file /sys/class/gpio/export. This tells Sysfs that you want to work with the specified pin:

```
echo "2" > /sys/class/gpio/export
```

A new file /sys/class/gpio/gpio2 will appear. You can then set the direction of the pin as either input or output by writing in or out to the file /sys/class/gpio/gpio2/direction. In the example we set it to output mode:

```
echo "out" > /sys/class/gpio/gpio2/direction
```

This effectively sets the registers that control the GPIO 2's mode. Setting the pin to high or low is then as simple as writing 1 or 0 to the /sys/class/gpio/gpio2/value file.

These Sysfs files are abstractions around the registers that control the GPIO pins. But the rust_gpiozero crate uses a more low-level crate, rppal, to interact with GPIO pins. For performance reasons, the rppal crate does not use the Sysfs interface. Instead, it works with the /dev/gpiomem directly. The /dev/gpiomem is a virtual device that represents the memory-mapped GPIO registers. If you call the mmap() system call on /dev/gpiomem, the GPIO registers will be mapped to the designated virtual memory addresses. You can then read or write the bits in memory to control the registers directly.

Tip   The /dev/gpiomem virtual device was created to overcome permission issues. Before /dev/gpiomem was available, you could only access the GPIO-related memory address with /dev/mem. However, /dev/mem exposes the whole system memory and requires root permission to access. But since GPIO access is so common on Raspberry Pi, every program that interacts with GPIO needed to use root access, which created a security hazard. Therefore, /dev/gpiomem was created to expose only the GPIO-related part of the memory with no special permission needed. In rppal source code, you can see it tries /dev/gpiomem first. If any error occurs, it falls back to /dev/mem but then requires root access.

If you look into rppal's source code, you can see that it uses an unsafe code block to mmap() the /dev/gpiomem device. Once it's mapped into the virtual memory, you can write bits to set the direction and value of pins with low-level memory manipulation. You can see the relevant part of the code from rppal's src/gpio/mem.rs file in Listing 8-1.

Listing 8-1. Rppal's `src/gpio/mem.rs`

```rust
const PATH_DEV_GPIOMEM: &str = "/dev/gpiomem";

const GPFSEL0: usize = 0x00;
const GPSET0: usize = 0x1c / std::mem::size_of::<u32>();
const GPCLR0: usize = 0x28 / std::mem::size_of::<u32>();
const GPLEV0: usize = 0x34 / std::mem::size_of::<u32>();

pub struct GpioMem {}

impl GpioMem {
    // ...
    fn map_devgpiomem() -> Result<*mut u32> {
        // ...
        // Memory-map /dev/gpiomem at offset 0
        let gpiomem_ptr = unsafe {
            libc::mmap(
                ptr::null_mut(),
                GPIO_MEM_SIZE,
                PROT_READ | PROT_WRITE,
                MAP_SHARED,
                gpiomem_file.as_raw_fd(),
                0,
            )
        };
        Ok(gpiomem_ptr as *mut u32)
    }
    #[inline(always)]
    fn write(&self, offset: usize, value: u32) {
        unsafe {
            ptr::write_volatile(
                self.mem_ptr.add(offset),
                value
            );
        }
    }
}
```

```rust
#[inline(always)]
pub(crate) fn set_high(&self, pin: u8) {
    let offset = GPSET0 + pin as usize / 32;
    let shift = pin % 32;
    self.write(offset, 1 << shift);
}

#[inline(always)]
pub(crate) fn set_low(&self, pin: u8) {
    let offset = GPCLR0 + pin as usize / 32;
    let shift = pin % 32;
    self.write(offset, 1 << shift);
}

pub(crate) fn set_mode(&self, pin: u8, mode: Mode) {
    let offset = GPFSEL0 + pin as usize / 10;
    let shift = (pin % 10) * 3;

    // ...

    let reg_value = self.read(offset);
    self.write(
        offset,
        (
            reg_value & !(0b111 << shift)) |
            ((mode as u32) << shift
        ),
    );
}
}
```

We won't go into detail here, but you can see the libc::mmap() call inside the map_devgpiomem() function. You can also see that all the operations you did have corresponding functions:

- Set direction: set_mode()

- Set pin to high: set_high()

- Set pin to low: set_low()

These functions write directly to memory with `std::mem::transmute()` inside `unsafe` blocks. You might wonder how they know which memory address is for which functionality. These are all defined in the manual of the Broadcom BCM2711 chip.[6]

8.5 Where to Go from Here?

This chapter only scratched the surface of physical computing with Rust. There are many directions you can explore further.

In Rust's core team, there are some domain-specific working groups. The *embedded devices working group* is responsible for overseeing the Rust embedded ecosystem. They also maintain a curated list of exciting projects and resources in the *Awesome Embedded Rust* repository.[7] They are also transparent in disclosing what is not that awesome yet in the *Not Yet Awesome Embedded Rust* repository.[8] If you wish to follow the latest developments and the working group's future direction, you might want to follow the issues on their coordination repository: `rust-embedded/wg`.[9]

The first thing you can try is to build up on top of the Raspberry Pi. You learned how to control LEDs and buttons, but there are many more kinds of hardware you can play with, such as the following:

- Buzzers

- Light sensors

- Sound sensors

- Orientation sensors

- Cameras

- Humidity and temperature sensors

- Infrared sensors

- Ultrasonic sensors

---

[6]`https://datasheets.raspberrypi.com/bcm2711/bcm2711-peripherals.pdf`
[7]`https://github.com/rust-embedded/awesome-embedded-rust`
[8]`https://github.com/rust-embedded/not-yet-awesome-embedded-rust`
[9]`https://github.com/rust-embedded/wg`

- Touch screens

- Servo motors

There are also add-on boards called "HATs" (Hardware Attached on Top). These are boards with a lot of the hardware components packed into a small form factor. They are designed so that they can mount directly on top of the Raspberry Pi board and connect with its GPIO pins. The board will also communicate with the Raspberry Pi board and configure the GPIO pins for you. This provides you with an easy way to try out many different kinds of hardware without worrying about wiring on a breadboard. You can find crates like `sensehat` that provide an abstraction layer for a specific HAT called the *Sense HAT*. There is also a tutorial accompanying the crate: `https://github.com/thejpster/pi-workshop-rs/`.

You can also explore other boards and platforms. Rust supports many different computer architectures, so there are many boards available. For instance, the Embedded Working Group published *The Embedded Rust Book*.[10] In the book, they teach you how to program an STM32F3DISCOVERY board, which runs an STM32F303VCT6 microcontroller. Many of the tutorials use the QEMU emulator, so, you don't need actual hardware to get started. You can build your code and run it on a hardware emulator.

You can also go deeper. One thing that we didn't mention is how to run Rust on a bare-metal platform. "Bare metal" means the Rust program runs directly on the hardware without an operating system. In such a case, you can't use the standard library because many of the standard library functions depend on the platform. Instead, you need to set the `#![no_std]` attribute on the crate to let the Rust compiler know that you can't use `libstd`. It will then use `libcore`, which is a platform-agnostic subset of `libstd`. This will also exclude many features you might not want in an embedded environment, like dynamic memory allocation and runtime. *The Embedded Rust Book* will get you started with bare-metal programming. If you are looking to go deeper, you can read the advanced book *The Embedonomicon*.[11] You might want to go even further to build your operating system, but you'll touch on that topic in Chapter 10. Finally, WebAssembly (WASM) could serve as an abstraction for the embedded devices. You can run a WASM runtime and develop WASM code for the embedded hardware. For example, Wasmer[12] is a Rust-based WASM runtime that promises to let you "Run any code on any client," including embedded devices.

---

[10] `https://docs.rust-embedded.org/book/`

[11] `https://docs.rust-embedded.org/embedonomicon/`

[12] `https://wasmer.io/`

CHAPTER 9

Artificial Intelligence and Machine Learning

Artificial intelligence and machine learning have always captured the imaginations of science fiction authors and the media. Begun in the 1950s, the field of artificial intelligence has been through multiple ups and downs. Recently, it has received more media attention again because of technology breakthroughs in deep learning and consumer-facing applications on the market, such as ChatGPT and other advanced online chatbots.

The terms *machine learning* (ML) and *artificial intelligence* (AI) are sometimes used interchangeably, but there is a subtle difference. Artificial intelligence focuses on "intelligence." An AI system tries to behave as if it possesses human intelligence, no matter what the underlying method or algorithm is. Machine learning, on the other hand, focuses on "learning," where the model is trying to learn the pattern in the data without a human explicitly programming in the knowledge. For example, one of the early ideas used to build AI is the "expert system" approach. In an expert system, the knowledge of a particular field is written down as a set of rules and programmed directly into the code so the system can answer questions or perform tasks as if it's a domain expert. This kind of system might appear to have some level of human intelligence, but it's not actually "learning" anything from data. So, an expert system can be called an AI system but not a machine learning system.

Researchers have tried many different strategies to build AI systems that aren't based on machine learning. But machine learning became a leading strategy due to a few technical advancements. First, the computing power of modern central processing units (CPUs) and graphics processing units (GPUs) has grown exponentially since the 1950s because of innovations in hardware technology. This means that previously intractable machine learning models can now be trained in a reasonable amount of time. The rise of Web 2.0 also means more and more data are collected at very low cost, so companies

© Shing Lyu and Andrew Rzeznik 2023
S. Lyu and A. Rzeznik, *Practical Rust Projects*, https://doi.org/10.1007/978-1-4842-9331-7_9

now have the huge amounts of data required to train machine learning algorithms, like deep neural networks. All of these factors are contributing to the current boom in machine learning applications.

9.1 Types of Machine Learning Models

There are two main branches of machine learning: supervised and unsupervised. In a supervised learning setting you give the model a fully labeled training dataset where the labels provide the "correct" answers for each example input. For example, if you are trying to distinguish cat pictures from dog pictures, you need to prepare a large number of photos with the label "cat" or "dog." Because the model can check its prediction against the label (which is sometimes referred to as "ground-truth"), the algorithm can learn from its errors and improve its predictions.

But a fully labeled dataset is not always easy to obtain. Unless there is an automated way of collecting the label with high accuracy, you have to fall back to manually labeling the dataset. This takes a tremendous amount of time and money. Therefore, when getting a high-quality, fully labeled dataset is not possible, you can try an unsupervised learning model to do the job. An unsupervised model takes a training dataset without labels and tries to learn the intrinsic patterns from the data itself. For example, if you wish to distinguish between flower species, you can let the model group the flowers by their color, shape, leaf shape, etc. But without ground-truth labels to check against, one model might cluster all the flowers of the same color in one category, and it wouldn't tell you exactly what type of flower it is. So for certain use cases, supervised learning is more suitable than unsupervised learning.

There are other categories of machine learning, like *semi-supervised learning*, which uses a partially labeled dataset to get high accuracy and has a low dataset-preparation cost. There is also *reinforced learning*, which takes feedback from the environment to correct future behavior. For example, a maze-navigating robot can get a reward every time it successfully reaches the end of a maze. It can learn the way to navigate a maze by seeking maximum reward and avoiding potential penalties. There is also *transfer learning*, which allows you to carry over the learnings from one model to another problem. For example, if you wish to build a model to identify certain kinds of cats from photos, it might be helpful to use an existing model trained on a dataset of common household pets, including cats, dogs, rabbits, etc. Then you further refine it on the cat photos you aim to identify. This not only reduces the time it takes to train the model, but also can achieve better accuracy with less training data. In this chapter, you'll be focusing on supervised learning and unsupervised learning.

9.2 What Are You Building?

You'll build one supervised learning model and one unsupervised learning model. First, you'll start with an unsupervised learning model that can identify different cat breeds. You'll generate fake body size measurements from three cat breeds: Persian, British shorthair, and ragdoll (Figures 9-1 to 9-3). Since these three breeds have a slightly different average body height and length, you'll run a K-means clustering model (explained in Section 9.3) on these two features. The trained model can cluster cat body measurements into different groups automatically. Because K-means can only see the similarity between the data points, it can group the cats into groups but cannot tell you exactly which group maps to which cat breed.

Figure 9-1. Persian cat

Figure 9-2. *British shorthair cat*

Figure 9-3. *Ragdoll cat*

The second example is for supervised learning. Similar to the previous model, you have a handful of body measurements, but this time from both cats and dogs. You have a label for each point that indicates if each body measurement is taken from a cat or a dog. Using this dataset, you'll construct a neural network model to learn how to tell a cat from a dog. In machine learning, this kind of job is called a classification problem. When the model is trained it can predict if a given body measurement is most likely from a cat or a dog, even if the data is not part of the training set. For simplicity's sake, you'll use only the height and body length as the inputs.

Model training and inference is just a small part of machine learning. There are many other tasks involved in the machine learning process, like data preparation, cleaning, and visualization. You'll also learn how to use Rust to generate artificial training data, write and read the data as CSV (comma-separated value) files, and visualize the data. The demo programs will consist of a few loosely related binary executables. They will not communicate directly but rather by passing CSV files. This way you can minimize the dependency between the different steps.

9.3 Introducing linfa and rusty-machine

The machine learning ecosystem in any programming language relies on a strong foundation. Building machine learning libraries involves not only the machine learning algorithm itself, but also many fundamental operations, like numerical computing, linear algebra, statistics, and data manipulation.

In this chapter, you are going to use the linfa and rusty-machine crates. The linfa crate contains many traditional machine learning algorithms implemented in Rust. Although deep learning is the hottest topic in machine learning now, there are no mature, purely Rust-based libraries yet. Most of the deep learning libraries in Rust now are bindings to libraries in other languages, so the API design is not very Rusty. While linfa has a lot of production-quality ML algorithms, it does not contain anything related to neural networks, and there are no major neural network libraries written in pure Rust that have widespread acceptance. We want to focus on building things in Rust and not the low-level details of writing Rust bindings to neural-network libraries. Deep learning models are also harder to understand intuitively because they involve more advanced mathematical theories, which might distract us from the code architecture and Rust API. Because of this, we'll use the well-accepted linfa crate for the first portion of this chapter, and then switch over to the older and currently deprecated rust-machine crate as a learning tool for neural networks.

Some of the machine learning algorithms `linfa` contains are as follows:

- Linear regression

- Logistic regression

- Generalized linear models

- K-means clustering*

- Gaussian process regression

- Support vector machines

- Gaussian mixture models

- Naive Bayes classifiers

- DBSCAN

- K-nearest neighbor classifiers

- Principal component analysis

The linfa crate uses the `ndarray` crate for linear algebra, which has come to be seen as the flagship linear algebra crate in Rust. It also contains useful data transformation tools for data pre-processing, and other utility functions.

9.4 Clustering Cat Breeds with K-means

Our first project will determining Cat Breeds with K-means clustering. This algorithm is relatively simply to reason about and easy to intuitively understand, so it lets us focus on the Rust aspects. In later sections we'll look at more powerful but complicated learning algorithms.

Introduction to the K-means Algorithm

You don't need to be a cat expert to identify different cat breeds. A Persian cat looks different from a British shorthair in many aspects: their coats are of different lengths, their faces look different, and their average sizes are also different. Categorizing things is a natural human activity that helps us make sense of this world. But machines don't have such instincts, so instead they must rely on mathematical methods of categorization provided to them. This kind of problem is called a clustering problem, and a popular algorithm to solve it is *K-means*.

Since this is a book for general Rust enthusiasts, not mathematicians, we are going to explain the concept in simple terms. You can easily find the formal mathematical definitions by searching for "K-means" online.

The goal of K-means is simple: in order to cluster a set of data points into k groups you need to split them such that the points in each group are close to each other, but far from points in other groups. The exact steps to achieve this are as follows:

1. Random initialization: Randomly assigns k points as the "centroids." A centroid is the center point of a cluster.

2. Assignment: For all the other points, assign them to the group of the nearest centroid.

3. Updating the centroids: For each group, find the center point (i.e., the mean) of all the points in the group and use this center point as the new centroid.

4. Repeat steps 2 to 3 until the centroids no longer move significantly.

As you can imagine, during each update the centroids will move toward the center of the points "cloud," and during the next assignment some points might be assigned to a new centroid because the centroid position has changed. You continue this process until the centroids no longer move significantly; this is when you say the model converges. You can see a graphical example in Figure 9-4.

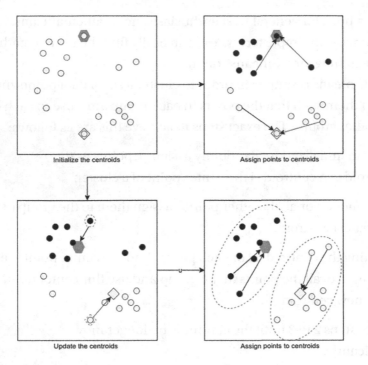

Figure 9-4. *An example of the K-means algorithm*

In practice, the initial location of the centroids matters a lot to the final result. If you assign the initial centroids suboptimally, the algorithm might converge to a result that is not ideal.[1] It might also take longer for the model to converge. You can use an algorithm called K-means++ to initialize the initial centroids better than random assignment. The intuition behind it is that you want to spread out the initial centroids as far as possible. The exact steps to do this are as follows:

1. Choose the first centroid randomly from all the points.

2. For each point x, calculate the distance to its nearest existing centroid as $D(x)$.

3. To find the next centroid, pick a point with a probability proportional to $D(x)^2$. What this means is that if a point x is farther away from any existing centroids, its $D(x)$ is larger, and it has a higher probability to be chosen as a new centroid.

4. Repeat steps 2 to 3 until all the centroids are picked.

---

[1] In mathematics, you say it converges to a local optimum, rather than the global optimum.

By using the K-means++ algorithm, the initial centroids are spread out as far away from each other as possible. This will usually lead to a better result. This is the default initialization method used by `linfa`.

The Training Data

To prepare the training data, you need to collect body measurements from many cats. Since you might not have access to thousands of cats, we'll generate some artificial cat body measurements for demonstration purposes. The body measurements you are going to generate are as follows:

- height: the height from the ground to a cat's shoulder

- length: the length from a cat's head to its bottom, excluding the tail.

The average measurements of the three breeds are as follows:

- Persian: height 22.5 cm, length 40.5 cm

- British shorthair: height 38.0 cm, length 50.0 cm

- Ragdoll: height 25.5 cm, length 48.0 cm

To have a fair amount of data points for demonstration, you can generate 2,000 samples per cat breed. These data points are generated using a normal distribution around the average with an arbitrarily chosen standard deviation of 1.8 cm. This standard deviation creates a nice cloud of data points with a little overlap, which will help us illustrate how K-means works.

To generate this training data, you are going to set up `ndarray` so that you can use it to easily work with the generated arrays. First, let's create a Rust project by opening a terminal and running the following command:

```
$ cargo new cat-breeds-k-means
$ cd cat-breeds-k-means
```

Add the following crates to the project:

```
$ cargo add linfa rand rand_distr ndarray
```

- `linfa`: the machine learning framework

- `rand`: for random number generation

- • rand_distr: for common probability distributions like the normal distribution

- • ndarray: for working with arrays and matrices

Because you are going to have multiple binaries in this project, you can't simply have an src/main.rs and run it with cargo run. Cargo has support for multiple binaries in a project. Simply add the files to src/bin/; for example, src/bin/generate.rs. Then you can run it with cargo run --bin generate.

In the src/bin/generate.rs file, copy and paste Listing 9-1.

Listing 9-1. Script for generating fake test dataset

```
// src/bin/generate.rs
use rand::thread_rng;
use rand::distributions::Distribution; // for using .sample()
use rand_distr::Normal; // split from rand since 0.7
use ndarray::Array2;
use std::error::Error;

fn generate_data(centroids: &Array2<f64>,
                 points_per_centroid: usize,
                 noise: f64)
                 -> Result<Array2<f64>, Box<dyn Error>> {
  assert!(!centroids.is_empty() , "centroids cannot be empty.");
  assert!(noise >= 0f64, "noise must be non-negative.");

  let rows = centroids.shape()[0];
  let cols = centroids.shape()[1];

  let mut rng = thread_rng();
  let normal_rv = Normal::new(0f64, noise)?; [2]

  let mut raw_cluster_data = Vec::with_capacity(
    rows * points_per_centroid * cols);

  for _ in 0..points_per_centroid { //[3]
    // generate points from each centroid
    for centroid in centroids.rows() {
      // generate a point randomly around the centroid
```

```
    let mut point = Vec::with_capacity(
        centroids.shape()[1]
    );
    for feature in centroid.into_iter() {
        point.push(feature + normal_rv.sample(&mut rng));
    }
    // push point to raw_cluster_data
    raw_cluster_data.extend(point);
    }
}

Ok(Array2::from_shape_vec((rows * points_per_centroid, cols),
            raw_cluster_data)?)
}
```

The core of this script is the function that generates training data around the given average with the normal distribution. It has the following signature (Listing 9-2):

Listing 9-2. Interface for data generation

```
fn generate_data(centroids: &Array2<f64>,
    points_per_centroid: usize,
    noise: f64)
    -> Array2<f64> { ... }
```

As you can see, it takes three parameters:

- An Array2 of f64 values. Each row is the average height and length of a cat breed. It should have a shape of (3 × 2) (3 cat breeds × 2 dimensions [height and length] per breed)

- The number of data points you want to generate for each cat breed.

- The standard deviation used for the normal distribution, a.k.a. the noise.

The return value will be an Array2 containing all the generated data points. It should have the shape (total number of samples × 2).

The logic is pretty simple; you have nested for loops that iterate through the three centroids and generate the required number of samples for each centroid. This is shown in Listing 9-1.

The first thing the function does is to validate that the centroids matrix is not empty and that the standard deviation is non-negative (Listing 9-3).

Listing 9-3. Validation for data generation

```
assert!(!centroids.is_empty() , "centroids cannot be empty.");
assert!(noise >= 0f64, "noise must be non-negative.");
```

Then, you initialize a `raw_cluster_data` vector with the expected capacity. You allocate the memory for the `raw_cluster_data` in advance so the vector does not need to resize when it grows (Listing 9-4).

Listing 9-4. Generating a Vector

```
let mut raw_cluster_data =
  Vec::with_capacity(rows * points_per_centroid * cols);
```

You then create the random number generator from the `rand` crate, and a normal distribution using `rand_distr::Normal`. This normal distribution has a mean (average) of 0 and standard deviation of `noise`.

```
let mut rng = thread_rng();
let normal_rv = Normal::new(0f64, noise).unwrap();
```

These two are later used together to draw random samples from the normal distribution like so:

```
normal_rv.sample(&mut rng)
```

Then comes the actual generation of samples. The outer for loop makes sure you repeat the generation n times, where n is the number of desired samples per centroid. In the inner loop, you iterate through the centroids, so you generate a sample for each. This ensures that you generate a total number of (number of centroids × number of sample per centroid) samples. In this case, you have 3 × 2000 = 6000 samples.

```
for _ in 0..points_per_centroid {
  // generate points from each centroid
  for centroid in centroids.rows() {
    // ...
  }
}
```

In the body of the loop, you create a temporary vector of size two to hold the height and length. For each dimension, you get a random number from the normal distribution you just initialized. This random number is generated around 0. Then, you add the random number to the average height or length, so you'll have samples that follow a normal distribution around the average height or length of the cat breed. Finally, this point is added to the raw_cluster_data vector as follows:

```
for _ in 0..points_per_centroid {
  for centroid in centroids.rows() {
    let mut point = Vec::with_capacity(cols);
    for feature in centroid.into_iter() {
      point.push(
        feature + normal_rv.sample(&mut rng)
      );
    }
    raw_cluster_data.extend(point);
  }
}
```

The vector will then become a large 1D array. If you use the symbol A_h to denote the height of cat A, and A_l for the its length, the raw_cluster_data vector for cats A, B, and C will look like the following:

$$\left[A_h, A_l, B_h, B_l, C_h, C_l \right]$$

But what you actually want is a matrix of samples, with one sample per row, like so:

$$\begin{bmatrix} A_h & A_l \\ B_h & B_l \\ C_h & C_l \end{bmatrix}$$

To convert this, you pass the 1D array to the `Array2::from_shape_vec` function. You can provide the desired shape (number of rows and columns), and `Array2::from_shape_vec` will reshape the 1D array into the matrix you want. Finally, you return this matrix as the training data as follows:

```
Array2::from_shape_vec(
  (rows * points_per_centroid, cols), raw_cluster_data
)?
```

Exporting as a CSV

In the `main()` function of the `src/bin/generate.rs`, we want to call the `generate_data()` function and output the data to STDOUT in the CSV format. CSV (comma-separated value) is a simple format for tabular data: rows are separated into lines, and columns are separated by commas. This format is supported in most programming languages and spreadsheet software (e.g., LibreOffice Calc or Microsoft Excel).

Although the CSV format is quite simple, it's still too error-prone to format it without the help of a library. Therefore, we are going to use the `csv` crate. Run the following command in your terminal:

```
$ cargo add csv
```

This should add the `csv` crate to the `dependencies` section of your `Cargo.toml`. Then in the `main()` function of `src/bin/generate.rs`, add the code to call `generate_data()` and write the output to a CSV file, as shown in Listing 9-5.

Listing 9-5. Writing a CSV

```
// src/bin/generate.rs
use std::io;
//..

// settings
const CENTROIDS:[f64;6] = [
```

```
    //Height, length
    22.5, 40.5, // persian
    38.0, 50.0, // British shorthair
    25.5, 48.0, // Ragdoll
];
const NOISE:f64 = 1.8;
const SAMPLES_PER_CENTROID: usize = 2000;

fn generate_data(...) // ... previous function

fn main() -> Result<(), Box<dyn Error>> {
    let centroids = Array2::from_shape_vec(
        (3, 2), CENTROIDS.to_vec()
    )?;

    let samples = generate_data(
        &centroids,
        SAMPLES_PER_CENTROID,
        NOISE
    )?;

    let mut writer = csv::Writer::from_writer(io::stdout());
    writer.write_record(&["height", "length"])?;
    for sample in samples.rows() {
        let mut sample_iter = sample.into_iter();
        writer.serialize((
            sample_iter.next().unwrap(),
            sample_iter.next().unwrap()
        ))?;
    }
    Ok(())
}
```

First, you convert the centroids from the const CENTROIDS vector into an array.
Ideally, all these parameters should be configurable from command-line arguments, but
we'll leave that for the next section. For now, you'll just hard-code the configurations as
consts at the beginning of the file.

Then, you call the `generate_data()` function and assign the generated training data to the variable `samples` as follows:

```
let samples = generate_data(
  &centroids,
  SAMPLES_PER_CENTROID,
  NOISE
)?;
```

For simplicity, you are going to write the CSV directly to STDOUT. You'll see more advanced usage of writing directly to files in Section 9.4. To write these samples into CSV format, you need to initialize a `csv::Writer`:

```
let mut writer = csv::Writer::from_writer(io::stdout());
```

To write a simple plain-text line to the CSV output, you can use the `writer.write_record()`. It takes a reference to an array of strings. So, you write the headers "height" and "length" to it. You can also provide a serializable (i.e., implements `serde::Serialize`) struct and let it be automatically converted to a valid CSV line. This can be done by `writer.serialize()`. So, you iterate through the rows of the sample array and write each line to a CSV as follows:

```
for sample in samples.rows() {
  let mut sample_iter = sample.into_iter();
  writer.serialize((
    sample_iter.next().unwrap(),
    sample_iter.next().unwrap()
  ))?;
}
```

Now, if you run `cargo run --bin generate` in a terminal, you'll see 6,001 lines (including a heading line) being printed to the screen. You can easily pipe it to a file by running the following:

```
$ cargo run --bin generate > training_data.csv
```

Moving the Configuration into a File

In the previous section, you hard-coded all the configurations as consts in the source code. This becomes an impedance when you want to experiment with many different configurations. Building a machine learning application involves a lot of experimentation. You usually need to try many different parameters and settings to get the best result. If you hard-code the parameters in the code, you'll need to change them and recompile the program every time. It's easier to put those configurations in a configuration file, then specify the configuration file using command-line arguments. This way, you can easily choose a configuration at runtime. Another benefit is that you can keep all the configuration files in the source code repository so that you can reproduce a specific experiment quickly.

There are many machine-readable configuration file formats to choose from; for example, TOML, JSON, YAML, and XML. We chose TOML because Cargo uses it, so it's widely accepted by the Rust community. Also, it has excellent parsing and deserialization support in Rust.

You can move the consts into a file named config/generate.toml (Listing 9-6). You'll notice that the syntax is slightly different from Rust, but it's still straightforward.

Listing 9-6. TOML configuration for centroids

```
# config/generate.toml

centroids = [ # Height, length
  22.5, 40.5, # persian
  38.0, 50.0, # British short hair
  25.5, 48.0, # Ragdoll
]
noise = 1.8
samples_per_centroid = 2000
```

But the value types in TOML do not map one-to-one to Rust types. How do you make sure the values are parsed into Rust as a [f64;6], f64, and usize? For that you can use the toml crate, which is a TOML parser that uses serde to deserialize a TOML file into a pre-defined Rust struct. You need to add the toml and serde crates to the project with the following commands:

```
$ cargo add toml
$ cargo add serde --features derive
```

Ensure the `Cargo.toml` file has the versions and features listed below:

```
# Cargo.toml

[dependencies]
# ...
toml = "0.7.3"
serde = { version = "1.0.159", features = ["derive"] }
```

Then, you can define the struct format for the TOML file at the beginning of the `src/bin/generate.rs` file, as in Listing 9-7.

Listing 9-7. Struct for centroid deserialization

```
// src/bin/generate.rs
use serde::Deserialize;
// ...

#[derive(Deserialize)]
struct Config {
    centroids: [f64;6],
    noise: f64,
    samples_per_centroid: usize,
}

// ...
```

You derived the `serde::Deserialize` trait on the `Config` struct, which gives the `toml` parser a hint on how to parse the TOML file into the `Config` struct. Then you can read the `config/generate.toml` file into a `String` and pass its reference to `toml::from_str()`, as in Listing 9-8.

Listing 9-8. Loading the config from disk

```
// src/bin/generate.rs
use std::fs::read_to_string;
// ...
```

```
#[derive(Deserialize)]
struct Config {
    //...
}

fn main() -> Result<(), Box<dyn Error> {
  let toml_config_str = read_to_string(
    "config/generate.toml"
  )?;
  let config: Config = toml::from_str(&toml_config_str)?;
  // ...
}
```

Because the variable config has the type Config, toml parses the string into a Config struct using the derived Deserialize implementation. Once it's parsed, you can access the individual fields using dot notation; for example, config.centroids, config.noise.

You can then remove all the consts and use the config instead. For example,

```
let centroids = Array2::from_shape_vec(
  (3, 2), config.centroids.to_vec()
)?;
let samples = generate_data(
  &centroids,
  SAMPLES_PER_CENTROID,
  NOISE
)?;
```

becomes

```
let centroids = Array2::from_shape_vec(
  (3, 2), config.centroids.to_vec()
)?;
let samples = generate_data(
  &centroids,
  config.samples_per_centroid,
  config.noise
)?;
```

Now you can run

```
$ cargo run --bin generate
```

and you should see the data being generated in the terminal.

Setting the Configuration File at Runtime

In the previous example, the path to the TOML file is hard-coded in the main()
function. You can use Clap, which you learned in Chapter 2, to make it a command-line
parameter. You need to add the clap dependency in Cargo.toml with the derive feature
by running the following command in the terminal:

```
$ cargo add clap --features derive
```

Then, in src/bin/generate.rs, add an parameter called --config-file as in
Listing 9-9.

Listing 9-9. Using clap to parse command-line arguments

```rust
// src/bin/generate.rs
// ...
use clap::Parser;

// ...

#[derive(Parser)]
struct Args {
  #[arg(
    short = 'c',
    long = "config-file"
  )]
  /// Configuration file TOML
  config_file_path: std::path::PathBuf,
}

fn main() -> Result<(), Box<dyn Error>> {
  let args = Args::parse();
  let toml_config_str = read_to_string(
```

```
    args.config_file_path
  )?;
  // ...
}
```

In the `main()` function, you can read the configuration file path dynamically from `Args::parse()` and pass it to `read_to_string()`. Then, to run the `generate` script, you can use the following command in the shell:

```
$ cargo run --bin generate -- --config-file config/generate.toml
```

If you want to try different configurations, simply copy-paste the `config/generate.toml`, change some parameters in it, and specify the new file name in the `–config-file` argument. You no longer need to recompile the `src/bin/generate.rs` script every time you change the configuration. This pattern is also beneficial when you do model training in the following section. One of the key processes in machine learning is hyperparameter tuning. This involves testing various hyperparameters for the machine learning model to find the best-performing combination. You can test with many different configuration files using this pattern. You can also easily recreate the model with the executable binary, configuration file, and training data.

Visualizing the Data

Before jumping into training a model, it's crucial to explore how the data looks. You can use a plotting library to visualize data and get some basic intuition for the results that come later. Rust didn't initially have any mature plotting libraries of its own and had to rely on bindings to other popular visualization tools, like gnuplot. This has changed recently, however, and a clear leader in the pure-Rust visualization space has arisen with the `plotters` crate.

You need to first install the `plotters` dependencies by running the following commands in the terminal:

```
$ sudo apt install pkg-config libfreetype6-dev
$ sudo apt install libfontconfig1-dev
```

Then, as usual, you'll need to add the `plotters` crate to `Cargo.toml` by running the following:

```
$ cargo add plotters
```

We'll use version 0.3.4. Let's create a new file in src/bin named plot.rs. Copy-paste the following code into the file to draw something on the screen (Listing 9-10).

Listing 9-10. Minimal plotters plot

```rust
use plotters::prelude::*;
use std::error::Error;

fn main() -> Result<(), Box<dyn Error>> {
  let mut x: Vec<f64> = Vec::new();
  let mut y: Vec<f64> = Vec::new();

  //TODO: read the CSV data into x and y

  let root_drawing_area = BitMapBackend::new(
    "plot.png", (900, 600)
  ).into_drawing_area();

  root_drawing_area.fill(&WHITE)?;

  let mut chart = ChartBuilder::on(&root_drawing_area)
    .build_cartesian_2d(15.0..45.0, 30.0..55.0)?;
    chart.configure_mesh().disable_mesh().draw()?;

  chart.draw_series(
    x.into_iter()
      .zip(y)
      .map(|point| Cross::new(
        point,
        3,
        Into::<ShapeStyle>::into(&BLUE).stroke_width(2)
    )),
  )?;
  Ok(())
}
```

In the `main()` function, you first create a drawing area that your plot will use. In this case a `BitMapBackend` is used, which will save the plot as a file. This is the simplest way to create a plot, but there are other backends available.[2] Next, create a `plotters` `ChartBuilder` struct and set various parameters about the chart. The cartesian 2D plotting area needs to be specified based on the region where you expect the data to be present. A mesh is configurd as disabled, which lets us just display the data without any axes for now. Finally, the `draw_series` method is used to draw the data. The x and y parameters are vectors holding the x-axis and y-axis coordinates of all the points. Once the figure is configured and the program exists, the chart will save the image file created when the `ChartContext` variable goes out of scope and it's destructor is called. Since both x and y are still empty vectors, you can only see a blank image.

One thing you missed in the previous example is how to get the x and y. Since you piped the generated CSV to STDOUT, you can read the data using STDIN. This way, you can easily pipe the CSV generated from the previous section into this `plot.rs` script:

```
cat training_data.csv | cargo run --bin plot
```

The CSV reading code is very similar to the writing case, just reversing the write with reading (Listing 9-11).

Listing 9-11. Reading in CSV data

```rust
// use ...
use std::io;

fn main() -> Result<(), Box<dyn Error>>{
  let mut x: Vec<f64> = Vec::new();
  let mut y: Vec<f64> = Vec::new();

  let mut reader = csv::Reader::from_reader(io::stdin());
  for result in reader.records() {
    let record = result?;
    x.push(record[0].parse()?);
    y.push(record[1].parse()?);
  }
```

---

[2] One of the major benefits of the `plotters` crate is that it can use various backends, and thus be used in web and other application contexts

```
// ... Drawing the figure

  Ok(())
}
```

First, you create a Reader that reads from io::stdin(). Then, you can easily iterate through the rows of the file by for result in reader.records(). However, the items yielded by the iterator (i.e., the result) have the type of Result<StringRecord, Error>, so you need to get the StringRecord out of the Result with the ? operator:

```
let record = result?;
```

You can access an individual column in a StringRecord using an index like record[0], which yields a str. Because the x and y require the type Vec<f64>, you can convert the str to f64 by calling .parse().unwrap(). You then can push the parsed x and y coordinate values into the x and y vector. The graph now looks like Figure 9-5.

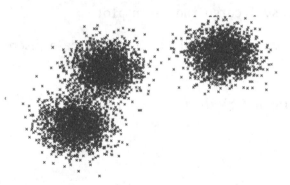

Figure 9-5. *A minimal plotters plot*

Details on Adding More Entries

To make the figure easier to understand, you can add titles, legend, and axes labels to the graph, as in Listing 9-12.

Listing 9-12. Adding axes, labels, and a legend

```
fn main() -> Result<(), Box<dyn Error>> {
  // ...
  let mut chart = ChartBuilder::on(&root_drawing_area)
    .caption("Cat body measurements", ("sans-serif", 30))
```

```
    .x_label_area_size(30)
    .y_label_area_size(40)
    .build_cartesian_2d(15.0..45.0, 30.0..55.0)?;
  chart
    .configure_mesh()
    .x_desc("height (cm)")
    .y_desc("width (cm)")
    .disable_mesh()
    .draw()?;

  chart
    .draw_series(
      x.into_iter()
        .zip(y)
        .map(|point| Cross::new(
          point,
          3,
          Into::<ShapeStyle>::into(&BLUE).stroke_width(2)
        )),
    )?
    .label("Cat")
    .legend(|(x, y)| Cross::new(
      (x, y),
      3,
      Into::<ShapeStyle>::into(&BLUE).stroke_width(2)
    ));

  chart
    .configure_series_labels()
    .position(SeriesLabelPosition::LowerRight)
    .background_style(&WHITE.mix(0.8))
    .border_style(&BLACK)
    .draw()?;
  Ok(())
}
```

Most of the function names are self-explanatory. Label areas are provided for the x-and y-axes. A caption is placed on the graph, and then axis labels are provided for the x- and y-axes. Finally, after creating the draw series and label, a legend with a label is created. You need to provide the symbol to draw for the legend as you would actually draw it. If you rerun the script, the generated figure will look like Figure 9-6.

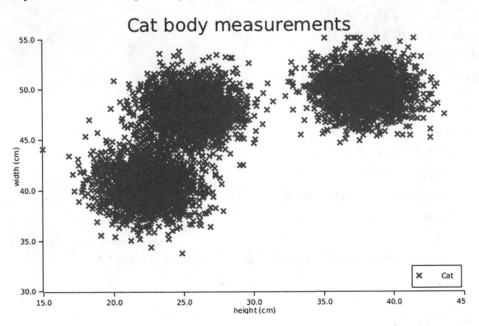

Figure 9-6. *The plot with title, legend, and axes labels*

Setting Up K-means

As you can see from Figure 9-6, the cat body measurements form three clusters. We'd expect the K-means algorithm to cluster them into three groups. The K-means model is located in the linfa_clustering crate and is called KMeans. All of the unsupervised models, including K-means, implement the linfa::traits::Fit and linfa::traits::Predict traits. These traits have a very simple interface, as shown in Listing 9-13.

Listing 9-13. Traits used for models in the linfa crate

```rust
pub trait Fit<
  R: Records,
  T,
```

```
    E: std::error::Error + From<crate::error::Error>>
{
    type Object;

    fn fit(&self, dataset: &DatasetBase<R, T>)
        -> Result<Self::Object, E>;
}
pub trait Predict<R: Records, T> {
    fn predict(&self, x: R) -> T;
}
```

The fit() function will take the training data dataset and learn from it. The "knowledge" is stored in the model itself. After the model is trained, you can use the predict() function to predict (in this case, cluster) new data based on the knowledge learned from the training data.

You'll need to add a few more linfa-related crates, as follows, before you can start writing the K-means code, along with ndarray for basic array structs:

```
$ cargo add linfa-nn linfa-clustering
```

The linfa-clustering crate includes the various models for clustering operations, while the linfa-nn crate contains definitions for how the distance from the centroid to each point should be calculated.

Before you can call fit(), you need to configure the K in the name K-means, along with some other secondary parameters. K is the number of clusters you expect it to cluster into. From Figure 9-6, you can clearly see there are three clusters. Therefore, you are going to set $k = 3$. As you mentioned in Section 9.1, you create a separate binary for the K-means training and clustering: src/bin/cluster.rs. You can start by writing a simple main() function, as in Listing 9-14.

Listing 9-14. Initial K-means setup

```
use std::error::Error;
use linfa::DatasetBase;
use linfa::traits::Fit;
use linfa::traits::Predict;
use linfa_clustering::KMeans;
```

```rust
use linfa_nn::distance::L2Dist;
use rand::thread_rng;

const CLUSTER_COUNT: usize = 3;

fn main() -> Result<(), Box<dyn Error>> {
  let samples = read_data_from_stdin()?; //To be added
  let training_data = DatasetBase::from(samples);
  let rng = thread_rng();

  let model = KMeans::params_with(CLUSTER_COUNT, rng, L2Dist)
      .max_n_iterations(200)
      .tolerance(1e-5)
      .fit(&training_data)?;

  // Assign each point to a cluster using the set of
  // centroids found using `fit`
  let dataset = model.predict(training_data);
  let DatasetBase {
      records, targets, ..
  } = dataset;

  export_result_to_stdout(records, targets)?; // To be added
  Ok(())
}
```

The steps in the main() function are pretty straightforward. You load the CSV data from STDIN using the helper function read_data_from_stdin(), which we'll discuss later. After converting the loaded Array2 to a DatasetBase and initializing a random number generator, you initialize a KMeans struct with the configuration K = CLUSTER_COUNT. You also set the max number of iterations and the tolerance before passing in the training data to generate a fit. Now the same training data can be passed to the trained model by using the predict function to classify each point. This generates a new DatasetBase containing the cluster ID label (i.e., the cat breed) for each data point. You then write the result to STDOUT using another helper function, export_result_to_stdout(). That's all you need for training a complicated mathematical model in Rust!

The helper functions for reading and outputting data are similar to the ones you saw in the generation and visualization scripts. The read_data_from_stdin() function

(Listing 9-15) is almost the same as the plot.rs function (Listing 9-11), except that you convert the output to an Array2. This is because KMeans expects a DatasetBase that can be easily generated from an Array2, while plotters expects iterators.

Listing 9-15. Reading in data for clustering

```
use std::io;
use ndarray::Array2;
// ...

fn read_data_from_stdin() ->
  Result<Array2<f64>, Box<dyn Error>>
{
    let mut points: Vec<f64> = Vec::new();

    let mut reader = csv::Reader::from_reader(io::stdin());
    for result in reader.records() {
        let record = result?;
        points.push(record[0].parse()?);
        points.push(record[1].parse()?);
    }

    let rows = points.len() / 2;
    let cols = 2;
    Ok(Array2::from_shape_vec((rows, cols), points)?)
}
// ...
```

The output function export_results_to_stdout() is also a simple call to a csv::Writer (Listing 9-16). The key in this function is that you want to output the original 2D body measurement data along with the classification data from the clustering result. Imagine you have three cats as follows:

$$\begin{bmatrix} 22.5 & 40.5 \\ 38.0 & 50.0 \\ 25.5 & 48.0 \end{bmatrix}$$

They are clustered into class 0, 1, and 2, respectively: [3]

$$\begin{bmatrix} 0 \\ 1 \\ 2 \end{bmatrix}$$

You want the output CSV to be the two matrixes "stitched" together:

$$\begin{bmatrix} 22.5 & 40.5 & 0 \\ 38.0 & 50.0 & 1 \\ 25.5 & 48.0 & 2 \end{bmatrix}$$

This is achieved by the line `points.iter_rows().zip(classes)`. The `.zip()` function does exactly the stitching you want. All you then need to do is arrange the data in tuples to be passed to the CSV writer.

Listing 9-16. Writing clustering results to stdout

```
use ndarray::Array1;

// ...

fn export_result_to_stdout(
  points: Array2<f64>,
  classes: Array1<usize>,
) -> Result<(), Box<dyn Error>> {
  let mut writer = csv::Writer::from_writer(io::stdout());
  writer.write_record(&["height", "length", "class"])?;
  for (point, class) in points
    .rows()
    .into_iter()
    .zip(classes.into_iter()) {
      let mut row_iter = point.into_iter();
      writer.serialize((
```

---

[3] The class IDs are arbitrary integers; they are categorical, so the number doesn't convey any mathematical meaning.

```
        row_iter
          .next()
            .unwrap(),
        row_iter
          .next()
            .unwrap(),
        class
      ))?;
  }
  Ok(())
}

// ...
```

You can export the result to a CSV file for visualization:

```
$ cat training_data.csv | cargo run --bin cluster > results.csv
```

To make it clear which point belongs to which class, you can use different point symbols and colors for different classes. You can tweak the original visualization script into Listing 9-17.

Listing 9-17. Plotting the clusters

```rust
use plotters::prelude::*;
use std::error::Error;
use std::io;

fn main() -> Result<(), Box<dyn Error>> {
  let mut x: [Vec<f64>; 3] = [
    Vec::new(), Vec::new(), Vec::new()
  ];
  let mut y: [Vec<f64>; 3] = [
    Vec::new(), Vec::new(), Vec::new()
  ];

  let mut reader = csv::Reader::from_reader(io::stdin());
  for result in reader.records() {
    let record = result?;
```

```rust
    let class: usize = record[2].parse()?;
    x[class].push(record[0].parse()?);
    y[class].push(record[1].parse()?);
}

let root_drawing_area =
    BitMapBackend::new("k-means-result-plot.png", (900, 600))
        .into_drawing_area();

root_drawing_area.fill(&WHITE)?;

let mut chart = ChartBuilder::on(&root_drawing_area)
    .caption("Cat body measurements", ("sans-serif", 30))
    .x_label_area_size(30)
    .y_label_area_size(40)
    .build_cartesian_2d(15.0..45.0, 30.0..55.0)?;
chart
    .configure_mesh()
    .x_desc("height (cm)")
    .y_desc("width (cm)")
    .disable_mesh()
    .draw()?;

chart
    .draw_series(x[0].iter().zip(y[0].iter()).map(|point| {
        Cross::new(
            (*point.0, *point.1),
            3,
            Into::<ShapeStyle>::into(&BLUE).stroke_width(2),
        )
    }))?
    .label("Cat breed 1")
    .legend(|(x, y)| Cross::new(
        (x, y),
        3,
        Into::<ShapeStyle>::into(&BLUE).stroke_width(2)
    ));
```

```
chart
  .draw_series(x[1].iter().zip(y[1].iter()).map(|point| {
    TriangleMarker::new(
      (*point.0, *point.1),
      5,
      Into::<ShapeStyle>::into(&GREEN).stroke_width(2),
    )
  }))?
  .label("Cat breed 2")
  .legend(|(x, y)| { TriangleMarker::new(
    (x, y),
    5,
    Into::<ShapeStyle>::into(&GREEN).stroke_width(2)
  )});
chart
  .draw_series(x[2].iter().zip(y[2].iter()).map(|point| {
    Circle::new(
      (*point.0, *point.1),
      3,
      Into::<ShapeStyle>::into(&RED).stroke_width(2),
    )
  }))?
  .label("Cat breed 3")
  .legend(|(x, y)| Circle::new(
    (x, y),
    3,
    Into::<ShapeStyle>::into(&RED).stroke_width(2)));
chart
  .configure_series_labels()
  .position(SeriesLabelPosition::LowerRight)
  .background_style(&WHITE.mix(0.8))
  .border_style(&BLACK)
  .draw()?;
Ok(())
}
```

Most of the code is the same as in Listing 9-10, with some duplication for additional plotting. In this version, the x and the y are a nested array of three individual arrays. Each sub-array contains the x (or y) coordinates for a specific cluster. For example, x[0] contains the x coordinates of the cat cluster 0, and x[1] is for cluster 1 and x[2] for cluster 2.

To plot the points using a different symbol and color, you can use some optional parameters, as follows:

- label("Cat breed 1") sets the caption for that cluster of points.

- ElementType like Cross, Circle, and TriangleMarker sets the shape of the datapoint; it's critical to not rely on color for differentiation.

- ShapeStyle is used to define the size and color of the shape, which are of secondary importance but are useful when color is available.

You can then pipe the data into the new plot command using

```
$ cat results.csv | cargo run --bin cluster > results.csv
```

This gives us Figure 9-7.

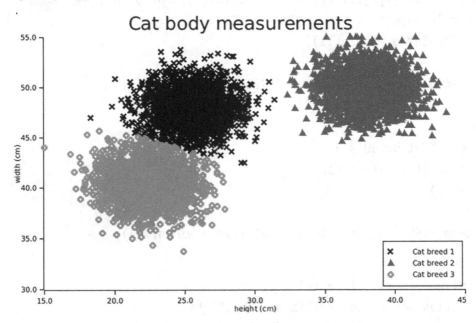

Figure 9-7. *Clustering result for the K-means algorithm*

If you zoom into the border between the breed 1 (x) and breed 3 (o), you can see the points are almost split by a straight line (Figure 9-8). A normal distribution will probably not look like this; some of the breed 2 points might fall in the breed 3 "cloud" and vice

354

versa. But this is an inherent limitation of K-means. Given only the height and length, without a proper ground-truth tagging, the algorithm can only predict breeds based on the nearest mean (i.e., centroid), resulting in a seemingly clear-cut line between the clusters.

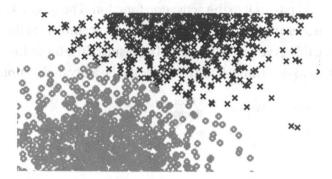

Figure 9-8.   *Clear-cut between breeds 1 and 3*

9.5 Detecting Cats Versus Dogs with a Neural Network

Now that we've written a simple K-means clustering as an unsupervised model, it's time to move on to a more complicated neural network as our supervised model. Neural networks are a lot more complicated that K-means clustering, but thanks to useful Rust libraries we can skip over the details here and focus on just using the code on our data. After a brief intro we'll write new code to generate training and tests datasets and use these for our new supervised model.

Introduction to Neural Networks

We've seen how unsupervised models work, so now we can shift our attention to a supervised model. The supervised model we are going to introduce is the artificial neural network (ANN) model, or neural network for short. Neural networks draw their inspiration from how a human brain works. The human brain consists of neurons, with each neuron taking stimuli and deciding if it should be "activated" or not. An activated neuron will send an electrical signal to other connected neurons. If you have a big network of interconnected neurons, they can learn to react to different inputs by adjusting the way they connect and how sensitive they are to the stimuli.

Modern neural network models use the same guiding principle but focus more on solving empirical questions using data rather than trying to model a human brain accurately. One of the key components of a neural network model is the neuron (sometimes called a *node*; shown in Figure 9-9). A node consists of one or more inputs (x_i), their weights (w_i), an input function, and an activation function.[4] The input function takes the weighted sum of all the inputs and passes it to the activation function. The weights are adjusted during the learning process to amplify or dampen signals according to the significance of the input signal to the things you want to learn. The result of the input function will pass to the activation function to determine if the node should be activated or not.

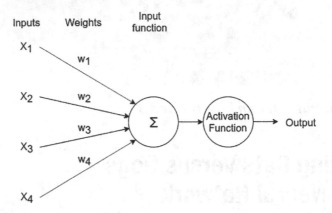

Figure 9-9. Structure of a neuron/node

The nodes need to be combined into a network. A simple example is Figure 9-10, which contains two input nodes, two nodes in the middle layer, and one output node. For the dog-or-cat example, you can send the height and length values to the two input nodes, and the output node should give you a signal to indicate if the input data belongs to a dog or cat. Each node will determine if it should be activated based on the input it got from the previous stage, combined with the weights.

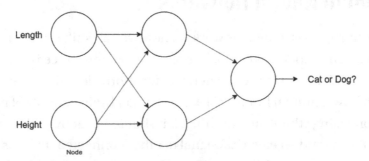

Figure 9-10. A simple neural network

---

[4] The rusty machine uses the Sigmoid function by default.

In the beginning, you can randomly set the weights, but this won't give any better results than merely guessing. You need to adjust the weights in the nodes according to the training data. You can compare the output of the neural network with the ground-truth answer you hold; if the output is far off, that means you need to adjust the weights to make a better prediction next time. You evaluate how good (or bad) the model is currently performing through a loss function. The rusty-machine default is the *binary cross-entropy* loss function, which will give a higher value if the output (cat or dog) does not match the ground-truth and a lower value vice versa. The goal is to adjust the weights to minimize the loss (i.e., make the loss function return the smallest value possible). To achieve this, you use an algorithm called *gradient descent*. Gradient descent will adjust the weight in a direction that will cause the loss to decrease.

After you provide a lot of initial data to the neural network, you can feed a small batch of test data in and check the network's output against the ground-truth answer. Then, gradient descent is used to adjust the weights to make the loss go down. This process of feeding in data and adjusting weights is repeated multiple times to better tune the network. Once all the data are fed in, the neural network should have nodes with weights that best capture the characteristics of the training data. When you get a new body measurement, you can feed it to the network, and the output should then tell you if the body measurement belongs to a dog or cat.

Preparing the Training Data and Testing Data

To get started on this next example, create a new project, change to the directory, and add the necessary crates, as follows:

```
$ cargo new cat-neural-net
$ cd cat-neural-net
$ cargo add serde --features derive
$ cargo add rand rand_distr ndarray csv toml
$ cargo add clap --features derive
```

To keep the example simple, you are going to use the same kind of input as the K-means example: height and length. You'll create 2,000 samples for cats and 2,000 for dogs. But there are some differences between this data and the K-means data:

- You'll need to provide the "answer," or the ground-truth labels, for each sample.

- You need to generate two sets of data: the training data and the testing data.

You need the ground-truth labels because a neural network is a supervised model, which means that it needs to learn by comparing its prediction with the ground-truth and try to improve its accuracy.

You also need to split the data into a training set and a testing set. The training set is used to train the model. The testing set is used to verify how accurate the trained model actually is. One key point is that the model should never see the data in the testing set during the training phase. Otherwise, it will already know the answer and can quickly achieve 100% accuracy by memorizing the testing data. Even if the algorithm doesn't intentionally memorize the answer, using the testing data in training will usually lead to overfitting. Overfitting is when the model tries to accommodate the particular training data set too much and fails to generate a model that is general enough to handle new but not identical data. That means the model will work very well on the same set of training data but fail miserably for any data that it hasn't seen before, even if it's only slightly off. You keep yourself honest by splitting off a testing set to confirm the training of your model.

The overall code structure to generate the training data looks similar to Listing 9-5. The only difference is in the generate_data() function, presented in Listing 9-18. You should copy this code into src/bin/generate.rs just as in the previous project.

Listing 9-18. Generating training and test data for the neural network

```
use clap::Parser;
use ndarray::Array2;
use rand::distributions::Distribution; // for using .sample()
use rand::thread_rng;
use rand_distr::Normal; // split from rand since 0.7
use serde::Deserialize;
use serde::Serialize;
use std::fs::read_to_string;
use std::io;
use std::error::Error;

#[derive(Deserialize)]
struct Config {
```

```rust
  centroids: [f64; 4],
  noise: f64,
  samples_per_centroid: usize,
}

#[derive(Debug, Serialize)]
struct Sample {
  // [1]
  height: f64,
  length: f64,
  category_id: usize,
}

fn generate_data(
  centroids: &Array2<f64>,
  points_per_centroid: usize,
  noise: f64
) -> Vec<Sample> {
  assert!(
    !centroids.is_empty(),
    "centroids cannot be empty."
  );
  assert!(noise >= 0f64, "noise must be non-negative.");

  let cols = centroids.shape()[1];

  let mut rng = thread_rng();
  let normal_rv = Normal::new(0f64, noise).unwrap();

  let mut samples = Vec::with_capacity(points_per_centroid);

  for _ in 0..points_per_centroid {
    // generate points from each centroid
    for (centroid_id, centroid) in centroids
      .rows()
      .into_iter()
      .enumerate() {
```

```rust
    // generate a point randomly around the centroid
    let mut point = Vec::with_capacity(cols);
    for feature in centroid.into_iter() {
      point.push(feature + normal_rv.sample(&mut rng));
    }

    samples.push(Sample {
      height: point[0],
      length: point[1],
      category_id: centroid_id,
    });
    }
  }

  samples
}

#[derive(Parser)]
struct Args {
  #[arg(short = 'c', long = "config-file")]
  /// Configuration file TOML
  config_file_path: std::path::PathBuf,
}

fn main() -> Result<(), Box<dyn Error>> {
  let args = Args::parse();
  let toml_config_str = read_to_string(args.config_file_path)?;
  let config: Config = toml::from_str(
    &toml_config_str
  ).unwrap();
  let centroids = Array2::from_shape_vec(
    (2, 2),
    config.centroids.to_vec()
  )?;
  let samples = generate_data(
    &centroids,
    config.samples_per_centroid,
```

```
    config.noise
  );

  let mut writer = csv::Writer::from_writer(io::stdout());
  for sample in samples {
    writer.serialize(sample)?;
  }
  Ok(())
}
```

Each row in the new data now has three columns: length, height, and the cat-or-dog label. The cat-or-dog label will be an integer; 0 represents dog, and 1 represents cat.[5] You can serialize all the fields into f64s, but the integer label will become 0.0 or 1.0 in the CSV file. To force it to serialize to a nice-looking 0 or 1, you need to define that desire in the schema. The schema is simply a struct that implements the serde::Serialize trait. You define this in the struct Sample. The generate_data() function will return a Vec<Sample> instead of a Matrix<f64>. When you call csv::Writer.serialize() with a Sample, it will use serde to serialize it to something like 25.24, 60.03, 1.

Listing 9-19. Configuration data for generating the initial cat and dog populations

```
# config/generate_cats_and_dogs.toml

centroids = [ # Height, length
    22.5, 40.5, # cat
    38.0, 50.0, # dog
]
noise = 1.8
samples_per_centroid = 2000
```

The code you wrote in src/bin/generate.rs will be used to generate the training and testing data by running it twice. You should generate a total of 4,000 training samples and 4,000 testing samples. You can go ahead and create a new file, config/generate_cats_and_dogs.toml, with two different centroids, as in Listing 9-19—one for cats and one for dogs.

---

[5] This number is assigned arbitrarily. There is no special meaning behind the numbers.

Go ahead and generate the training and testing data by running the following:

```
$ cargo run --bin generate -- \
--config-file config/generate_cats_and_dogs.toml \
 > training_nn.csv
$ cargo run --bin generate -- \
--config-file config/generate_cats_and_dogs.toml \
 > testing_nn.csv
```

Setting Up the Neural Network Model

After the training and testing data are generated, you need to build the model training and predicting code. You are going to put them in a new binary, `src/bin/train_and_predict.rs`. This binary has to do the following:

- Read and parse the training data into a `Vec`, and shape it into an `Array`.

- Normalize the training data.

- Initialize the neural network model.

- Feed the normalized training data into the model for training.

- Read and parse the testing data into a `Vec`, and shape it into an `Array`.

- Normalize the testing data using the same parameter for normalizing the training data.

- Use the trained model to make predictions on the testing data.

Since Rust doesn't have any major crates written in pure Rust that provide an implementation of a neural network, we are going to use the now pretty old `rusty-machine` crate for this example. This crate and its accompanying linear algebra crate `rulinalg` are fairly old and currently are not actively updated. However, their interface is the simplest for learning neural networks in Rust. Once you understand the basics of neural network models you can go ahead and use Rust bindings to pytorch or tensorflow, which are two popular deep learning frameworks written in C++. These frameworks are pretty advanced, so we chose not to start with them here.

To get the necessary crates, run the following on the command line:

```
$ cargo add rusty-machine
```

You'll discuss each neural network subtask in the following sections.

Reading the Training and Testing Data

In the K-means example (Listing 9-15), you read the CSV input from STDIN. However, in a supervised model, you need two input files: the training data and the testing data. So this time you are going to give the CSV files' paths as CLI arguments and read them directly from the file. Using the clap crate and code you introduced in Chapter 2, you can create two arguments: training_data_csv and testing_data_csv (Listing 9-20).

Listing 9-20. Neural network CLI argument parsing

```rust
use clap::Parser;
use std::error::Error;

#[derive(Parser)]
struct Args {
  #[arg(short = 'r', long = "train")]
  /// Training data CSV file
  training_data_csv: std::path::PathBuf,

  #[arg(short = 't', long = "test")]
  /// Testing data CSV file
  testing_data_csv: std::path::PathBuf,
}

fn main() -> Result<(), Box<dyn Error>>{
  let args = Args::parse();
  // ...
  Ok(())
}
```

You might recall how to serialize the data from a Rust struct into a CSV from Section 9.4 when working with K-means. Now you need to do the opposite: deserialize the CSV data back to Rust structs. For this, you need to define the same data schema in a Rust struct and provide it to csv::Reader (Listing 9-21).

Listing 9-21. Reading training data from CSV

```
use serde::Deserialize;
use rusty_machine::linalg::Matrix;

// ...

#[derive(Debug, Deserialize)]
struct SampleRow { // [1]
  height: f64,
  length: f64,
  category_id: usize,
}

fn read_data_from_csv(
  file_path: std::path::PathBuf,
) -> Result<(Matrix<f64>, Matrix<f64>), Box<dyn Error>> {
  let mut input_data = vec![];
  let mut label_data = vec![];
  let mut sample_count = 0;
  let mut reader = csv::Reader::from_path(file_path)?; // [2]
  for raw_row in reader.deserialize() { // [3]
      let row: SampleRow = raw_row?;
      input_data.push(row.height);
      input_data.push(row.length);
      label_data.push(row.category_id as f64);
      sample_count += 1
  }

  let inputs = Matrix::new(sample_count, 2, input_data);
  let targets = Matrix::new(sample_count, 1, label_data);
  return Ok((inputs, targets));
}

fn main() -> Result<(), Box<dyn Error>>{

  let options = Args::parse();
```

```
let (training_inputs, training_label_data) =
  read_data_from_csv(options.training_data_csv)?;
// ...
Ok(())
}
```

The schema you define is the struct `SampleRow` ([1]) is exactly the same as in `generate_data.rs`. But this time, you derive the `Deserialize` trait from it. You created the utility function `read_data_from_csv()` to read the data from the CSV file path. The line that actually reads the CSV file is on [2], where you use `csv::Reader::from_path()`. The path parameter is the `PathBuf` you get from the CLI options. Once the file is loaded into memory, you loop through the rows obtained by calling `reader.deserialize()` ([3]). This will deserialize the CSV line into `Result<SampleRow, Error>`.

In the loop, you put the rows into two vectors, `input_data` and `label_data`. You put the height and length into `input_data`; and you put the `category_id` into `label_data`.[6] These two vectors are then converted to the `Matrix` types that the `rusty-machine` model accepts.[7]

Normalizing the Training Data

Before you feed the data into the neural network model, there is a less obvious step you have to take that will significantly speed up the training and accuracy of the model. This step is called *normalization*. The goal of the normalization is to shift and scale the input data so it has a mean of 0 and a standard deviation of 1. This is very helpful for models like a neural network because when you do gradient descent, a normalized dataset means the optimization process will not be dominated by one single dimension that has a much larger scale than the others. It also means that the cost function will have a smoother shape, which means the gradient descent process will be faster and smoother.

The normalization process involves the following steps:

---

[6] You might notice that you convert the `category_id` from `usize` to `f64`. You might wonder why you don't just use `f64` in the CSV format. That's because this is a categorical integer. If you use `f64` in CSV, they'll become `0.0`, `1.0,` and so on, which doesn't look nice if you want to check the training/testing data with spreadsheet software.

[7] `rust-machine` was created before `ndarray` became the de facto standard matrix library in Rust, and has its own linear algebra library `rulinalg` and its own array type `Matrix`.

- Calculate the mean of the dataset and subtract it from all data points. This shifts the mean of the dataset to 0.

- Calculate the standard deviation of the dataset and divide each data point's coordinates by the standard deviation. This scales the dataset to a standard deviation of 1.

You must keep the mean and standard deviation of the *training* data at hand. When you normalize the *testing* data you'll use the mean and standard deviation from the *training* data. This is because all the parameters in the neural network model will be trained for the normalized training data. If the testing data has a different mean and standard deviation, the model's prediction might be off.

You don't need to write this part of the code by yourself. The `rusty-machine` contains a handy `rusty_machine::data::transforms::Standardizer` struct. The `Standardizer` implements the `Transformer` trait, which defines a shared interface for commonly used data pre-processing transformations.

The `Standardizer` can be initialized with the `new()` function with two options: the desired mean and the standard deviation. The normalization process we described requires a mean of 0 and a standard deviation of 1, but the `Standardizer` can scale the data to any other mean and standard deviation. The `Standardizer` instance has the following functions defined by the `Transformer` trait:

- `fit()`: Calculates the mean and standard deviation from the input data and stores it inside the `Standardizer` instance.

- `transform()`: Performs the transformation on the provided data using the mean and standard deviation learned in the `fit()` step.

You can see the `Standardizer` in action in Listing 9-22.

Listing 9-22. Normalizing input data

```
use rusty_machine::data::transforms::Transformer;
use rusty_machine::data::transforms::Standardizer;
// ...

fn main() -> Result<(), Box<dyn Error>>{
  let options = Args::parse();
```

```
let (training_inputs, training_label_data) =
read_data_from_csv(options.training_data_csv)?;

let mut standardizer = Standardizer::new(0.0, 1.0);

standardizer.fit(&training_inputs).unwrap();
let normalized_training_inputs =
  standardizer.transform(training_inputs).unwrap();

// ... Train the model with normalzied_training_inputs ...

// Read the testing_inputs
let (testing_inputs, expected) =
  read_data_from_csv(options.testing_data_csv)?;
// Normalize the testing data with training data
let normalized_test_cases =
  standardizer.transform(testing_inputs.clone())?;

// ... Run the prediction with normalized_test_cases ...

Ok(())
}
```

You first run `Standardizer.fit()` with the training data to learn its mean and standard deviation. Then you use this configuration to run `Standardizer.transform()` on both the training data and the testing data. You then feed the model with the normalized data instead of raw data directly read from the CSV files.

Training and Predicting

Finally, after all these efforts for reading, parsing, and normalizing data, you are ready to build the neural network model. The neural network model takes a little more configuration than the K-means, which only has one configuration parameter: the k. For the neural network model, you have the option to set the following:

- The number of layers and the number of nodes per layer

- The criterion, including an activation function and a loss function

- The optimization algorithm

The rusty_machine::learning::nnet::NeuralNet struct has a ::default() function. If you look under the hood, it chooses configurations like in Listing 9-23.

Listing 9-23. Training the neural network

```
use rusty_machine::learning::nnet::{NeuralNet, BCECriterion};
use rusty_machine::learning::optim::grad_desc::StochasticGD;
use rusty_machine::learning::SupModel;

fn main() -> Result<(), Box<dyn Error>>{
  // ... Loading training data and pre-processing ...

  let layers = &[2, 2, 1]; // [1]
  let criterion = BCECriterion::default(); // [2]
  let gradient_descent = StochasticGD::new(0.1, 0.1, 20); // [3]
  let mut model = NeuralNet::new(
    layers,
    criterion,
    gradient_descent
  );

  model.train(
    &normalized_training_inputs,
    &training_label_data
  )?;

  // ... Testing

  Ok(())
}
```

Let's break this down line-by-line. In [1], you define the layers as [2, 2, 1], which means a three-layer architecture. The first layer has two input neurons, the middle layer has two neurons, and the output layer has one neuron. By default, the NeuralNet chooses the binary cross-entropy criterion (BCECriterion)([2]), which uses the Sigmoid activation function and the cross-entropy error as the loss function. Finally, stochastic gradient descent (`StochasticGD`) is chosen as the optimization algorithm in [3]. The stochastic gradient descent has three parameters:

- Momentum (default: 0.1)

- Learning rate[8] (default: 0.1)

- Number of iterations (default: 20)

All these parameters have some impact on how the neural network model performs. Since this is not a book on machine learning we are not going to discuss how to tune them in detail, and you will stick to the defaults. A vital skill for a machine learning expert is to understand the mathematical meaning of these parameters and how to tune them to make the model accurate and robust.

You can collect all of these configurations (layers, criterion, and gradient descent algorithm) and pass them to `NeuralNet::new()` to create the model. The `NeuralNet` model implements the `SupModel` trait. `SupModel` also implements `.train()` and `.predict()` functions. The only difference between `SupModel` and `UnSupModel` is that the former's `.train()` function takes an extra `target` parameter, which contains the ground-truth labels, as follows:

```
pub trait SupModel<T, U> {
  fn train(&mut self, inputs: &T, targets: &U) -> // ...
  //                              ^---------- extra parameter
  // ...
}

pub trait UnSupModel<T, U> {
    fn train(&mut self, inputs: &T) -> LearningResult<()>;
    // ...
}
```

Therefore, you can train the model by calling the following:

```
model.train(&normalized_training_inputs, &training_label_data)?;
```

This step will usually take some time to run because the neural network is doing all the complicated mathematical computations and training the model. Once trained, it will store all the learned weights and other parameters inside itself, and you are ready to use it to make predictions.

---

[8] Actually, the second argument is the square root of the raw learning rate.

Making the Prediction

To check if the model is trained properly, you prepared 4,000 new data points using the generate_data.rs script. This time you are only going to pass the height and length to the trained neural network model. The neural network model will pass these inputs into the network and calculate all the signals all the way to the output node. Then, the output node will give us a signal between 0 and 1. A 0 means the model believes that the input is most likely a dog, and a 1 means it's a cat. You can compare this prediction with the provided answer and see if the model is correct.

You load the testing data from CSV and normalize it using the Standardizer you created during training. Then you can use model.predict() on it to get a list of predicted labels (Listing 9-24).

Listing 9-24. Using the neural network to make predictions

```
use rusty_machine::linalg::BaseMatrix;
use std::io;
// ...

fn main() -> Result<(), Box<dyn Error>>{
  // Training the model

  // Testing ====================
  let (testing_inputs, expected) = read_data_from_csv(
    options.testing_data_csv
  )?;

  // Normalize the testing data using the mean and
  // variance of the training data
  let normalized_test_cases = standardizer.transform(
    testing_inputs.clone()
  )?;

  let res = model.predict(&normalized_test_cases)?;

  let mut writer = csv::Writer::from_writer(io::stdout());
  writer.write_record(&[
```

```
      "height",
      "length",
      "estimated_category_id",
      "true_category_id",
   ])?;

   for row in testing_inputs
     .iter_rows()
     .zip(res.into_vec().into_iter())
     .zip(expected.into_vec().into_iter())
   {
     writer.serialize((
         row.0 .0[0], row.0 .0[1], row.0 .1, row.1
     ))?;
   }

   Ok(())
}
```

With the code written you can then run the following command to train and then test your predictions:

```
$ cargo run --bin train_and_predict -- \
   --train training_nn.csv \
   --test testing_nn.csv > results.csv
```

The `res` generated by `model.predict()` will be a list of labels 0 or 1, which is the result you are looking for. You then can print this data back out to a CSV as we did before, now including both the estimated and expected category IDs as additional columns. Notice that you only use the height and length parts of the testing data (i.e., `testing_inputs`) in the estimation. The actual label `expected` is not given to the neural network. Otherwise, it'll know the answer. If you compare `res` with `expected` by looking at the third and fourth columns you'll see that almost all predictions are correct. This is not usually the case in real-life applications. The reason that you can achieve a 100% accuracy is that the training and testing data are artificially generated to be easy for a neural network model, and it's free of noise. Still, this example shows us the core steps in training a supervised neural network model using `rusty-machine`.

9.6 Alternatives

As you can see from the examples in this chapter, machine learning is not just about training the model. There are many data-related operations before and after you train the model. These kinds of operations include the following:

- Reading and writing CSV or other structural data formats

- Pre-processing the data (e.g., normalization)

- Setting and loading model configurations and parameters

- Visualizing the data

It's not really practical to write all this code from scratch for every machine learning application. You need a strong ecosystem with many pre-built crates to help quickly and efficiently implement the learning part without worrying about fundamental tasks like linear algebra and data manipulation. Similar to other fields in Rust, there's an "Are you learning yet?" page[9] tracking how the ecosystem is doing. As stated on the page, the machine learning landscape in Rust is "ripe for experimentation, but the ecosystem isn't very complete yet." There's also the Awesome-Rust-MachineLearning Github repo,[10] which is a condensed and updated list of crates that are currently usable in Rust for various machine learning purposes.

For the foundational mathematical crates, `nalgebra` and `ndarray` have come to be seen as the de-facto standard. They provide linear algebra and array/matrix operation, similar to the `numpy` in Python. Many machine learning algorithms also rely on code from high-performance computing (HPC), which harnesses more of the hardware (CPU, GPU, etc.) and parallelism. There is much experimentation in this field, like `std::simd`, `RustCUDA`, and `rayon`, just to name a few.

If you consider traditional machine learning ("traditional" in the sense that it's not deep learning), the `smartcore` and `linfa` crates are both leading and relatively comprehensive. They both have implemented several commonly used traditional machine learning models and continue to do so, also putting a large emphasis on interoperability with crates like `ndarray`.

---

[9] https://www.arewelearningyet.com/
[10] https://github.com/vaaaaanquish/Awesome-Rust-MachineLearning

As for deep learning, there is no mature library built from scratch using Rust. We used `rusty-machine` here since it was easy to set up and use for learning purposes, but the library is no longer actively maintained. So to tap into the field of deep learning, the best bet now is to use Rust bindings to mature libraries written in other languages. There are Rust bindings to the TVM project, which is an open-source deep learning compiler stack. There is also `tensorflow/rust` for TensorFlow and `tch-rs` for PyTorch, which are two mainstream deep learning frameworks and probably the most popular tools for deep learning with Rust at this time.

Rust has excellent potential to enable high performance and safe machine learning applications, but there is still much more work to get the ecosystem ready for production use. If you are interested, we encourage you to reach out to an open source project and start working on it; often the best way to deeply understand something is to implement some of it yourself.

9.7 Conclusion

In this chapter, you learned about how Rust can be used in machine learning and artificial intelligence. You first created a supervised model using K-means clustering, where you classified cats into breeds based on measurement data. Then you shifted to an unsupervised model, where you used a neural network to analyze cat and dog measurement data and determine the species of new unknown data points. We also shared a few other libraries for the still young AI/ML ecosystem in Rust.

## CHAPTER 10

What Else Can You Do with Rust?

10.1 The End Is Just the Beginning

We've taken an exciting journey through the world of Rust together. We've learned how to build a CLI, a GUI, a web application frontend, a REST API, a serverless website using AWS, a game, a program to control hardware, and machine learning models. What next steps can you take? What other exciting applications can you build with Rust? We'll briefly walk you through some other areas that weren't covered in this book.

10.2 Server-side Rendered Website

In the previous chapters you learned how to build a single-page application (SPA) frontend and a REST API in Rust. This combination, sometimes called *client-side rendering*, is currently the most popular architecture in modern web development. However, there is an older architecture for building dynamic websites called *server-side rendering*, which is still viable and in some places coming back into favor. In a server-side rendered website, the backend is responsible for constructing the HTML and sending it back to the frontend. There are several reasons that server-side rendering is still relevant:

- Simplicity: For simple websites, the user interface (HTML and CSS) is written in the same place as the business logic. The frontend also does not need to make complex API calls to the backend to receive data.

© Shing Lyu and Andrew Rzeznik 2023
S. Lyu and A. Rzeznik, *Practical Rust Projects*, https://doi.org/10.1007/978-1-4842-9331-7_10

- Performance: Because the browser receives HTML from the backend directly, it doesn't need to wait until the JavaScript is loaded and wait for the JavaScript to render the screen. There is potentially a performance gain. Although some frameworks that use isomorphic rendering can also accelerate the performance in client-side rendered pages,[1] this adds more complications that can be done without to keep the codebase simpler (and generally there aren't production-ready Rust libraries currently available).

- Search engine optimization (SEO): Search engines use programs called crawlers to scan through web pages and build up their search index. Some crawlers might not have the capability to run JavaScript, so a server-side rendered website is more friendly to the browser engine crawlers. Nowadays, major search engines all have some capability of handling client-side rendered websites, but it can still be useful to consider SEO when designing a new site.

The actix-web framework you used in Chapter 5 can be used for server-side rendering. Other current frameworks that support server-side rendering include Axum (`https://github.com/tokio-rs/axum`) and Rocket.[2]

10.3 Web Browser and Crawler

When people discuss the web in terms of frontend and backend, they often omit what sits in between: the web browser. The reason people often omit it is because there are only a handful of browsers available on the market, so they are considered something set in stone. You might protest that there are hundreds of browsers you can find on Wikipedia,[3] but in fact most modern browsers are powered by three browser engines:

- Blink: powers Chromium, Google Chrome, Microsoft Edge, Opera

- Gecko: powers Firefox

- WebKit: powers Safari

---

[1] `https://en.wikipedia.org/wiki/Isomorphic_JavaScript`

[2] `https://rocket.rs/`

[3] Wikipedia, "List of web browsers," `https://en.wikipedia.org/wiki/List_of_web_browsers`

The history of Rust is tied deeply to browser engines. There is also a browser engine prototype written in Rust from the ground up, called Servo.[4] Servo is historically one of the most significant projects written in Rust. The Servo project started in 2012, and now has roughly 2.6 million lines of code (not all in Rust, but still impressive). Servo started as a research project at Mozilla. In 2017, Servo's CSS engine matured and was merged into Gecko, the browser engine that powers Mozilla's Firefox. The rendering component of Servo, called WebRender, was integrated into Firefox later as well. So, if you are using Firefox right now, you are also executing a big chunk of Rust code.

Servo has had a significant impact on Rust itself. The two projects shared some core developers, and the core contributors worked closely with each other because they both started as research projects under Mozilla Research. Many of Servo's needs drove the development of new features in Rust, and Rust's design also heavily influenced how Servo was architected. If you are interested in seeing Rust in large-scale projects, Servo is definitely a fun piece of work to dive into. In 2020, the Servo project was moved from Mozilla to Linux Foundation.[5] As vindication of the success of Rust in web browsers, the Chromium project has decided to formally support calling Rust code from their C++ libraries.[6]

Browsers are for human beings. However, many other programs also consume web pages. These programs are usually referred to as *web crawlers*, *scrapers,* or *spiders*. They "crawl" through web pages and extract information from them. A use case might be when you want to compare prices listed on different e-commerce websites, but these websites don't provide APIs. We can utilize a crawler to crawl through their web pages and extract the price information from the HTML. There are a few frameworks for building web crawlers, for example `spider`[7] and `website-crawler`.[8] If you want more fine-grained control over the crawling and parsing process, you can use the `reqwest`[9]

---

[4] https://github.com/servo/servo

[5] https://www.linuxfoundation.org/press-release/open-source-web-engine-servo-to-be-hosted-at-linux-foundation/

[6] https://security.googleblog.com/2023/01/supporting-use-of-rust-in-chromium.html

[7] https://crates.io/crates/spider

[8] https://github.com/a11ywatch/crawler

[9] https://crates.io/crates/reqwest

HTTP client library to download the HTML page, and use an HTML parsing/querying library to parse the page and extract data. Some popular HTML parsing/querying libraries include html5ever,[10] scraper,[11] and select.[12]

10.4 Mobile

In Chapter 3, we talked about how to build a GUI for desktop. But we didn't talk about how to build GUIs for mobile devices (i.e., apps). The dominant mobile platforms are Google's Android and Apple's iOS. Android apps are written with Java or Kotlin, while iOS apps are written in Objective-C or Swift. On Android, Rust is officially supported as a platform language for working directly on the Android OS.[13] Sadly, however, Rust can't be a drop-in replacement for these natively supported languages when it comes to developing a user-facing application. But both Android and iOS have some mechanism for invoking (and being invoked by) C or C++ libraries. These mechanisms are crucial for performance-critical applications that build the user interface in Java/Kotlin/Objective-C/Swift and offload the computation-intensive part to C/C++ libraries. Since we can compile Rust to a library that looks and feels like a C library, we can also use this mechanism to build an app that has business logic written in Rust.

For Android, the process will be as follows:[14]

- Install Android Studio (containing the Android SDK). This is the official development environment for Android apps.

- Install the Android NDK (Native Development Kit). This toolkit allows us to compile Rust into a library that can work on Android and interact with Java/Kotlin.

---

[10] https://github.com/servo/html5ever

[11] https://crates.io/crates/scraper

[12] https://crates.io/crates/select

[13] https://source.android.com/docs/setup/build/rust/building-rust-modules/overview

[14] Mozilla published a post that guides you through the process step by step: https://mozilla.github.io/firefox-browser-architecture/experiments/2017-09-21-rust-on-android.html

There is a `cargo ndk`[15] command you can install to simplify the compilation process.

- Use `rustup` to install the Android targets; for example `armv7-linux-androideabi`.

- Build your Rust library project and compile it to a library file. You need to expose your Rust code to Java through JNI (Java Native Interface); there is a `jni`[16] crate that helps you with that.

- Import the Rust library into your Java/Kotlin Android app project and call the library inside your Java/Kotlin code.

The steps for iOS[17] are very similar, as follows:

- Install Xcode, which is the official development environment for iOS apps.

- Use `rustup` to install the iOS targets; for example `armv7-apple-ios`.

- Build your Rust library project and compile it to a library file. You also need to expose a C-style header file so iOS can consume the Rust library as if it's a C library.

- Import the Rust library into your XCode and call the library inside your Objective-C/Swift code.

If you are looking for purely Rust mobile applications, you can try using Tauri. Tauri provides an engine for running JavaScript and WASM-based UI's in the desktop and as of recently, also on mobile.[18] We saw in Chapter 4 how you can make a single-page web application purely in Rust using WebAssembly. This same code can be run, with minimal modifications, using Tauri, thus turning it into a desktop or mobile app. Besides using Tauri or another JavaScript/WASM-based runtime, you can write a simple Java application that starts an OpenGL or Vulkan window, and write Rust code that directly

---

[15] https://github.com/bbqsrc/cargo-ndk

[16] https://crates.io/crates/jni

[17] Here is the Mozilla post on running Rust on iOS: https://mozilla.github.io/firefox-browser-architecture/experiments/2017-09-06-rust-on-ios.html.

[18] https://github.com/tauri-apps/tauri-mobile

renders the UI, but this will require writing a lot of this rendering code from scratch. Previously, crates have existed for doing this kind of low-level rendering on Android, like `android-rs-glue`,[19] but these have largely been abandoned as the community has shifted its focus to WebAssembly.

Another alternative is to use a game engine that handles the rendering by itself. For example, the macroquad[20] game engine allows you to write applications in Rust and build them for Android and iOS. The downside of this route is that you don't have access to platform-native UIs and you have to render the UI by yourself.

Note   The idea of compiling Rust into a shared library and using it inside other programming languages using their FFI (foreign function interface) mechanism can be applied not only in the mobile realm. The Rust FFI Omnibus website[21] collects such examples for various programming languages:

- C

- Ruby

- Python

- Haskell

- Node.js

- C#

- Julia

It can also work the other way around. Rust can call libraries written in other languages supporting the C language ABI, such as C and C++. You can reference the section "Using extern Functions to Call External Code"[22] from "The Rust Programming Language" by Steve Klabnik and Carol Nichols to learn more.

---

[19] https://github.com/rust-windowing/android-rs-glue

[20] https://github.com/not-fl3/macroquad

[21] http://jakegoulding.com/rust-ffi-omnibus/basics/

[22] https://doc.rust-lang.org/book/ch19-01-unsafe-rust.html#using-extern-functions-to-call-external-code

10.5 Operating Systems and Embedded Devices

As we mentioned at the end of Chapter 8, there are many more things you can do on the hardware level than just blinking an LED. There are simply too many hardware platforms and peripherals out there, and writing bare-metal Rust programs for each and every one of them from scratch is virtually impossible. Thankfully, there are some software abstractions already defined at various layers. At the bottom layer, there are peripheral-access crates that contain register definitions and low-level details of the micro-controllers. On top of that, there is the embedded-hal layer. The -hal suffix stands for Hardware Abstraction Layer. The embedded-hal is a few traits that define a hardware-agnostic interface between a specific HAL implementation and drivers. Drivers can be written against the embedded-hal traits without worrying about hardware-specific details. This enables developers to build portable drivers, firmware, and applications on top of this abstraction layer. You can find many embedded-hal crates and their implementations by searching the keyword "embedded-hal" or "embedded-hal-impl" on crates.io.

Building on top of embedded-hal there are driver crates and board-support crates. Drivers give you platform-agnostic support for a specific class of device, like sensors, modems, LCD controllers, etc. Board-support crates give you support for a specific development board.

Many Rust developers also take on the challenge of building or extending operating systems in Rust. A relatively mature one is Redox OS[23] (Figure 10-1), which is designed with a micro-kernel architecture. It already has a GUI and some useful applications running on it. There is also Tock,[24] which is targeting IoT (Internet of Things) devices with low-memory and low-power constraints. Another recent low-level open-source Rust-based OS is Hubris[25] by Oxide Computer Company. And finally (and probably most important), Rust has become the first language after C to be added to the Linux kernel, starting with the ability to write drivers.[26]

---

[23] https://www.redox-os.org/

[24] https://www.tockos.org

[25] https://github.com/oxidecomputer/hubris

[26] https://rust-for-linux.com/

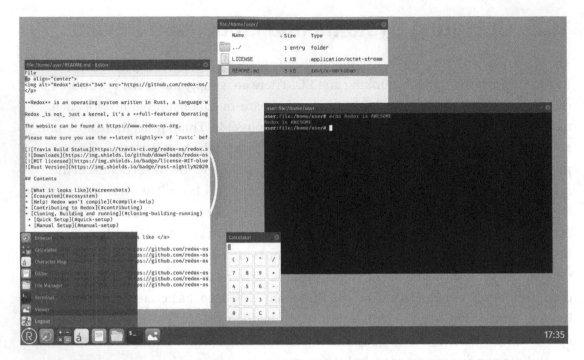

Figure 10-1. *Redox OS. Image retrieved from the Redox OS GitLab repository. MIT License*

There are OSes for teaching purposes, like Blog OS.[27] There are also a few less-active ones that take a language-based approach, which means their focus is to build a minimal OS that can run a Rust program.

10.6 The Cloud

In Chapter 6, you built an application on the AWS cloud using Rust. But do you know that part of the services that make up the AWS cloud are also built in Rust? For example, the Firecracker VM,[28] the lightweight virtualization technology that powers AWS Lambda and AWS Fargate, is written in Rust. The micro-virtual machines (microVMs) launched in Firecracker have a fast startup time and low memory overhead, without trade-offs in security or efficiency.

---

[27] https://os.phil-opp.com/. It's named *Blog OS* because it was a series of blog articles by Philip Opperman on how to build an OS in Rust.

[28] https://firecracker-microvm.github.io/

AWS also developed Bottlerocket,[29] a Linux-based operating system that is purpose-built to run containers. You can use it on the host machine that runs containers. It contains only the essential software to run containers, so it reduces the attack surface and improves security. It's also written in Rust.

AWS Nitro Enclaves is another service that uses Rust. AWS Nitro Enclaves allows you to create isolated compute environments in your Amazon Elastic Compute Cloud (Amazon EC2) instances. By running the most sensitive data processing applications, such as those involving personally identifiable information (PII), financial, and health care details in a Nitro Enclave, you can improve the security of your application.

As you can see, Rust plays a big part in building secure applications for cloud computing. Other services like Amazon Simple Storage Service (Amazon S3), Amazon Elastic Compute Cloud (Amazon EC2), and Amazon CloudFront also use Rust internally.[30]

10.7 Blockchains and Cryptocurrencies

Rust has caught a lot of attention in the world of blockchain and cryptocurrency because of its safety and performance. There are two levels of usage for Rust in blockchains: using Rust to build the blockchain itself, or using Rust to write smart contracts on a blockchain.

There are several high-profile blockchains that are built with Rust: Solana,[31] Polkadot,[32] and Hyperledger Sawtooth.[33] The failed cryptocurrency *Diem*[34] (formerly *Libra*, created by Meta) was also built with Rust.

These blockchains also allow you to write smart contracts in Rust. These smart contracts run inside the blockchain's virtual machine, and most of the time they require some kind of cross-compilation into WebAssembly or custom bytecode format. For example, the NEAR Protocol allows you to use ink!, an embedded domain-specific language (DSL) that allows you to write smart contracts in Rust. Solana also allows you to write its smart contracts (called Programs) in Rust.

---

[29] https://aws.amazon.com/bottlerocket/

[30] https://aws.amazon.com/blogs/opensource/sustainability-with-rust/

[31] https://solana.com/

[32] https://polkadot.network/

[33] https://www.hyperledger.org/blog/2019/01/18/safety-performance-and-innovation-rust-in-hyperledger-sawtooth

[34] https://www.diem.com/

Blockchain is a fast-evolving domain. You can follow the latest developments from the curated list of Rust blockchain projects, Awesome Blockchain Rust,[35] and newsletters, like *Rust in Blockchain*.[36]

10.8 Unlimited Possibilities of Rust

Besides the topics we discussed in previous chapters and sections, there are many more applications of Rust. Here is a non-exhaustive list:[37]

- Compression

- Cryptography and Security: `ring`,[38] `openssl`,[39] `sodiumoxide`[40]

- Database implementations[41]

- Emulators: game consoles and other hardware

- Multimedia: images, audio, and video manipulation; rendering 2D/3D content

- Language parsers

- Scientific applications: mathematics, bio-informatics (e.g., Rust-Bio[42]), geo-information, physics, and chemistry simulation

Rust is a wonderful tool for building almost any kind of application. Although at this moment, some fields might not have mature, production-ready Rust libraries or user bases, with support from the passionate and friendly community, we can expect to see many more applications of Rust. From mini IoT sensors running on low-power micro-controllers, to cutting-edge AI running on massive supercomputers, the future of Rust is wide open and looks bright. Have you found anything you would like to build with Rust? Let's all work together to grow Rust and unleash its full potential!

---

[35] https://github.com/rust-in-blockchain/awesome-blockchain-rust

[36] https://rustinblockchain.org/

[37] This list in alphabetical order. The order does not indicate popularity or maturity.

[38] https://crates.io/crates/ring

[39] https://crates.io/crates/openssl

[40] https://crates.io/crates/sodiumoxide

[41] https://crates.io/categories/database-implementations

[42] https://rust-bio.github.io/

Index

A

B

© Shing Lyu and Andrew Rzeznik 2023

S. Lyu and A. Rzeznik, *Practical Rust Projects*, https://doi.org/10.1007/978-1-4842-9331-7